I0831724

Narrating the Prison

Narrating the Prison

Role and Representation in Charles Dickens' Novels, Twentieth-Century Fiction, and Film

Jan Alber

CAMBRIA
PRESS

Youngstown, New York

Printed in the United States of America

Library of Congress Cataloging-in-Publication Data

Alber, Jan, 1973-

Narrating the prison: role and representation in Charles Dickens' novels, twentieth-century fiction, and film / Jan Alber.

p. cm.

ISBN 978-1-934043-60-8 (alk. paper)

1. Dickens, Charles, 1812-1870—Film and video adaptations. 2. Prisons in literature. 3. English fiction—20th century—History and criticism. 4. American fiction—20th century—History and criticism. 5. Film adaptations—History and criticism. 6. Prisons—England—History. 7. Prisons—United States—History. 8. Motion pictures and literature. I. Title.

PR4575.A43 2007
823.009'3556—dc22

2007006227

Dedicated to Monika Fludernik
on the occasion
of her fiftieth birthday

Contents

Foreword

Largely in response to Foucault's work on surveillance, literary and cultural historians of the early 1980s start revisiting the modern representations of "carcerality," so much so that within years punishment as discipline gives rise to a whole discipline *of* punishment, imprisonment, and penal confinement. The discipline was not entirely new. Nor was it one but several rolled in one rather, and that was precisely what made it innovative, capable to take another look at an otherwise longstanding object of inquiry. In other words, the field was, and has remained, interdisciplinary. It is to this institutionally fluid, methodologically complex, and epistemologically demanding domain that Jan Alber's *Narrating the Prison* belongs, lodged as it stands at the shifting crossroads of literary and film analysis, Victorian scholarship, sociology, legal studies, Frankfurt School-inspired critical theory, imagology, and narratology. I list the focus on imaginary and narrative structures last, but it certainly comes first and defines, I think, the bulk of Alber's contribution to the study of carceral modernity in Dickens and later, twentieth-century British and American fiction and film.

Impressive as a whole, his toolkit is nevertheless employed selectively. Its use is characteristically geared toward uncovering a certain ideology of literary form, where form is either a dominant figure, a particular configuration of recurrent tropes, or narrative strategy such as omniscience. The best discussions of things ideological, the most effective *Kritik* generally obtain, as far as I am concerned, on a bottom-up model that operates inductively by drawing on incidents of "style"—a recurring image or storytelling device—and working itself up into broader considerations that bring together the textual and the contextual. To be sure, this is precisely where the ideological plays out, where it comes into being and holds sway over our lives: not inherently "in" specific cultural forms and formations or completely outside them but on their outer edge, where they and their environment seem to dovetail naturally and, as a result, inquiry, questioning, and revaluation may appear superfluous.

In dwelling on modernity's fictional production of "carceral topography," as Monika Fludernik calls it, *Narrating the Prison* shows that closing out such deliberations is ideologically ambiguous at best in that it projects carcerality as a self-evident carce-reality whose social meanings and roles are in no need of public debate. This is exactly the kind of collective projection Dickens takes to task in *Little Dorrit*, *A Tale of Two Cities*, and *Great Expectations*. Oddly enough, his critique is perhaps more insistent than that of later writers such as Robert E. Burns (*I Am a Fugitive from a Georgia Chain Gang*, 1932), Thomas E. Gaddis (*Birdman of Alcatraz*, 1955), Anthony Burgess (*A Clockwork Orange*, 1962), Stephen King ("Rita Hayworth and Shawshank Redemption," 1982), and Lorenzo Carcaterra (*Sleepers*, 1995), not to mention the directors who made movies (hence catered to larger audiences) based on these texts. In their works, Alber points out, a good deal of "naturalizing" cover-up goes on, that is to say, a whole constellation of prison tropes and narrative devices are deployed to the effect that prison stories end up corroborating a number of extant "certainties" about convicts, society, the judicial system, and the sociopolitical status quo such beliefs uphold.

It is only in his conclusion that the author tackles issues of literary history head-on, but the concern is in play throughout and asks repeatedly, directly and indirectly, what kind of critical narrative can we put together if we zero in on prison literature with Victorians at one end and American pop culture masters at the other? What developments, literary and otherwise, do we register, what shifts do we notice in the artistic and, more broadly, social perception of disciplinary confinement? At last, given the strong imprint Dickens left on this perception—so strong that it has become virtually impossible to talk about modern incarceration without referring or alluding to Dickens—how can we evaluate his posthumousness, his critical-humanist legacy in this all-too-contested area? *Narrating the Prison* raises all these important questions, and the answers are both compelling and intriguing.

I will not spoil its readers the pleasure of discovering these answers for themselves as they work their way through Alber's careful readings of novels, novellas, film, and nonfiction. "Close" as they necessarily are, showcasing some painstaking attention paid to detail, these readings are far from formalist. As noted earlier, they dwell on form to tease out its commitment to specific sociopolitical and ethical arrangements (or rearrangements). There is no question in my mind that both narrative studies and the New Historicism need this kind of approach, eclectic in the best sense, keen on stylistic details from narrative viewpoint to cinematic technique as much as on these details' cultural and political inflections. Consistently applied across a century and a half of prison literature and film, this methodology fits its object like glove. It helps us see, for instance, how and why post-Dickensian representation of correctional landscapes gives way to an uncritical exceptionalism of sorts with the protagonist (such as Stephen King's) set up as an "exception" to the grim rule of the prison and the imprisoned others. It is these others whom he must fight and thus prove himself as a man and as an "individual" in a racially and homosocially threatening environment that otherwise filters outside phobias associated with race, sexual choice, and class. Alber's discussion of *The Shawshank Redemption*, which I have just outlined, is emblematic for how his analysis works to uncover a rather cynical or, as I say above, uncritical strain in recent carceral discourses that bespeaks the breakdown or shift of former prison-world-at-large homologies. While Dickens and other realists fancied society itself as one big prison and the latter as a microcosm of the former, a significant number of authors and movie directors closer to our time appear to buy into the notion of prison as "social necessity" and violent arena that retroactively legitimates our apprehensions and further shores up "consensus" around the dominant correctional mindset. For sure, these are all controversial problems of urgent interest inside and outside the academy. *Narrating the Prison* deals with them systematically, without preconceptions. Thoroughly researched, the book sheds refreshing light on prison literature and film.

Professor Christian Moraru
University of North Carolina, Greensboro

Acknowledgments

This book is a substantially revised version of my PhD thesis, submitted to the University of Freiburg in 2005. First of all, I would like to thank Prof. Dr. Monika Fludernik who has supervised my doctoral thesis and provided me with invaluable comments on work in progress. I want to thank her for profound discussions about prisons, metaphors, films, narratological questions, Foucault, Dickens, and other Victorian authors. The discussion climate could not have been better. I also want to thank her for the continuous trust that she has placed in me and my work. This book is dedicated to her on the occasion of her fiftieth birthday.

Second, I am indebted to Prof. Dr. Paul Goetsch and Prof. Dr. Hans-Helmuth Gander for co-examining my thesis, and for making very helpful comments and suggestions.

Third, I would like to thank my colleagues from the Deutsche Forschungsgemeinschaft (DFG) research project, "Law, Norm and Criminalization." This project analyzes the connections between the creation of norms, the legal punishment of non-normative behavior, and the exclusion of forms of deviance from the norm through discursive means. I want to thank Prof. Dr. Hans-Jörg Albrecht,

Prof. Dr. Hans-Helmuth Gander, and their teams for most stimulating debates about the situation in real prisons as well as the relationship between prisons and prison narratives.

This book also owes its existence to the financial support I have received. I would like to thank the German Academic Exchange Programme (DAAD), the Wissenschaftliche Gesellschaft in Freiburg e.V. and the Sonderforschungsbereich 541 "Identitäten und Alteritäten" for the funding of my two stays at the British Film Institute (bfi) in London.

Furthermore, I would like to thank Prof. Dr. Hans-Jörg Albrecht, the Director of the Max Planck Institute for Foreign and International Law in Freiburg, for granting me access to the library of his institute. In particular my historical analyses of the prison experience have greatly benefited from the material in this library.

I am also indebted to Dr. Rebecca Davies, Dr. Kerstin Fest, Jon Harty, Dr. Manfred Jahn, Frank Lauterbach, Dr. Thomas Lederer, Dr. Miriam Nandi, Neal O'Donoghue, and Dr. Greta Olson for their comments and encouragement.

My thanks are also due to Dr. Jochen Petzold who drew my attention to Cambria's new series in Literature, Film, and Theory. I would also like to thank C.A. Murphy, Toni Tan, and others at Cambria Press, as well as the anonymous readers of the manuscript, for their invaluable guidance during the process of turning the manuscript into a book.

Moreover, I want to thank Anja, Quirin, and my parents, Barbara and Wolf-Dietrich Alber, as well as Andi, Axel, Beate, Dieter, Helge, Irmi, Katerina, Kathi, Katrin, Luise, Matthias, Miriam, Neumi, Sandra, Thomas, Ursula, and Valeska for being there. Finally, I am indebted to my brother Jörg, whose way of looking at things I have always greatly admired. My greetings go to him and the people of Escanda in the north of Spain.

Narrating the Prison

CHAPTER ONE

INTRODUCTION

This book investigates the ways in which Charles Dickens' mature fiction, prison novels of the twentieth century, and prison films narrate the prison.[1] In other words, it looks at the depiction of British and American institutions that hold captives. Since most people lack first-hand experience of the prison and gain their 'knowledge' through indirect means, it is of primary importance to deal with fictional representations of the prison to get an understanding of how the prison has entered the cultural subconscious. For good or ill, prison narratives influence the cognitive categories of their recipients and thus the popular understanding of the prison.

This study looks at prison novels and films from four interrelated perspectives and addresses the ideological underpinnings of these prison narratives; the representation of the prison experience; the role of prison metaphors; and narratological questions concerning similarities, differences, and continuities between Dickens' mature novels, twentieth-century fiction, and films.

This book deals with the ideological underpinnings of prison novels and films, i.e., the question of whether they generate cultural understandings of the legitimacy or illegitimacy of the prison.

Prison narratives spread certain images of prisons and their inmates and these pictures always correlate with a certain type of ideology in the sense of James H. Kavanagh. Kavanagh argues that an ideology "has the function of producing an *obvious* 'reality' that social subjects can assume and accept, precisely as if it had not been socially produced and did not need to be 'known' at all" (311). Dickens' mature fiction participates in a philanthropic discourse that constructs prisoners as the innocent victims of an evil society. Dickens represents the prison as an instrument of a fundamentally unjust society which is to be blamed for the existence of criminals. Twentieth-century novels and films, on the other hand, usually legitimate the prison as a social institution by arguing that irreclaimably depraved criminals exist and need to be punished. They participate in a conservative discourse of pro-prison propaganda that presents the prison as a societal necessity.

My investigation of the ideological underpinnings of prison narratives naturally also comprises an analysis of the ways in which novels and films narrate the prison experience. Since fictional prison narratives always transform and distort the actual prison experience, I pay particular attention to the ways in which novels and films depart from the experiential realities of prison life. In a second step, I interpret these narrations (or 'misrepresentations') against the foil of historical and criminological analyses of the prison experience in British and American prisons of the nineteenth and twentieth centuries.

While Dickens narrates the prison experience in terms of the unjust suffering of *many* idealized and sympathetic inmates, prison novels and films of the twentieth century tend to focus on *one* newcomer who is sent to prison because he committed a trivial crime and then suffers under a brutal system. And while they represent the fate of this 'unique' character as being terrible and unjust, the attitude toward the mass of ordinary prisoners is complicit with the common view that 'real' criminals have to be imprisoned. Prison narratives of the twentieth century only invite us to sympathize with the quasi-innocent prisoner-hero but do not allow us to empathize with the 'deviant' rest of the prison population and thus implicitly sanction the existence of prisons.

Furthermore, these delimitations are connected with other cultural delineations. The newcomer is typically a member of the white and heterosexual middle class, and has to go through a process of symbolic 'feminization' in prison that threatens his masculinity[2] (violent and sadistic guards, 'homosexual' rapes, and time in the 'hole' normally play an important role). Also, twentieth-century narratives typically counter the ill-treatment of this prisoner-hero by means of his escape and restore his manliness and, by extension, the phallic power of the white middle class. Such narratives do not address the situation of the actual prison population in British and American prisons. Rather, they present us with stories about the unjust victimization of 'innocent' members of the white and heterosexual middle class, and they additionally code colored and homosexual inmates as 'real' criminals who belong where they are.

The ideological underpinnings of prison narratives also closely correlate with the use of prison metaphors and similes. I treat similes and metaphors as being more or less equivalent because I am concerned with the results of the mapping process. In both cases, the recipient starts to correlate aspects of the source and the target domain and creates a complex understanding of their conjunction to generate new meaning structures. Like Fludernik ("The Prison as World," "Metaphorics"), I discriminate between three types of prison metaphors. First, metaphors of imprisonment (PRISON IS X) that describe the prison in terms of another domain of human experience usually play an important role with regard to the rendering of the prison experience. Second, the 'prison-as-world' simile operates by means of a homological structure between the prison and society and accentuates that certain attitudes or societal eccentricities are reproduced in prison. Third, proper prison metaphors (X IS PRISON) project the image of the prison onto domains outside a legal or penal context and are normally used to critique a certain segment of society.

Since my analyses of prison metaphors aim at semantic significance, they contribute to my investigation of ideological underpinnings. Dickens' mature fiction focuses on 'negative' metaphors of imprisonment that describe the prison as a tomb, a cage, or in terms of hell. By means of these metaphors, which highlight the inmates' agony, Dickens condemns the prison system as such. Twentieth-century narratives, on the other hand, only critique discipline-based institutions but argue in favor of rehabilitative penal styles. More specifically, they describe the former by using 'negative' metaphors and the latter through positive ones that invite us to see the prison as a womb, a matrix of spiritual rebirth, a catalyst of intense friendship, or as an 'academy.' Furthermore, prison narratives of the twentieth century suggest that society needs such reformative prisons for colored and homosexual inmates, while members of the white and heterosexual middle class do not belong there.

Finally, since this study deals with the ways in which novels and films narrate the prison, I also address similarities, differences, and continuities between filmic and novelistic narration. With regard to the depiction of crucial features of the experience of imprisonment, the book wishes to gain an understanding of the possibilities of the media novel and film. Furthermore, Dickens' mature fiction anticipates prison narratives of the twentieth century in a wide variety of ways. First, Dickens' panoramic visions in the authorial novels[3] *Little Dorrit* and *A Tale of Two Cities* foreshadow prison films of the twentieth century. Both Dickens' novels and twentieth-century prison films correlate with a third-person perspective, extremely detailed descriptions of prison settings, and various attempts to simulate the inmates' internal states through external details. Second, the embedded first-person confessions, letters and diaries in *Little Dorrit* and *A Tale of Two Cities* as well as the pseudo-autobiography *Great Expectations,* written immediately after *A Tale of Two Cities*, anticipate the increasingly narrower and internal visions of first-person prison novels in the twentieth century.

Since this study discusses prison novels and films, it makes sense to provide definitions of the prison novel and the prison film before moving on to a more specific account of the corpus. According to W.B. Carnochan, "literature of the prison includes, on the one hand, fictions written about prison experience and, on the other, writing of every sort by inmates" ("Literature" 431). Following this definition, prison literature deals with the experience of imprisonment and its consequences. Indeed, this book concentrates on novels that centrally address the prison experience, i.e., the dynamic interrelationship between the prisoner and his surroundings, the prison world. More specifically, it focuses on narratives that deal with "the crucial position of the prison subject" as well as the subject's resulting "identity crisis" (Fludernik "Carceral Topography" 46).

This takes me to a definition of the prison film. As Paul Mason has shown ("Screen Machine" 282), the prison film is not a proper genre like the western or the science fiction film. Following Mike Nellis ("British Prison Movies" 2), one may characterize prison films as fiction films which take the experience of imprisonment and its consequences as a primary theme, and which are usually (but not always) set in a penal institution. Hence, western films or science fiction movies may qualify as prison films if they centrally address the prison experience and/or its consequences.

Which prison novels and films serve as the book's corpus? First of all, this study focuses on Dickens' mature fiction because in novels like *Little Dorrit*, *A Tale of Two Cities*, and *Great Expectations*, prisons, prisoners, and prison metaphors are of paramount importance. Generally speaking, and in comparison with other nineteenth-century novels, it is in Dickens' fiction that the prison figures most prominently.[4] Charles Dickens' father John Dickens was imprisoned for debt in the Marshalsea in 1824, and many of his books deal with the subject at length. But even without any knowledge of the biographical background, the dominance of the prison theme in Dickens' work is obvious. The decision to concentrate on Dickens was also motivated by the lack of film adaptations of other nineteenth-century novels. Dickens' novels, on the other hand, appear perennially attractive to filmmakers. According to Marsh, "more films have been made of works by Dickens than of any other author's" (204).

In comparison with nineteenth-century texts, prison novels of the twentieth century focus much more extensively on inside views of prisoners. Many 'newer' prison novels are written from the perspective of an imprisoned first-person narrator and offer us access to the narrator's thoughts, feelings, and motivations. This book focuses on prison novels that have been read by a vast audience and have influenced the popular understanding of the prison. Therefore, the book's corpus contains novels that may be classified as high literature but also works that may be categorized as popular literature.

Even though one cannot verify the influence of prison narratives on the citizen's image of prisons as such, certain indications exist that suggest a link between the representation of prisons in certain narratives and the public idea of imprisonment. Sometimes one can be fairly certain that many recipients must have read or viewed a prison narrative. For instance, Mike Poole points out that serial publication ensured Dickens' novels "a cultural currency greatly in excess of its merely literary reputation" (150). Indeed, when the publication of Dickens' *Great Expectations* was halfway through its run in *All Year Round*, the magazine was selling approximately one thousand copies a week. This figure is significant because it represented many more copies than the daily circulation of the London *Times* (Carlisle "Critical" 445). Hence, the instalments of Dickens' novels must have shaped the popular understanding of the prison in a significant way. Also, on the Internet Movie data base of the top 250 films of all times, female voters rate the film *The Shawshank Redemption* (1996) as the best (<http://www.imdb.com/chart/female>) and male voters as the second best film of all times (<http://www.imdb.com/chart/male>). One can conclude that a huge number of people have viewed this film and this must have influenced their perception of the prison as well. Furthermore, cases exist in which prison narratives actually caused social action. For example, the film *I Am a Fugitive from a Georgia Chain Gang!* played a central role in the campaign to abolish the chain gangs in the south of the US. Also, the novel *Birdman of Alcatraz* led to the formation of the *Committee for Release of Robert F. Stroud*. "Thousands of letters were written through the efforts of the committee's bulletins, to President Eisenhower and other federal officials" (Gaddis *Birdman* 255). Such prison narratives are important because they clearly influenced the public's perception.

In this context, it is perhaps worth noting that my corpus includes one famous and heavily fictionalized autobiography, namely Robert E. Burns' *I Am a Fugitive from a Georgia Chain Gang!* This narrative is a classical prison autobiography and reads like a sensationalist novel. In contrast to Lejeune (1994), who argues that we can differentiate between novels and autobiographies on the basis of the so-called *pacte autobiographique*, this study assumes that an absolute separation between novels and autobiographies is impossible. The prison experience in autobiographies is always reinvented and fictionalized. Also, the fact that the magazine *Time* points out that Burns "admitted he had never been chained or whipped in Georgia" (qtd. in Campbell 17) even though he claims this in his narrative, justifies the treating of Burns' text as a novel rather than an autobiography.

This book also focuses on prison films because today, most individuals gain their knowledge of prisons from films or television shows about them. The criminologists Wilson and O'Sullivan point out that they

> [...] cannot assume that the general public have more access to and interest in factual information about the nature of prison rather than its fictional representation. If anything, the reverse is likely to be true. Given this assumption, we need to consider the possibility that fictional representations of prison are an important source of these ideas and understandings. (14)

At the beginning of the research for this book, I viewed about one hundred prison films at the British Film Institute in London.[5] The choice of movies focused on was then primarily based on their wider availability. Also, the films I discuss cover different decades ranging from the 1930s up until the 1990s.

Moreover, the desire to get a comprehensive picture of British and American prison institutions motivated the selection of narratives for my corpus. Hence, this book looks at narratives that represent British debtors' prisons, penal colonies, convict prisons, and borstals but also at novels and films that narrate American reform schools as well as state and federal penitentiaries. For example, Dickens' *Little Dorrit* and Christine Edzard's two-partite 1987 film adaptation are set at the Marshalsea debtors' prison; Dickens' *Great Expectations* and David Lean's 1946 film adaptation deal with Newgate Prison, the hulks and penal colonies; the film *Wilde* narrates Oscar Wilde's time in Victorian prisons; the novella "The Loneliness of the Long-Distance Runner" and its 1964 film version are set at an English borstal; and the novel *A Clockwork Orange* and its 1971 film adaptation deal with a futurist British prison (including a special psychiatric unit). The American autobiography *I Am a Fugitive from a Georgia Chain Gang!* and the 1932 film version present us with a chain gang in the south of the US; the novella "Rita Hayworth and Shawshank Redemption" and the film version *The Shawshank Redemption* are set at the so-called Shawshank State Prison, while the movie *Down by Law* (1986) deals with the Orleans Parish Prison; the novel *Birdman of Alcatraz* and its 1962 film adaptation are set at the federal penitentiaries at Leavenworth and Alcatraz; and the novel *Sleepers* and its 1996 film version present us with the Wilkinson Home for Boys, a reform school in New York.

This takes me to prison narratives that I have excluded from the corpus. First, the book focuses on narratives that were produced *after* the 'birth' of the 'new' prison system at the beginning of the nineteenth century. Second, the book restricts itself to a discussion of narratives about male prisoners. This is so because the prison population in real and fictional prisons has been and still is predominantly male. Furthermore, an analysis of female inmates and prison narratives would yield a slightly different account of the experience of imprisonment than the one given in this study. For example, women may be forced to give birth in prison, and they may be shackled during their pregnancy, "during transport to a hospital, throughout labour, and again immediately after the child is born" (Schulz 33). This is of course a humiliating component of the prison experience men do not have to go through. In contrast to prison narratives about male prisoners, which frequently reproduce traditional masculinity (or tough-guy ideals), the deconstruction of gender roles appears to be one of the most central concerns of prison narratives about imprisoned women. For instance, in women-in-prison (WIP) films, female prisoners like Marie Allen (Eleanor Parker) in *Caged* (1949) use the prison as a cultural space to subvert, and break out of, traditional gender roles. At the end of the film, Marie is unsuited to domestic life, symbolically throws her wedding ring away, and, accompanied by joyful jazz music, emerges from the prison door to become a self-determined and happy crook.

Surprisingly, even the many WIP films of the 1970s that shade off into sexploitation movies like *Caged Heat* (1974) question traditional gender roles by constructing a type of a female masculinity. With regard to such films, Judith Halberstam notes that "the scenes of rebellious women in prison films always allow for the possibility of an overt feminist message that involves both a critique of male-dominated society and some notion of female community" (201). Similarly, prison autobiographies by women—such as the anonymous *Female Convict* (1934) or Edna O'Brien's *So I Went to Prison* (1938)—foreground community feeling among women and view imprisonment as the logical outcome of exploitation by men. Since WIP narratives focus on the exploitation of women by the patriarchal system or construct the prison as a counter-site that allows women to deconstruct traditional gender roles, they require a different analytical framework and call for a separate study (rather than a single section or an afterthought in a book about male prisoners).

What is new about the present study? While earlier studies of prison narratives focus on the dialectical relationship between physical incarceration and mental flight,[6] more recent work concentrates on ideological questions from the perspective of Michel Foucault's *Discipline and Punish* (1975), and addresses the alleged importance of Jeremy Bentham's plans for a *Panopticon* (1791).[7] These newer studies link narrative structures (like authorial narration, first-person narratives or neutral filmic narration) to structural attributes of the penitentiary and/or the idea of panoptic vision.[8] Thus, certain narratives are considered to be conservative and autocratic because their formal features are argued to reproduce the prison. And, by extension, these structures are supposed to infiltrate us with a pro-prison ideology.

This book investigates the ideological underpinnings of prison narratives as well. However, in contrast to critics like Seltzer, Bender, Miller, Hale, and Grass, I do not link these understandings of the prison to narrative structures but to the way in which prison novels and films as a whole narrate the prison. More specifically, I analyse the representation of the prison experience, i.e., the interaction between prisons and their inmates, and the use of prison metaphors. In order to determine whether prison narratives critique or buttress the prison, questions like the following will be addressed: Is the major protagonist a criminal or not? Is he likeable or not? How is the relationship between the major protagonist and the 'rest' of the prison population depicted? How is the interaction between prisoners and prison officers envisioned? Which prison metaphors are used?

This study also transcends the traditional Foucauldian or *Panopticon*-centered paradigm by demonstrating how narrations of imprisonment work in relation to the discursive delimitations of cultural categories like race and gender. More specifically, the book shows that in contrast to Dickens' novels, most prison narratives of the twentieth century implicitly code colored and homosexual inmates as 'real' criminals. Hence, they sanction the existence of prisons because evil villains are argued to exist. In a second step, they also make relatively clear statements concerning the question of who belongs into prison and who does not. In other words, they do not only constitute a form of pro-prison propaganda. They additionally describe colored and homosexual prisoners as criminals, and are openly racist and homophobic systems of representation.

Since well-known prison novels and films are far more likely to be an important source of the public's ideas about prisoners and prisons than government reports or campaigning documents, this book discusses fictional narratives that were read or viewed by a significant number of recipients. An investigation of the way in which they narrate the prison is necessary to demonstrate how prison novels and films construct popular 'misunderstandings' of the prison. The investigation of prison metaphors essentially follows the same purpose.

By showing what associations the prison evokes and by illustrating what aspects of the prison are highlighted in prison metaphors, this study attempts to gain a deeper understanding of how the prison has entered the cultural subconscious. Furthermore, this study looks at metaphors that have so far been neglected by metaphor studies, namely cinematic (or film) metaphors. The book presents a new taxonomy of film metaphors, i.e., the various ways in which films may evoke metaphorical readings, and thus contributes to an area of film studies that is still largely under-researched.

Finally, it is worth noting that many scholars have already dealt with the proto-cinematic quality of Dickens' novels. However, up until now no study has drawn the obvious thematic and stylistic link between Dickens' prison novels and prison films of the twentieth century. This book shows how Dickens' mature fiction anticipates the representation of prisons in twentieth-century novels and films.

Endnotes

1. It deals with Dickens' *Little Dorrit* (1855–57); *A Tale of Two Cities* (1859); and *Great Expectations* (1860–61) as well as their film adaptations. The book also analyzes Robert E. Burns' *I Am a Fugitive from a Georgia Chain Gang!* (1932); Thomas E. Gaddis' *Birdman of Alcatraz* (1955); Alan Sillitoe's "The Loneliness of the Long-Distance Runner" (1959); Anthony Burgess' *A Clockwork Orange* (1962); Stephen King's "Rita Hayworth and Shawshank Redemption" (1982); and Lorenzo Carcaterra's *Sleepers* (1995) as well as their film versions. Finally, the book also looks at the films *Down by Law* (1986) and *Wilde* (1997).
2. Since it is certainly reductionist to speak of 'masculinity' in the singular, I wish to stress that various different forms of masculinity exist. Gender roles are never stable or fixed but hyper-legible and artificial. Traditional masculinity correlates with a clear preference for heterosexual practices (as opposed to homosexual ones) and sometimes even homophobia. Also, traditional manliness correlates with toughness as well as a stress on activity (as opposed to passivity) and dominance (as opposed to submission).
3. In authorial novels, the story is told by and presented from the perspective of an authorial or 'omniscient' narrator who is not present as a character in the story. An authorial narrator is typically overt, i.e., clearly recognisable as a speaker or writer (Stanzel *Theory*).
4. Other nineteenth-century novels that deal with imprisonment include Charles Reade's *It Is Never Too Late to Mend* (1895), George Eliot's *Adam Bede* (1859) and the so-called Newgate novels by Edward Bulwer Lytton (1803–73) and William Harrison Ainsworth (1805–82). Forms of metaphorical imprisonment can be found in Charlotte Brontë's *Villette* (1853) and Wilkie Collins' *Armadale* (1866).
5. See my list of British and American prison films in the bibliography.
6. See, for example, Victor Brombert's *The Romantic Prison* (1975), W.B. Carnochan's *Confinement and Flight* (1977), Sigrid Weigel's *"Und selbst im Kerker frei...!"* (1982) and Christa Karpenstein-Eßbach's *Einschluß und Imagination* (1985).
7. Bentham envisioned the Panopticon as a circular prison with a central tower at the center, from which the inspectors can observe all cells located on the outer perimeter. Strategically positioned venetian

blinds on the central watchtower prevent the prisoners from observing the guards, while allowing the prison officers an unobstructed view of the prisoners. The idea behind this arrangement was to inculcate compliance, self-surveillance and self-control in the inmates by subjecting them to the fiction of permanent surveillance.

8. See Mark Seltzer's *Henry James and the Art of Power* (1984), John Bender's *Imagining the Penitentiary* (1987), D.A. Miller's *The Novel and the Police* (1988), and the debate between Dorrit Cohn ("Optics" and "Reply"), Seltzer ("The Graphic") and Bender ("Making") in *New Literary History*. See Hale ("Punishment") for the link between filmic narratives and the *Panopticon*, and Grass for the connection between first-person narration and Victorian prisons.

Chapter Two

What is a Prison?

The 'Old' and the 'New' Prison System in Great Britain

Since this book deals with the ways in which prison novels and films narrate British debtors' prisons, penal colonies, convict prisons, and borstals, a brief history of these institutions is in order. Although in eighteenth-century Britain whippings, brandings, the pillory, and the gallows were employed as forms of punishment, confinement also played a central role in the judicial process. Three types of prison-like institutions existed at the time, namely the *jails*, which contained felons and debtors as well as those held for trial or awaiting the execution of a sentence, the *houses of correction*, which were intended to suppress idleness and vagrancy, and the *debtors' prisons*.

All of these 'old' institutions were dark, filthy, and disorderly places. The debtors, who were either held in debtors' prisons or confined together with felons in jails, were particularly unruly elements. Their imprisonment was not meant as punishment but used to secure the debtor until the debt was paid. "The largest and most notorious debtors' prisons, Ludgate, King's Bench, the Fleet and the Marshalsea, were in London" (Ignatieff 29).[1] At the time, a debt of even a few shillings could mean imprisonment for life. Since debtors were not proper felons, the prison authorities had only limited control over them. In both jails and debtors' prisons, debtors often brought their wives and children with them, thus contributing to the typical disorder of these institutions. All eighteenth-century prisons were open to people from outside, who visited these institutions with the observational curiosity and nonchalance of zoo visitors. For example, after 8 a.m., the gates of the Marshalsea "were open to almost anybody, with very few restrictions" (Philpotts 140) so that, at that time, imprisonment was still a public matter. In jails and debtors' prisons, the prison officers were supposed to derive their income from the fees owed by prisoners for various services (like the buying of food or drinks outside). Furthermore, the jailers had almost no staff and tolerated a wide measure of self-government on the part of those confined: "The usual complaint about prisons was that occupants passed their time in games, gambling and drunkenness. [...] Life in an eighteenth-century prison could be tumultuous, but it would be a mistake to confuse disorder with anarchy" (McGowen "The Well-Ordered" 83).

Between 1718 and 1775, about thirty thousand felons were transported to the American penal colonies, where they were sold to private masters for the whole term of their sentence. The interruption of transportation following the independence of the American colonies and increasing numbers of convicted criminals produced a crisis that led to the Penitentiary Act of 1779. However, it is worth noting that even before the American Revolution, fewer convicts were shipped to the American colonies so that more and more prisoners remained 'at home.' According to Beattie (546), between 1772 and 1775, sentences to transportation declined by more than 40 per cent in Surrey, while the proportion of sentences to imprisonment at the same time quadrupled.

The interruption of transportation in 1775 offered an opportunity to rethink the arrangements for dealing with prisoners. The development of the 'new' reformative penitentiary—based on separation, religion, and work—was heavily influenced by the thoughts of early penologists. Cesare Beccaria's *An Essay on Crimes and Punishment* (1764), Jonas Hanway's *Solitude in Imprisonment* (1776), and John Howard's *State of the Prisons in England and Wales* (1777) were the most influential works. Beccaria did not explicitly argue in favor of penitentiaries. Rather, he believed that certainty of punishment in combination with 'milder' forms of punishment would effectively prevent criminal action. Hanway and Howard, on the other hand, were much more explicit with regard to the material goals that would distinguish prisons of the past from the penitentiary. The 'new' prison would lead to the moral reformation of the inmate. Solitary confinement in 'therapeutic' cells would produce feelings of guilt so that the prisoner would begin to reflect upon 'the errors of his ways.' Hanway believed that the remedy for all crimes lay in the isolation of the individual soul. Solitary confinement would promote the internalization of more exacting rules for regulating private conduct. While Hanway concentrated on the offender, Howard was much more interested in the construction of a 'healthy' and efficient prison institution.

The Penitentiary Act of 1779 introduced many of the features Howard had proposed: solitary confinement, religious instruction, and a strict labor regime. However, it still took thirty-seven years until the first 'new' *convict prison*, the General Penitentiary at Millbank on Thames, was opened in 1816. After the loss of the American convict depositories in 1776, the government extended its holdings of *hulks*, i.e., disused and decommissioned warships that had been used to hold convicts awaiting transportation to the penal colonies. "Put to dockyard, arsenal, and similar work during the day, the convicts returned to the hulks in order to eat and sleep" (McConville "Victorian" 134). Ultimately, the irremediable condition of the hulks proved to be rather unsatisfactory so that in 1779, the House of Commons set up a committee that was supposed to look for alternative options of transportation to rid Britain of convicts. In 1786, the government decided on Botany Bay in New South Wales, a harbor discovered by James Cook on his voyage along the eastern coast of Australia.[10]

When the first convict prison was finally opened at Millbank in 1816, thousands of convicts were still being transported to Australia each year. It is also worth noting that even though Millbank used solitary cells and attempted to isolate prisoners from their fellows to prevent 'contamination,' Millbank did not become a truly reformative penitentiary. In part the problem arose from the increase of prisoners which overwhelmed the arrangements.[11]

In 1842, another convict prison was established at Pentonville. This prison also opened as an experiment in the so-called Philadelphia (or 'separate') system, in which the prisoners had to remain in permanent solitary confinement. Pentonville relied heavily on attempts to turn its prisoners into Christian citizens, and isolated the inmates completely. Prisoners had to wear hoods when they emerged from their cells; the construction of the walls hindered communication between prisoners; and only the governor, prison officers and the chaplain were allowed to see the individual inmate in the cell. In the early 1840s, all prisoners who entered Pentonville were to be transported to Australia after a severe test of eighteen months of solitary confinement. The prison authorities eventually reduced this test to nine because of the toll it took on physical health and sanity. Once the prisoner was in a compliant state, he was taught the basics of a handicraft trade, indoctrinated by the prison chaplain and otherwise prepared for life overseas. The 'best behaved' were still transported to Australia but granted a certificate that allowed conditional release, while the 'ill-conducted' were delivered in chains to a penal colony for years of debilitating toil, harsh conditions of living, and crushing discipline (McConville "Victorian" 136). More and more convicts stayed in Britain, until in 1853, this informal practice was put on a legal footing and called 'penal servitude.'

As Grass has shown (33–36), in the nineteenth century, the prison chaplains began to write down the stories of individual prisoners, and ensured that these accounts would say the 'right thing' about the usefulness of the 'therapeutic' separation in prison. More specifically, prison authorities wished to hear first-person accounts that began in depravity and ended in the 'glorious' religious awakening engendered by solitary confinement, and this official propaganda was precisely what they were presented with.[12] Hence, at that time, fictionalized first-person narratives began to be used as ideological means of justifying and legitimating the existence and work of prisons. In contrast to Grass (11), this book does not see a necessary link between first-person narration and the prison. It is rather the case that all narrative structures can be used to express various different attitudes toward the prison. Nevertheles, it is of course true that many fictional prison narratives of the nineteenth and twentieth centuries actually legitimate the prison.

By the early 1860s, two types of prisons existed in Britain, namely the *convict prisons* on the one hand, and the *local prisons* on the other. The convict prisons held offenders who had been sentenced to a minimum of three years, while petty offenders were sent to the local prisons for very short periods. The Prison Act of 1865 created the *local prison* by amalgamating the *jail* and the *house of correction*. After 1865, the local prisons like Newgate Prison performed the functions of jails in the American sense and simultaneously served as places of punishment for those sentenced for terms of up to two years. Before 1877, local prisons were administered by county and borough magistrates, while convict prisons were run by the central government. Under the 1877 Prison Act, the local prisons were brought under central government administration together with the convict prisons. A year later, administrative power was transferred from the local magistrates to the Prison Commission in Whitehall, working under the chairmanship of Sir Edmund Du Cane.[13]

The major reason for the nationalization of local prisons was a (typically Victorian) cry for uniformity. The obligation to enforce hard labor was a major feature of the 1865 Prison Act. Du Cane thus appointed a medical and scientific prison committee which, for example, decided that prisoners sentenced to hard labor should daily ascend 8,640 steps on the treadwheel. The fact that the inmates' toil was entirely wasted provided an additional psychological complement to the physical torment. Furthermore, the law established a progressive dietary which was so meagre in its early stages as to constitute deliberate starvation. According to Oscar Wilde, Du Cane's officials and scientists issued detailed instructions on how to cook meals in such a way that they had a smell, taste and consistency so repulsive that some prisoners began to feel nauseous or suffer from diarrhea ("Don't Read This" 1046; McConville "Victorian" 149). It is also worth noting that the 1865 Prison Act made the 'separate' system, i.e., absolute solitary confinement, compulsory in local prisons. Hence, inmates were strictly separated and the solace of reading was restricted to the Bible or books of religious exhortation to cause the prisoners to repent and reflect upon 'the errors of their ways.'

The disillusionment with Du Cane's regime led to the Gladstone Report of 1895, which reinvented the idea of rehabilitation. Certain offenders like women, children, alcoholics, and first offenders were accorded different, more humane treatment. Du Cane was then replaced as Chairman of the Prison Commission by Sir Evelyn Ruggles Brise, who defined the purpose of imprisonment as being for "the humanisation of the individual" (qtd. in Bryan and Wilson 2). Prisoners were allowed to do 'useful work'; the 'separate' system was abolished; and psychologists were introduced into prison. In 1910, Churchill provided a very clear condemnation of punitive imprisonment:

> The mood and temper of the public in regard to the treatment of crime and criminals is one of the most unfailing tests of the civilisation of any country. A calm and dispassionate recognition of the rights of the accused against the state and even of convicted criminals against the State, a constant heart-searching by all charged with the duty of punishment, a desire and eagerness to rehabilitate in the world of industry all those who have paid their dues in the hard coinage of punishment, tireless efforts towards the discovery of curative and regenerating processes, and an unfaltering faith that there is a treasure, if you can only find it, in the heart of every man—these are the symbols which, in the treatment of crime and criminals, mark and measure the stored-up strength of a nation, and are a sign and proof of the living virtue in it. (qtd. in Collins *Dickens and Crime* 23)

In 1922, the reform-minded Alexander Paterson, who made much of his aphorism that "men are sent to prison as a punishment, not for punishment," was appointed to the Prison Commission. He was to remain a Commissioner until 1946 and his influence was immense. For example, in the 1930s, Paterson introduced the open prison system.

These changes notwithstanding, twentieth-century imprisonment in Britain was marked by a tenacious Victorian inheritance. The 'separate' system required special buildings, which were particularly difficult to adapt to new types of discipline allowing prisoners to congregate. At the beginning of the twentieth century, British prisons were "caught between inadequate funding and increased demands" and "declined to levels of sordidness that would have appalled and shamed Victorian administrators, politicians and public alike" (McConville "Victorian" 155). The Criminal Justice Act of 1948 formally abolished 'penal servitude,' thus removing some of the last vestiges of the dual prison system. Only flogging as prison punishment survived up until 1967. It is perhaps also worth noting that between 1946 and 1986, the prison population increased from 15,000 to 45,000, which posed severe problems of order and overcrowding. Ramsbotham points out that the prison population exceeded 70,000 in 2002 so that the possibility of doing anything useful with inmates has been progressively undermined. Today, two and sometimes three British prisoners have to share a cell that was originally designed for one. Also, today's prisons no longer try to instil morality or penitence into the prisoners so that the experience of imprisonment correlates with boring and monotonous routines.

Finally, I would like to mention the so-called *borstals*,[14] which were placed on a statutory footing in 1908 to fight juvenile delinquency in Britain. In the course of the hearings of the 1894–95 Gladstone Committee on Prisons, the call for central government to get involved in juvenile reformation was made. The novel feature of the system, which came to be called the *borstal* system, was that criminals between the ages of sixteen and twenty-one, who were convicted of offences for which they could be sent to a local or convict prison, might instead be sent to a borstal for between one and three years. Alexander Paterson, who administered the borstals as Prison Commissioner between 1922 and 1946, replaced the military type of training of the early borstals with delegated authority and encouragement of personal responsibility.

On the public (i.e., private) school model, cellblocks were designated as 'houses' and institutional loyalty was cultivated through inter-house sports, house-based recreational and social activities. Furthermore, all staff wore civilian clothes, and subordinates were encouraged to get to know the trainees individually (McConville "Victorian" 159). In 1982, the administration of Margaret Thatcher formally abolished the borstal system, and replaced it by a determinate sentence of imprisonment for young people, which came to be called "Youth Custody."[15] Finally, as a result of the Criminal Justice Act of 1988, so-called "Young Offenders Institutions" were founded (Horne 110). Between 1908 and 1982, British reform schools made extensive use of sports and gymnastics as part of their system of discipline. According to a 1934 study of the borstal system, all kinds of physical exercise were important aspects of the inmates' recreative training. In this study, Barman argues that such training gives the trainees

> [...] an alertness and an agility in movement not before experienced. The previous dull, aimless, shuffling gait gives place to a carriage that betokens elastic muscles and supple joints. The faces soon lose the dull and stolid look which they usually wear upon arrival at the institutions, and assume a more intelligent expression, while the eye gains a brightness and clearness that before was conspicuous by its absence. With physical culture and improvement, there comes a mental alertness, a cerebral activity never manifested in their lives. (44)

At the same time, borstals laid great stress upon the communication of moral and religious truths—and this combination of physical and moral exercise, which one might see as a remnant of Victorian times, was supposed to reform the trainees.

The 'Birth' of the Penitentiary in the United States

Since this book also deals with the way in which novels and films narrate American reform schools as well as state and federal penitentiaries, we shall move on to a historical analysis of these types of prisons. Both state and federal prisons receive offenders sentenced to imprisonment for more than one year. Norval Morris argues that "the distinction between federal offenses and state offenses has never been clear, other than the obvious and formal point that the former reflects a breach of federal law, the latter of state law" (238). Generally speaking, a federal crime, like drug trafficking, transcends the borders of a single state.

The American penitentiary was invented during the Jacksonian era. The creation of the penitentiary in the US was influenced by the thoughts of Cesare Beccaria (1764) and John Howard (1777) as well as Benjamin Rush's essay "An Inquiry into the Effects of Public Punishments upon Criminals and Upon Society" (1798). All three proposed to house criminals in a place of solitude where they could engage in a prolonged period of self-examination that would lead to their reformation. These influences notwithstanding, one has to note that the idea of the 'new' prison had already been present in American culture. The Jacksonian Americans "believed that crime was posing a fundamental threat to the stability and order of republican society" (Rothman 115). In the 1820s, the Auburn (or 'silent') system and the Philadelphia (or 'separate') system emphasized a steady routine of hard labor and moral instruction in the context of a regime of silence intended to prevent criminal 'contamination.' Both systems were modeled on the example of religious orders and their practice of penitence and monastic isolation. The outcome of both types of prison was to be a reformed, responsible citizen who had seen 'the error of his ways.' Under the Auburn plan, prisoners slept alone but came together to eat and work in the prison shops. However, the strict rules prohibited all talking and even the exchange of glances.

Pennsylvania set out a slightly different system in which prisoners were sent to individual cells for the whole period of their confinement. They worked, ate and slept in solitary confinement and were allowed to see only selected visitors. The Quaker designers of the Pennsylvania system believed solitary confinement to be beneficial to convicted criminals. More specifically, they thought that repentant criminals would refrain from further criminal action upon release. The 'separate' system in particular attempted to prevent the danger of criminal 'contamination' amongst prisoners. It is believed that many prisoners were driven to insanity by these extreme conditions of solitary confinement. Moreover, in both types of prisons, the inmates had to wear uniforms with stripes in order "to keep the men humble and to increase the likelihood of recapture in case of escape" (Rothman 122).

Ultimately, the Auburn system became the role model of a finely functioning 'social machine' and was adopted by almost all the states of America. However, by 1865, the elements of the original Auburn design, based on regimentation, silence, religious conversion, and steady labor, had been subverted by overcrowding, corruption, and cruelty. The prison experience at that time was medieval-like in character and included brutal corporal punishments. Progressive reformers sought to modernize prisons by abolishing corporal punishment as well as the lockstep and striped uniforms, liberalizing correspondence and visitation policies, and abolishing once and for all the rule of silence. Nevertheless, some states continued to whip or flog their inmates, and solitary confinement of very long duration was commonly used during the 1920s and 1930s. Although progressive reform fell far short of its goals, it did mitigate some of the most destructive practices of the inherited system. Progressive reform resulted in the abolishing of the vestiges of the Auburn system such as striped uniforms, lockstep marching and the rules of silence. In order to eliminate the abusive forms of corporal punishment and prison labor prevailing at the time, the so-called 'Big Houses' were founded. The 'Big Houses' were large prisons (like San Quentin in California, Sing Sing in New York, Stateville in Illinois and Jackson in Michigan) that held on average 2,500 men. The dominant features of the 'Big Houses' were "stultifying routines, monotonous schedules, and isolation" (Rotman 185). These state prisons coexisted with other state prisons—like the chain gangs in the southern parts of the United States—that maintained late nineteenth-century practices.

The sight of prisoners in chains became common in the postbellum south beginning in North Carolina in 1866, with most other southern states following suit in the next decade. The life of inmates of the state prisons in the American south was extremely hard. The prisoners lived in semi-mobile tents or wooden barracks. States like Georgia and Mississippi leased the inmates to entrepreneurs who exploited their labor, treating them like slaves. The surveillance of inmates was an important element of chain gangs. During the day, armed white guards continuously watched over the (mostly African-American) prisoners[16] who were organized into chain gangs, i.e., chained together in groups of five to seven, and typically had to build and repair roads or work in the quarries. The suffering of the members of such chain gangs was exacerbated by the debilitating heat. Furthermore, sick and injured convicts accused of malingering were frequently whipped until they returned to work. At times, they were even beaten to death. The food supplied for these chain gangs was so poor that it was barely enough to sustain the inmates' existence. "Every meal was the same: a square of corn pone, three slices of fried pig fat, and a dose of sorghum. The only variation was that on holidays there were only two meals instead of three" (McShane "Chain Gangs" 72). Eventually, in the 1930s, the inhumane treatment of prisoners in the southern states started to be criticized in public. Georgia was the last holdout in the US and finally closed its chain gangs in 1945.

Before 1890, *federal prisons* did not exist in the US. Until the end of the nineteenth century those convicted of federal crimes, i.e., criminal offenses against congressional statutes, were sent to state institutions which were in turn allowed to contract them to private employers. At the end of the nineteenth century, the number of federal prisoners began to rise, from 1,027 in 1885 to 2,516 in 1895 (Rotman 186). In 1887, Congress outlawed the practice of using federal prisoners in their prison labor system. Consequently, many state penitentiaries began to refuse federal prisoners. The Three Prisons Act of 1890 authorized the building of federal prisons at Leavenworth, Kansas; Atlanta, Georgia; and McNeil Island, Washington. These federal prisons were run as separate entities without any central organization. The problems caused by prison congestion and the need for a more efficient record-keeping led to the creation of the *Federal Bureau of Prisons* in 1929. Finally, the increase in federal prisoners, which was presumably caused by the crime waves associated with Prohibition and the Depression, forced the Bureau to open a prison of last resort, a prison for 'the worst of the worst' (ibid. 187). Alcatraz, a rocky little island in San Francisco Bay, was destined to become "the most memorable image of a penitentiary in American penal history" (Ward "Alcatraz" 82). When Alcatraz opened in July 1934, the following rules were instituted:

1. Inmates would not be directly committed to the island; they would be received only in transfer from other prisons.
2. There would be no parole directly from Alcatraz; inmates had to earn transfers to other prisons from which they could be paroled.
3. Inmates were told, 'You are entitled to food, clothing, shelter, and medical attention. Anything else you get is a privilege.'
4. The privileges were a chance to work and earn good time, to take correspondence courses and to borrow books from the prison library, to go to the yard for two hours on weekend days and holidays, and to receive unlimited amounts of roll-your-own tobacco.
5. No commissary was established and no newspapers, no radio, and only approved magazines (with all stories related to crime, criminals, and sex removed) were allowed.
6. No visits, not even visits with lawyers, were allowed for the first three months; thereafter, lawyers could visit as necessary, and an inmate could have one visit for one hour per month with blood relatives through a bulletproof window with all conversation monitored by guards.
7. Correspondences (except with attorneys) was limited to family members and consisted of one letter per week, written on no more than three sheets of paper, on one side only. All letters, including those written to attorneys, were censored and retyped.
8. Silence was to prevail at meals, in the cellhouse, and on the job. (ibid. 84)

Alcatraz consisted of one building, which contained two cell blocks back to back, each of which followed a three-story structure, and

D-Block, a 'special treatment unit.' The prisoners were permanently observed and strictly separated. Each prisoner occupied a five by nine foot cell and was informed upon entering the prison that he was there to serve time only. That is to say, there was not even any pretence at rehabilitation. Prisoners who did not conform to the rules and regulations of Alcatraz were sent to the isolation unit on D-Block, known as 'the hole.' A stay in one of the cells meant a complete loss of privileges and total isolation. "There was no light, sound, or human contact, and most inmates found this punishment almost unbearable" (Davis "Alcatraz" 22).[17] Alcatraz housed a number of famous convicts like Al Capone; "Machine Gun" Kelly; Robert F. Stroud, the so-called 'Birdman of Alcatraz'; Henri Young; and Frank Morris, who managed to escape from Alcatraz with the Anglin brothers in 1962. The cost of maintaining high-risk inmates, coupled with the massive deterioration of the prison, resulted in the closing of Alcatraz in 1963. After its closure in 1963, Alcatraz was replaced by the federal penitentiary at Marion, Illinois, which had none of the drama of its predecessor.

While inmates in nineteenth- and early twentieth-century American penitentiaries were subjected to extremely hard labor, the problem in the twentieth century has been quite different, namely to find sufficient work to keep the inmates occupied. Norval Morris points out that for the great bulk of American prisoners of the twentieth century, the pattern of daily life consists of a relentlessly unchanging, grimly gray routine (227). For instance, Mumia Abu-Jamal argues that "the most profound horror of prisons lives in the day-to-day banal occurrences that turn days into months, and months into years, and years into decades" (53). Usually, there is no attempt to morally reclaim the inmates so that the prison experience primarily correlates with boring routines. It is also worth noting that a gross racial imbalance exists in the American prison population. In the United States as a whole, the differential rate of imprisonment of African Americans to Caucasians, proportional to population, is in excess of 7.5 to 1. Furthermore, the differential rate of imprisonment of those with Hispanic surnames in proportion to Caucasians is about 5 to 1 (Morris "Contemporary" 240).[18]

Finally, I would like to mention the so-called *reform schools*, which were founded to fight juvenile delinquency. The New York House of Refuge, which opened in 1825, is generally acknowledged to be the first of the early reformatories in the US. The number of reform schools in America grew from only three in the 1840s to over fifty in the 1870s (Schlossman 367). In the nineteenth century, the work required of reform school inmates was less demanding than that prescribed for adult prisoners. However, like older prisoners, juvenile delinquents were whipped or placed in solitary confinement for failing to conform to the daily regimen. At the beginning of the twentieth century, the number of American reformatories grew steadily, while the average length of stay declined from two years to one. The reform schools relied somewhat less on corporal punishments and paid more attention to monitoring the post-release experiences of inmates. Nevertheless, Schlossman points out that "these changes notwithstanding, to enter most reform schools in America [...] in the mid-twentieth century was to return to a remnant of the Dickensian era" (374).

The prison experience in 'new' prisons of the nineteenth and twentieth centuries primarily correlates with two important elements. On the one hand, the prisoner's body is subjected to the almost ineluctable gaze of the prison guard, who acquires external knowledge about him. On the other hand, the prison system normally attempts to gain access to the inmate's mind in order to transform him into a law-abiding citizen. Grass is certainly right in arguing that

> [...] the exercise of power in the Victorian prison had very little to do with surveillance. Rather, it had to with locking the self in solitude, inscribing guilt upon it, forcing it to account for its own disordered identity and guilty desire, and seizing the power to subject that self-account to the inventive power of the authorial other. (219)

However, it is worth noting that "the internal regimes of most modern prisons are remarkably deficient in 'moral tone' and rarely adopt any serious attempt to instil virtue or morality beyond the basic demands of obedience and discipline" (Garland 261). Indeed, most prisons of the twentieth century expose their inmates to monotonous routines and treat "prisoners primarily as bodies to be counted and objects to be administered" (ibid.). Since prisons are shrouded in secrecy and law-abiding citizens are excluded from any 'participatory' relation to punishment, prison narratives clearly serve as some sort of surrogate because they allow us to 'view' an alien world that we do not usually see. More specifically, prison films (and authorial prison novels) allow us to observe the bodies of prisoners from a third-person perspective, while first-person prison novels even allow us access to the minds of prisoners.

The Experience of Imprisonment

This section develops a list of crucial features of the prison experience in 'old' British debtors' prisons and 'new' prisons in Britain and America. Later sections will then address the question of how these features are narrated in novels and films.

The induction process is an important feature of the experience of imprisonment that seems to have undergone no fundamental alteration. For instance, Michael Ignatieff describes the reception of a convict at Pentonville Prison in the nineteenth-century as follows:

> On the day of his conviction, he [the convict, J.A.] was brought from the courtroom to the reception wards at Pentonville and made to strip naked. His clothes and possessions were taken from him, and the contents of his pockets [...] were emptied into an envelope. His street clothes were bundled together and sent to the ovens for fumigation. The naked convict was led into a wade-in bath and immersed in waist-high water smelling of carbolic acid. After drying himself, the convict marched to a desk behind which sat a prison officer with a large register before him. While this officer copied down the information, another officer inspected the prisoner's body for scars, deformities, tattoos, and other 'visible distinguishing marks.' [...] After his identity had been fixed in the state record system, the prisoner was led to the doctor for medical inspection.

> [...] Next, the prisoner's head was shaved and he was issued with his prison uniform. The final act in the ritual of initiation was the issue of his prison number. He was no longer George Withers, but HF 4736. (6–7)

Similarly, the criminologist Victoria R. DeRosia describes the induction process in an American prison of the twentieth century:

> You will be whisked away from court by cruiser or sheriff's car or DOCS bus on your first day as prisoner. You barely had time to say goodbye to your friends and relatives. On the van, you are shackled to each other, or to the van itself, while being glared at by time-hardened armed guards. As you pass through double rows of 12-foot, chain-link fence topped with the sharpest razor wire you have ever seen, you pull up to a mammoth brick and concrete edifice. The stark structure, where every window, what there are of them, is covered with bars, shows you one steel door into the place—all that stands between you and freedom. You enter like cattle and are counted and recounted several times. You feel as though you entered a foreign land, and all of a sudden, you know nothing. As your morning progresses you are shaved, photographed, given a hair cut, issued a number (which later, you learn, is the new you), a uniform, black shoes, some bedding, asked all kinds of questions, made to sign all sorts of forms, given a prison rulebook. In all likelihood, you will be strip-searched, or worse, and deloused. It is all so dehumanizing. You feel your identity slipping away—inmate #05701—you are in a shock, not yet having reached terrified. (17–18)

The purpose of the meticulous documentation in the course of this process has always been to provide the newcomers with an initial shock—even in early debtors' prisons. In the course of this process, the newcomers are transformed into numbers, files and statistics, and become the objects of individual descriptions and biographies.

Surveillance and the wish to inspire moral reform did not play any role in British debtors' prisons because the debtors were not proper felons. On the other hand, the near-continuous observation of the inmate's body and the attempt to transform the criminal into a law-abiding citizen became two of the most important features of the prison experience in the 'new' prisons in Britain and America.

Furthermore, while the inmates in debtors' prisons primarily indulged in idleness, games, gambling, and drunkenness, life in nineteenth and twentieth-century prisons was regulated by strict time-tables and routines. Historically speaking, the *form* of these daily routines, i.e., the grinding repetitions, has presumably always led to a sense of deadening sameness for the prisoners. However, in the course of time, the *content* of these rules and regulations changed fundamentally. The most important change from the nineteenth to the twentieth century was a move from forcing prisoners to undergo hard labor to a situation in which prisoners suffer from feelings of monotony and boredom.

In the 'old' British system, the prison staff had only some degree of control over the inmates and did not punish 'unruly' debtors. It was the 'birth' of the 'new' prison system which led to the use of corporal forms of punishment. In all nineteenth-century prisons, inmates were whipped or flogged if they did not conform to prison regulations. Even today, those who enter a prison enter a world of violence. In contemporary British and American prisons, outbreaks of physical violence between prison officers and inmates as well as between prisoners happen frequently.

In the nineteenth century, 'troublemakers' were either punished corporally or sent to dark solitary cells. At the beginning of the twentieth century, disobedient or violent prisoners were no longer whipped or flogged. Solitary confinement gradually became the most extreme punishment in prison. The so-called 'hole' was a dark and unventilated cell where 'troublemakers' were deprived of decent food, exercise and all human contact. In order to increase the prisoners' suffering, such cells had no mattress, no washbasin and no toilet. In the twentieth century, the use of dark dungeons as a form of punishment was gradually reduced. Today, prisoners who disturb the prison routine are still separated from the rest of the prison population and sent to solitary cells in the punishment block. A former inmate of Ohio State Penitentiary who was placed in solitary confinement for an inhumane length of time comments on the horror in the 'hole' as follows:

> I was recently released from solitary confinement after being held therein for thirty-seven months. The silence system was imposed on me and if I even whispered to the man in the next cell resulted in being beaten by the guards, sprayed with chemical mace, black jacked, stomped, and thrown into a strip cell naked to sleep on a concrete floor without bedding, covering, washbasin, or even a toilet [...] I know that thieves must be punished, and I don't justify stealing even though I am a thief myself. But now I don't think I will be a thief when I am released. No, I am not rehabilitated either. It is just that I no longer think of becoming wealthy or stealing. I now only think of killing—killing those who have beaten me and treated me as if I were a dog. (qtd. in Zimbardo "The Stanford" 40)

Moreover, the inmates of many nineteenth-century prisons were held in permanent solitary confinement, which contrasts with the relatively free association of prisoners in twentieth-century institutions. The current situation almost constitutes a return to eighteenth-century Britain, where the prisoners also associated freely with others and even had regular contact with the outside world. More specifically, they were usually joined by their families and surrounded by curious visitors.

One crucial problem in contemporary prisons is that weak and unpopular inmates face the danger of being beaten up or raped by their fellow inmates. Incidences of inmate-on-inmate violence and 'homosexual' rapes[19] are typical of twentieth-century prisons. Statistically, in contemporary prisons, violent outbreaks between inmates occur much more frequently than violence between prisoners and prison officers.[20] A rape is a particular type of prisoner-on-prisoner violence. Joanne Mariner's comprehensive study (2001) suggests that in American prisons of the twentieth century, male inmate-on-inmate sexual abuse is no aberrational occurrence but a deeply-rooted, systemic problem. For instance, in 1996, an inmate of an American prison sent the following letter to Human Rights Watch:

> When I first came to prison, I had no idea what to expect. Certainly none of this. I'm a tall white male, who unfortunately has a small amount of feminine characteristics. And very shy. These characteristics have got me raped so many times I have no more feelings physically. I have been raped by up to 5 black men and two white men at a time. I've had knifes [*sic*] at my head and throat. I had fought and been beat [*sic*] so hard that I didn't ever think I'd see straight again. One time when I refused to enter a cell, I was brutally attacked by staff and taken to segregation though I had only wanted to prevent the same and worse by not locking up with my cell mate. (Mariner xv)

By contrast, the situation in British prisons as well as custodial sexual misconduct against male prisoners appear to be largely under-researched.[21] It is worth noting that consensual practices of homoeroticism also exist in prison. Büssing points that people's fantasies about sex in prison "almost exclusively revolve around gang rape, sadism, and total degeneracy." She points out that "there is infinitely more to eroticism in jail than such manifestations of 'sledgehammer sex'" (14).

Finally, while in debtors' prisons, prisoners only occasionally suffered from lack of food, the food in most nineteenth-century prisons was hardly enough to keep the inmates alive. Debtors who could afford it were even allowed to buy food from outside, though usually, they cooked their food in the communal kitchen. The inmates of nineteenth-century prisons, on the other hand, were exposed to extremely meagre diets. Today, most institutions employ qualified food administrators. On the other hand, in *Going Up the River* (2001), Hallinan points out that in many American prisons, the food is bad-tasting low-calorie food and lacks vitamins so that one can only speak of a gradual improvement.

The following chart lists a number of important features of the experience of imprisonment in ‘old’ debtors’ prisons and ‘new’ prisons of the nineteenth and twentieth centuries:

‘old’ debtors’ prisons	**‘new’ 19th-century prisons**	**‘new’ 20th-century prisons**
no surveillance but free movement within prison	surveillance of the prisoner’s body	surveillance of the prisoner’s body
securing of debtors until debt is paid	attempt to inspire moral reform	attempt to inspire moral reform
induction process as initial shock	induction process as initial shock	induction process as initial shock
games, gambling and drunkenness	strictly regulated daily routines	strictly regulated daily routines
idleness and boredom	monotony of soul-breaking physical labor	lack of activity; monotony and boredom (of doing time)
limited control of prison officers, dissolute behavior and disorder	corporal punishments like whippings, floggings, etc.; use of the ‘hole’	fewer bodily punishments; occasional outbreaks of violence; use of the ‘hole’ as most extreme punishment
free association of prisoners, contact with family and visitors	permanent solitary confinement in the cell during the day or silent communal labor	free association of prisoners with the result of inmate-on-inmate violence; rapes and riots
richer people bought food outside; otherwise use of the kitchen	extremely bad food in small quantities (‘scientific starvation’)	slightly better food quality; frequently bad-tasting and high-calorie food (no vitamins)

ENDNOTES

1. John Howard's prison tour in the early 1770s revealed that 60 percent of all inmates were debtors. In 1842, the Marshalsea and the Fleet were abolished by Act of Parliament, and the Queen's Bench, renamed the Queen's Prison, became the sole place of confinement for debtors and bankrupts. See also Dixon (1985/1850). Imprisonment for debt was finally given up in 1869.
2. Up until the 1840s, convicts were transported to Botany Bay. The Bay was then replaced by Van Diemen's Land (now known as Tasmania), which was closed in 1853.
3. The enormous increase of convicted offenders is usually attributed to the end of the Napoleonic Wars in 1815 which left thousands of soldiers unemployed. In the aftermath of the Napoleonic Wars, the Quakers renewed the prison question. Like Howard and Hanway, they strongly believed in the power of faith to reform the convict.
4. As examples, Grass mentions the *Memoirs of Convicted Convicts* (1853) which were published by H.S. Joseph, the chaplain of Chester Castle Gaol, and the biography *The Prison Chaplain: A Memoir of the Reverend John Clay* (1861), which excerpts hundreds of pages of John Clay's notes from his conversations with individual inmates.
5. Under local government, between 1836 and the late 1860s, there had been a vigorous and effective system of prison inspections. In 1878, Du Cane slammed the doors against the magistrates and society at large: "Since 1878 the prison has become 'a silent world,' shrouded so far as the public is concerned in almost complete darkness" (Webb and Webb 235). It was only in the 1970s and 1980s that reasonable access to British prisons became again regularly available to journalists and investigators.
6. "The name [borstal, J.A.] came from the village in Kent where the scheme got its first full-scale trial" (McConville "Victorian" 158).
7. The Home Office Research Study *'Tell Them So They Listen': Messages from Young People in Custody* (2000) by Lyon et al. provides some insight into the experience of 'Youth Custody' from the perspective of the inmates.
8. Rotman points out that in the southern chain gangs, African Americans made up more than 75 percent of the inmates (176).

9. Ward claims that James A. Johnston, the first warden of Alcatraz, even "allowed for the confinement of particularly troublesome inmates in several cells located under the floor of the main cell-house—the so-called dungeon. Here inmates were locked up in alcoves behind a barred grille with only a pail for bodily functions. In some cases inmates were handcuffed to the grille door so that they had to remain standing during the workday hours" (Ward "Alcatraz" 85; see also Becker-Kavan 91). Warden Johnston himself says about these dungeons that in "the few instances when" he "did use them," the men had to be chained "to keep them from breaking out and running amuck" (253).
10. Morris argues that it is extremely difficult to account for this gross racial skewing. It might reflect racial prejudice on the part of the police, the prosecutors, the judges and juries with the consequence that African-American and Hispanic offenders are more likely to be arrested by the police and are more likely to be dealt with severely by the courts ("Contemporary" 241). Another reason might be that African-American and Hispanic offenders frequently lack money for their defence.
11. The inverted commas are used to stress that the perpetrators of rapes in prison typically view themselves as heterosexuals. In order to preserve a heterosexual identity while engaging in homosexual behavior, the aggressors 'feminize' their victims, placing men who play 'female' roles in submissive positions. From this perspective the crucial point is not that they are having sex with a man; "instead it is that they are the aggressor, as opposed to the victim—the person doing the penetration as opposed to the one being penetrated" (Mariner 70).
12. For instance, in 1996, there were approximately 29,000 inmates assaulted by other inmates and 70 were killed out of over 1.2 million persons incarcerated in American prisons (DeRosia 22).
13. For example, a fairly recent British study of inmate victimization by Ian O'Donnell and Kimmett Edgar (1998) makes no reference to 'homosexual' rapes at all.

Chapter Three

The Dark Dungeons in Charles Dickens' Novels and Their Film Adaptations

The Prison as All-Embracing Shadow in *Little Dorrit*

Prisons, Inmates, and the Prison Experience

The novel *Little Dorrit* presents us with two prison settings, namely a dungeon-like jail in Marseilles and the Marshalsea debtors' prison in London. From the novel's beginning on we are confronted with the 'lens' of an authorial narrator[1] which can bring details carefully into focus:

> Thirty years ago, Marseilles lay burning in the sun, one day. A blazing sun upon a fierce August day was no greater rarity in southern France then, than at any other time, before or since. Every thing in Marseilles, and about Marseilles, had stared at the fervid sky, and been stared at in return, until a staring habit had become universal there. Strangers were stared out of countenance by staring white houses, staring white walls,

> staring white streets, staring tracts of arid road, staring hills from which verdure was burnt away. The only things to be seen not fixedly staring and glaring were the vines drooping under their load of grapes. These did occasionally wink a little, as the hot air barely moved their faint leaves. [...] The universal stare made the eyes ache. [...] Everything that lived or grew, was oppressed by the glare; except the lizard, passing swiftly over rough stone walls, and the cicala, chirping by his dry hot chirp, like a rattle. The very dust was scorched brown, and something quivered in the atmosphere as if the air itself were panting. (15)

While the sun is looking down upon this scene, the people of Marseilles attempt to protect themselves by closing their "blinds, shutters, curtains, awnings [...] to keep out the stare" (16). Everybody tries to flee from the sunshine which kills and subjects people to its glare and gaze.

When we then move on to a description of the gloomy prison in Marseilles, we are not presented with an institution that is entirely different from the world outside. Rather, the tomb-like prison is even more life-denying than the scorching whiteness outside. It is said to be "so repulsive a place that even the obtrusive stare blinked at it, and left is to such refuse of reflected light as it could find for itself" (16). The narrator describes the prison, which houses the inmates Rigaud and Cavaletto, as follows: "Besides the two men, a notched and disfigured bench, immoveable from the wall with a draught-board rudely hacked upon it with a knife, a set of draughts, made of old buttons and soup-bones, a set of dominoes, two mats, and two or three wine bottles" (16). 'He' then points out that "that was all the chamber held, exclusive of rats and other unseen vermin, in addition to the seen vermin, the two men" (16).[2]

The classification of the two prisoners as vermin is interesting because we expect to be presented with two vicious criminals who clearly justify the existence of prisons. However, in the case of Cavaletto the narrator is completely mistaken. Cavaletto is only a harmless smuggler, and turns out to be one of the liveliest presences in this sombre novel. Later on, he is described as "a chirping, easy, hopeful little fellow" (295). Even in jail, he joyfully sings songs with the prison officer's daughter (21), whom one might see as an anticipation of Little Dorrit.[3] Nevertheless, the narrator at first continues to depict him as a wild animal. When Rigaud is led to his trial, Cavaletto jumps upon the ledge "like a lower animal—like some impatient ape, or roused bear of the smaller species" (27). For the narrator, the caged inmate then turns into a desperate gorilla:

> Excited into still greater resemblance to a caged wild animal by his anxiety to know more, the prisoner leaped nimbly down, ran round the chamber, leaped nimbly up again, clasped the grate and tried to shake it, leaped down and ran, leaped up and listened, and never rested until the noise, becoming more and more distant, had died away. (Ibid.)

While Cavaletto can hardly be classified as 'vermin,' the prisoner Rigaud remains entirely enigmatic. On the one hand, he claims to be a "gentleman" (22), while on the other hand, he tells Cavaletto that he killed a man, married his rich widow and then killed her (24–25). If this story is true, Rigaud might be classified as a monster and his existence may serve as an argument in favor of prisons. The situation in prison is bad—prison is like a tomb or hell[4]—but society needs prisons because of the irreclaimable depravity of criminals like Rigaud who suffers no remorse, guilt or fear for what he did. In the words of Trilling, Rigaud deprives us of the comfortable, philanthropic thought that prisons are nothing but instruments of injustice (56). The idea that prisons are a societal necessity is also expressed by the landlady of a lodge in Chalon. She points out

> [...] that there are people who have no human heart, and who must be crushed like savage beasts and cleared out of the way. They are few, I hope; but I have seen (in this world here where I find myself, and even at the little Break of Day) that there are such people. And I do not doubt that this man—whatever they call him, I forget his name [they are talking about Rigaud, J.A.]—is one of them. (131)

However, when Cavaletto and Rigaud meet again outside prison (134–38), we do not learn whether Rigaud, who hides his identity by calling himself Blandois and Lagnier, has actually committed any crime. Also, the question of how he managed to get out of prison remains unanswered. Maybe he was "deeply wronged" (136) and finally released; or he was guilty but managed to escape; or he was guilty but pronounced not guilty. Since we are not in a position to find out whether Rigaud is a real criminal, the landlady's statement could also be read as a critique of the ways in which law-abiding citizens classify other people as criminals. The assumption that Rigaud has "no human heart" seems to be based on prejudice rather than verifiable facts. The narrator's classification of the inmates as 'vermin' may also be a critical comment on the ways in which law-abiding citizens stigmatise prison inmates without knowing anything about them.

When the narrator turns to the Marshalsea debtors' prison, we learn that 'he' is rather critical of this institution. In an authorial aside, 'he' tells us that "it is gone now, and the world is none the worse without it" (68). We are then presented with a very detailed description of the Marshalsea which

> […] was an oblong pile of barrack building, partitioned into squalid houses standing back to back, so that there were no back rooms; environed by a narrow paved yard, hemmed in by high walls duly spiked at top. Itself a close and confined prison for debtors, it contained within it a much closer and more confined jail for smugglers. Offenders against the revenue laws, and defaulters to excise or customs, who had incurred fines which they were unable to pay, were supposed to be incarcerated behind an iron-plated door, closing up a second prison, consisting of a strong cell or two, and a blind alley some yard and a half wide, which formed the mysterious termination of the very limited skittle-ground in which the Marshalsea debtors bowled down their troubles. (68)

The prison is in a rotten state "because the time had rather outgrown the strong cells and the blind alley" (68). The imprisonment of debtors like William Dorrit and Arthur Clennam is represented as being unjust. Both are imprisoned for debt[5] under laws that are completely impolitic because imprisoned debtors are not in a position to earn any money to pay their debts. It is worth noting that "the inmates of the Marshalsea are there because they owe money they can't pay, not because they are guilty of murder, theft or grievous bodily harm" (Wall viii).

The novel's critical attitude toward the prison (and on society which punishes debtors too harshly) is intensified by the fact that most of the Marshalsea inmates are likeable characters. Amy Dorrit, who is not an actual inmate but lives in prison with her father, is an example of such a character. She may even constitute a symbol of hope because of her love for Arthur and her devotion to her father, whom she selflessly rescues from despair. The saint-like girl turns to her father's wasted heart "a fountain of love and fidelity that never [runs] dry or waned" (227). Moreover, most of the inmates of the Marshalsea suffer severely in prison. For instance, throughout the novel, the prisoners complain about the lack of air in the Marshalsea, which is presumably a psychological effect rather than a physical symptom. This hypothesis is corroborated by the depiction of the effects of imprisonment on Arthur Clennam:

> The sensation of being stifled, sometimes so overpowered him, that he would stand at the window holding his throat and gasping. At the same time, a longing for other air, and a yearning to be beyond the blind blank wall, made him feel as if he must go mad with the ardor of the desire. Many other prisoners had had the experience of this condition before him, and its violence and continuity had worn themselves out in their cases, as they did in his. Two nights and a day exhausted it. It came back by fits, but those grew fainter and returned at lengthening intervals. A desolate calm succeeded; and the middle of the week found him settled down in the despondency of low, slow fever. (721)

Arthur's suffering in prison is stressed in other ways, too. When Arthur arrives in prison, his identity is transformed, and he feels as though he were removed from his former life "into another stage of existence" (689). Furthermore, the structure of Arthur's memory sequences evokes the boring circularity of time in prison: "it was not remarkable that everything his memory turned upon should bring him round again to Little Dorrit" (689). On the other hand, Arthur also learns something in prison. The "unnatural peace" of "the dangerous resting-place [i.e., the Marshalsea, J.A.]" (689) may sometimes bring into focus the implications of our past actions, producing the 'right' perspective on our lives. The narrator tells us that "none of us clearly know to whom or to what we are indebted in this wise, until some marked stop in the whirling wheel of life brings the right perception with it" (689). Ironically, it is in prison that Arthur gains the 'right' perspective on Amy because the turnkey John Chivery tells him of Amy's love for him (698).

Other inmates suffer in prison as well. At one point, William Dorrit observes that new inmates cry when they have to leave their visitors, and we learn that he experiences his time in prison as a voyage on a ship: "[...] now he was like a passenger aboard ship in a long voyage, who has recovered from sea-sickness, and is impatient of that weakness in the fresher passengers taken aboard at the last port" (222). The point of this simile is to stress that the weeping newcomers are tossed on the waves of adversity just like new passengers become sea-sick because of tempests at sea, but after some time, they get used to it. In this case, the aspect of survival is mapped on from the source (voyage on a ship) to the target domain (prison).

On the other hand, even though Old Dorrit clearly suffers in prison—he is said to be "now boasting, now despairing" because he is "a captive with the jail-rot upon him" (227)—he simultaneously experiences the Marshalsea in terms of a place of "refuge" (74) that protects him from the world outside: "Crushed at first by his imprisonment, he had soon found a dull relief in it. He was under lock and key; but the lock and key that kept him in, kept numbers of his troubles out" (73). In contrast to his brother Frederick, who is lost in the "the labyrinthian world" (219) outside, William knows that he is "safe within the walls" (223). This safety is an ambivalent one because it also infantilizes the prisoner by making him powerless and dependent on the prison. Generally speaking, in *Little Dorrit*, metaphors of imprisonment serve to illustrate the inmates' suffering in prison.

We also learn that the prison determines the prisoners' mindsets. The novel's prisoners either get so used to the prison that they cannot live without it or they permanently try to conceal their 'deviant' prison identity. For example, Tip cannot cope with life outside prison, and returns to jail again and again. He begins to depend on the prison:

> Wherever he went, this foredoomed Tip appeared to take the prison walls with him, and to set them up in such trade or calling; and to prowl about within their narrow limits in the old-slip-shod, purposeless, down-at-heel way; until the real immoveable Marshalsea walls asserted their fascination over him, and brought him back. (84)

Similarly, when Little Dorrit is locked out of the Marshalsea, "she is locked out of her home, and so spends the night more aware than usual of the fact that she belongs nowhere else" (Cockshut 41). Once Amy is released, she begins to miss the Marshalsea and longs for its security and protection. And later on, when she visits Arthur in prison, the prison even evokes the association with a womb: "the Marshalsea walls, during a portion of every day, again embraced her in their shadows as their child [...]" (766). Obviously, Little Dorrit wishes to see her lover in prison but her returning to prison may at the same time be an expression of her longing for security, stability or perhaps even a nurturing mother (Duncan 28–29).[6]

The prison also influences the psychological states and behavior of its inmates in so far as they continuously try to conceal their prison identity. In other words, the prisoners depend upon the prison and simultaneously attempt to deny that this is the case. When the Dorrits are still incarcerated, Amy gradually realizes that it is not 'normal' to live in prison and attempts to hide the prison taint from others. The narrator informs us that it is hard to tell "at what period of her early life, the little creature began to perceive that it was not the habit of all the world to live locked up in narrow yards surrounded by high walls with spikes at the top" (78). When Little Dorrit begins to work for Mrs. Clennam as a seamstress, she has already learned that it is not 'normal' to live in prison. She finds it "necessary to conceal where she lived, and to come and go as secretly as she could, between the free city and the iron gates, outside of which she had never slept in her life" (86). Once the Dorrits have been released from prison, they all wish to erase their former prison identities. Edward tells his sister, whom he loves "with that Marshalsea taint upon his love" (230): "You needn't call me Tip, Amy child, [...] because that's an old habit, and one you may as well lay aside" (437). Also, upon release, William Dorrit orders "that his old clothes should be taken from him and burned" (408) in order to destroy the prison taint, which will of course not work out. When the Dorrits travel over the Alps to Venice and Rome, Old Dorrit urges his children to set the prison aside—as he thinks he is successful in doing:

> If *I* can put that aside, if *I* can eradicate the marks of what I have endured, and can emerge before the world a—ha—gentleman unspoiled, unspotted—it is a great deal to expect—that my children should—hum—do the same, and sweep that accursed experience off the face of the earth. [...] I am hurt that she [Amy Dorrit, J.A.] should—ha—systematically reproduce what the rest of us blot out; and seem—hum—I had almost said positively anxious to announce to wealthy and distinguished society, that she was born and bred in—ha hum—a place that I, myself, decline to name. But there is no inconsistency—ha—not the least in my feeling hurt, and yet complaining principally for your sake, Amy. (461–62)

The novel also presents us with numerous prison-like settings so that the prison metonymically transcends its borders and begins to 'infect' the world outside prison. For instance, at the beginning of the novel, we are confronted with the prison-like quarantine barracks where we get to know Tattycoram and Miss Wade, who both suffer from neurotic repression and might be classified as prisoners of their own minds. The conversation we witness at the quarantine barracks is also dominated by the prison. When Mr. Meagles argues that "a prisoner begins to relent towards his prison, after he is let out" (34), Miss Wade expresses her anger about prisons as follows: "If I had been shut up in any place to pine and suffer, I should always hate that place and wish to burn it down, or raze it to the ground. I know no more" (35). Meagles also draws a nice parallel between other people's suspicions that he might have the plague and the prison taint: "I have had the plague continually, ever since I have been here. [...] I came here as well as ever I was in my life; but to suspect me of the plague is to give me the plague. And I have had it—and I have got it" (29).[7] Finally, the autumnal atmosphere at the Swiss Alps of the Great Saint Bernard is also reminiscent of a prison or tomb because the scene is dominated by "barrenness and desolation" while "blackened skeleton arms of wood" beckon the travellers to the convent (418). Inside the convent, the travellers are presented with "gloomy vaulted rooms" (419) and the convent's "bare white walls" are "broken by an iron gate" so that Amy Dorrit thinks that "the place [is] something like a prison" and the rooms appear to be "cell[s]" (428; 432).

Little Dorrit presents us with a very complex view on prisons. Most importantly, the novel critiques the prison by representing certain types of imprisonment in the Marshalsea debtors' prison (e.g., the incarceration of William Dorrit and Arthur Clennam) as being grossly unjust. Second, we are confronted with numerous settings that resemble the prison so that we get a sense that the prison is everywhere. The novel's critique of the prison is intensified by showing that the prison determines the inmates' psychology and mindset. Many prisoners depend upon the static world of the prison or try to conceal their prison identity (or both at the same time). Also, we are confronted with numerous metaphors of imprisonment that express the inmates' suffering in prison. Finally, *Little Dorrit* perhaps also implies that society needs prisons because evil criminals like Rigaud exist. However, since we never learn whether he is an actual criminal, it is more likely that the novel hints at caution with regard to the identification of criminals because our judgments may be based on nothing but prejudice.

Christine Edzard's 1987 film version of *Little Dorrit* consists of two parts (*Nobody's Fault* and *Little Dorrit's Story*). Part One presents us with the story and 'point of view' of Arthur Clennam (Derek Jacobi), who feels disoriented in a maze-like and materialistic

London. Part Two concentrates on Amy Dorrit's (Sarah Pickering) story and 'point of view,' and investigates Amy's reactions to the discovery of her father's (Alec Guinness) riches and of Clennam's descent into poverty and imprisonment. 'Point of view' does here not mean that we are presented with POV-shots only. Rather, the camera undermines the distinction between internal and external focalization[8] so that we see Amy and Arthur (from an external perspective) while the images of Part One clearly imitate Arthur's perception, and the images of Part Two reproduce Amy's world view. Some critics argue that the film adaptation is a complete failure (Smith *Dickens* 146), while others consider it to be an outstanding artistic achievement (March; Giddings et al. 82). I would like to place myself in between these two critical camps. The adaptation is interesting from a film-theoretical perspective but from the point of view of entertainment, it is a failure. The repetition of moments from Part One as Amy sees them becomes quite wearisome after some time.

Edzard's film adaptation concentrates on the Marshalsea and its inmates. Pointer argues that "the dank, cramped misery of the Marshalsea prison, with its dispiriting squalor, [is] presented in claustrophobic detail" (107). The film omits the Marseilles jail, Rigaud, Cavaletto, the Marseilles jailer's daughter, Miss Wade, Tattycoram, the quarantine barracks, and the convent of the Great Saint Bernard. Edzard has decided to focus on the mental confinement of Amy and Arthur on the one hand, and the destructive and imprisoning power of money on the other.

How is the experience of imprisonment represented in the film? In *Nobody's Fault*, which concentrates on Arthur's perspective, Arthur's suffering in the debtors' prison is accentuated by a variety of visual details. In other words, his internal state is alluded to by means of external features. First of all, claustrophobia dominates the scene in which he enters his room at the Marshalsea. The ceiling bears down upon Arthur as if to crush him. Additionally, we see sweat on his pale face. Longing for air, Arthur opens the window and walks around his room in circles, which evokes the circularity of time in prison. His state of confusion is also conveyed through an imagined and surreal scene of Pancks (Roshan Seth) in a growing cloud of smoke which is followed by a montage sequence of Arthur's past. Later on, when Arthur views the bunch of flowers on his table and his visitor Little Dorrit behind, we are not sure whether the close-up of Amy's face is an illusion or part of the film's primary reality.

The film also uses cinematic metaphors to convey the suffering in prison. For example, at the end of *Nobody's Fault*, the juxtaposition of the sick inmate Arthur with a withered pot plant on his windowsill allows us to see him *as* a withering plant. This juxtaposition links the prison experience to some kind of (perhaps spiritual) death, and, by extension, codes the prison as a tomb. Also, at the beginning of *Little Dorrit's Story*, the Marshalsea is juxtaposed with close-ups of flies that fall into a water pot where they die. These close-ups might be a comment on the squalor of prison, while at the same time, the juxtaposition of the prisoners with flies defines the inmates *as* insignificant insects. Later on, one of the Collegians tells Arthur: "We got to the bottom and we can't fall. And what have we found? Peace." In this case, the interplay between the auditory and the visual channel codes the Marshalsea *as* a peaceful and sheltered place of refuge.

At first glance, the film suggests that Amy and Arthur remain relatively untouched by their surroundings in gerenal and the bleakness of the Marshalsea in particular. It is also worth noting that their lack of egotism and greed distances them from all the other characters in the film. However, upon closer inspection, one realizes that Amy and Arthur are not free from the taint of the prison because they are prisoners of their own minds. More specifically, the two-partite film adaptation suggests a prison of solipsism, of being trapped in one's perception. Both *Nobody's Fault* and *Little Dorrit's Story* ambivalently waver between internal and external focalization. In other words, the camera perspective and the *mise-en-scène* suggest that external knowledge is always tainted by internal (or subjective) assumptions so that every 'reading' of the world becomes a 'misreading.' The film's camera consistently 'misrepresents' the world because the 'external' camera perspective is tainted by Amy's and Arthur's world view. This technique may perhaps be seen as the cinematic version of free indirect discourse[9] because we see things from a third-person perspective while the images we are confronted with stay very close to Amy's or Arthur's perception of the world. For instance, the Marshalsea room in *Little Dorrit's Story* is bigger and brighter than the room we see in *Nobody's Fault*. According to March, "the walls of the set have been bodily moved out by several feet; the set has been repainted, redressed in slightly brighter colors; potted plants blossom [...]; Dorrit's bare chair grows a cover, and his dressing gown sprouts tendrils of embroidery" (255). And these two perspectives on the Marshalsea and its 'Father' are supposed to reflect Arthur's and Amy's perception. While Arthur has a pessimistic world view and feels oppressed in the room, Amy has become accustomed to the prison and has a more optimistic world view. For me, this almost subliminal change of the film set suggests that Amy is mentally restricted or confined. More specifically, this change implies a critique of her idealized view of her pompous and abusive father.[10]

Amy is metaphorically imprisoned by her naive and one-sided world view. She only perceives what she wishes to perceive and is unaware of the fact that her father exploits her economically and psychologically. Little Dorrit also idealizes Arthur, who is a child-cum-father like her own father. For instance, when she visits him in his room with Maggy (Pauline Quirke), Amy perceives a large room illuminated by comfortable firelight. By contrast, in Part One, we see Arthur in a much smaller room, holding a newspaper over the fire to make it draw. Throughout the film adaptation, Amy's mental confinement is suggested by her 'tunnel-vision' bonnet and further visual clues of imprisonment. We are repeatedly presented with shots of her being framed by windows (in which she sits sewing), by doorways, or by the bars of the Marshalsea. The juxtaposition of Amy with metonyms of the prison (like bars) also alludes to her metaphorical imprisonment. At the beginning of *Little Dorrit's Story*, the turnkey Bob (Howard Goorney) takes the child Amy (Susan Tanner) outside to show her the fields. When she asks him, "Was father ever here?," her face is covered by a bunch of flowers which effectively reworks the bars of the prison, thus alluding to her mental confinement. Even at this early stage, she cares more about her father and not so much about herself.

While Little Dorrit is imprisoned by her naive and idealized vision, the melancholy Arthur is trapped by his self-centeredness. To begin with, he does not care about the egotistical materialism that surrounds him. For example, in the "Slapbang Restaurant" scene, the rent-collector Pancks gets more and more angry about the materialist Casby and asks Arthur, "How can I squeeze them [the inhabitants of the Bleeding Heart Yard, J.A.], Mr. Clennam, if they're dry? They haven't got any money!" Arthur is not interested in Casby's money-mania, Pancks' moral problems, or the poverty of the Yard inhabitants and prefers to slip into a daydream of Little Dorrit. Arthur also appears to be rather oblivious to Amy's feelings. For example, in Part Two, we see Little Dorrit turn white when Arthur tells her that he used to be in love with the beautiful Minnie Meagles (Sophie Ward). By contrast, in Part One, Arthur is so ignorant of Amy's emotional reaction that we do not learn how she reacts to the news at all. Similarly, in one scene of Part Two, Little Dorrit is ashamed of the shabbiness of her shoes and the camera focuses on them, while in Part One, Arthur's gaze is absorbed by Amy's face, and the outworn shoes are not shown on the screen. This omission also suggests that he does not see her as she is but rather as he wishes to see her.

The general impression of mental confinement is intensified by the film adaptation's static framing. As Smith (*Dickens* 146–47) has shown, the camera remains in a fixed position throughout the two parts of the film adaptation, and frames the 'action' in a persistent medium shot that is varied only by modest panning movements and occasional close-ups. For me, the framing is a stylistic embodiment of the film's imprisoning world which unfortunately also correlates with a rather boring viewing experience.

The Prison as World and Forms of Metaphorical Imprisonment

In this section, I comment on the ways in which *Little Dorrit* and its film adaptation represent the relationship between the prison and the world outside. The novel draws a homological structure between prison and society that gradually turns into a critique of society, and defines society as a prison. Like all debtors' prisons, the Marshalsea contains a wide variety of inmates who associate freely and indulge in gambling and drinking. The prison population, which consists of a heterogeneous crowd of inmates, represents a cross-section of society and contains various ranks or classes: "landlord, waiter, barmaid, potboy" (95), and at one point even a "dancing-master" (81). Also, when the Dorrits leave the prison, the prison yard is full of "the usual chorus of people proper to such a place" (411).[11]

Like society, the debtors' prison consists of an 'aristocratic side' and a 'poor side.' While William Dorrit receives tips inside prison, crooks like Merdle and Casby ruin other people's lives outside prison by taking away their money. From this perspective, the Marshalsea seems like society in a reduced form, "a chimera of a class system contingent on what the odd shilling will buy: warmth, food, and even space" (Philpotts 144). Furthermore, in order to uphold his pride, William Dorrit exploits his daughter, whose work sustains her family economically. It is worth noting that Amy's selflessness borders on self-denial. She is unable to eat in the knowledge of her father's unhappiness and masks her own emotions for the sake of Old Dorrit. William Dorrit's exploitation of his daughter is clearly a private variety of the public morality that governs the novel's society: the society in *Little Dorrit* is dominated by criminals like Merdle or the shoals of Barnacles who run the Circumlocution Office and hinder all individual invention on the basis of the philosophy of How Not To Do It. The novel thus argues that people's manners and moral values are the same inside and outside prison.

The description of prison in terms of society gradually develops into an imputation of corruption to society, and begins to describe society as a prison, i.e., a society of criminals. The novel represents various domains in the world outside prison in terms of imprisonment. *Little Dorrit* confronts us with various prison metaphors which highlight that even in the 'free' world, people may be confined, restrained or metaphorically imprisoned. For instance, when Arthur sits in a coffee-house on Ludgate Hill, he speculates how the disembodied spirits of the former inhabitants of the surrounding houses "must pity themselves for their old places of imprisonment" (43). Similarly, at one point, Gowan states that his mother lives "down in that dreary red-brick dungeon at Hampton Court" (304). The "dull and dark" (64) Clennam house is repeatedly described as a prison or tomb as well.[12] In her house, Mrs. Clennam lies on a "black bier-like sofa, propped up by her black angular bolster that was like the headsman's block" (729), dressed in perpetual widow's black "as if attired for execution" (345). For her, time seems to have come to rest (as in prison). Memories of the world outside have become "controllable pictures" that deny "the rush of reality" (751). Her harsh Calvinism correlates with an all-seeing, powerful, and vindictive God who already in this world imprisons people through anticipatory punishment. Mrs. Clennam lives in a state of voluntary self-imprisonment, punishing herself and everyone else for some guilt of which her son cannot discover the true nature. Arthur speculates that her imprisoning illness is the price she pays for the guilty gratification of keeping the Dorrits in prison:

> A swift thought shot into his [Arthur's, J.A.] mind. In that long imprisonment here, and in her long confinement in her room, did his mother find a balance to be struck? I admit that I was accessory to that man's captivity. I have suffered for it in kind. He [William Dorrit, J.A.] has decayed in his prison; I in mine. I have paid the penalty. [...] When he [Arthur, J.A.] awoke, and sprang up causelessly frightened, the words were in his ears, as if her voice had slowly spoken them at his pillow, to break his rest: 'He withers away in his prison; I wither away in mine; inexorable justice is done; what do I owe on this score.' (96)

Miss Wade lives in a similar type of voluntary self-imprisonment. She is a frustrated, passionate, violent and potentially lesbian orphan who has withdrawn from society. Her house in Calais is reminiscent of a prison or tomb, too. Miss Wade lives in "a dead sort of house, with a dead wall over the way and a dead gateway at the side" (627). Also, Miss Wade is fiercely protective of Tattycoram, whom she persuades to run away from the Meagles family. The relationship between Miss Wade and Tattycoram is in fact reminiscent of the relationship between guards and inmates in prison. At one point, Tattycoram accuses Miss Wade of imprisoning her:

> And because I have nobody but you to look to, you think you are to make me do, or not do, everything you please, and are to put any affront upon me. You are as bad as they [the Meagleses, J.A.] were, every bit. But I will not be quite tamed and made submissive. (634)

The various prison-like settings, prison metaphors, and metaphorically imprisoned characters in the novel undermine the distinction between the prison and the 'free' world. In *Little Dorrit*, people suffer everywhere, i.e., both inside and outside prison.

Let me turn to the 'prison-as-world' simile and prison metaphors in the film. The social criticism of the novel is sucessfully reproduced and perhaps even intensified in Edzard's film adaptation. In the film, society's egotistical materialism is shown to imprison people inside and outside prison. The two-part film version focuses on the destructive power of money and its corrupting (or imprisoning) effects on the personality. The film adaptation thus makes a stronger statement against society's materialism than the novel. It is not only the obstructive bureaucracy of the Circumlocution Office which is to be blamed for the misery of the characters in the filmic world but also, and perhaps more importantly, society's egotistical materialism.

First of all, the recurring sound of clinking coins, which is reminiscent of clinking chains in prison, defines London as a materialist city and, by extension, as a prison. The recurring sound of buzzing flies additionally codes the prison-like materialist city as a cadaver or tomb.[13] The interplay between the visual and the auditory channel allows us to see London as a materialist prison or tomb. The target domain (London) is present visually, while the source domains (materialism, prison, and death) are substituted by sound. The film adaptation also critiques society's materialism in a dialogue Dickens never wrote. Toward the end of Part Two, Arthur argues that financial disasters like the Merdle crash are "nobody's fault,"[14] which is his standard response to almost every problem or conflict. In contrast to Arthur, Little Dorrit puts the blame on society and almost urges political activism. She argues that financial crashes, which lead to poverty and imprisonment, are "everybody's fault. Everyone who was at Mr. Merdle's feast was a sharer of the plunder, everybody there assented, accepted and approved." Also, after a near-fatal accident at his factory in Part One, Arthur says that "it's nobody's fault, and no one can be blamed for it." By contrast, the inventor Daniel Doyce (Edward Burnham) detects a mistake in the construction of his machines and argues that "the belts are to be blamed." One might extend this statement and read it as a critique of society's machinery, i.e., the general set-up of a materialist society which is to be blamed for the destruction of its citizens. Hence, the title *Nobody's Fault* may be read as an ironic comment on Arthur's misguided perception of the evil materialism that surrounds him.

Edzard's film adaptation stresses the corrupting power of money in other ways, too. In the novel, Arthur is released from the Marshalsea due to the generosity of his engineering partner, Doyce. In the film version, on the other hand, Doyce dies before Arthur's speculation which ruins the factory. Instead, Arthur's debts are paid off with money that had been sent to his real mother as remittances from his father and intercepted by Mrs. Clennam (Joan Greenwood) to provide credit for the Clennam business. The obvious parallel with the Merdle swindle suggests that money is always fraudulent. Edzard here sharpens Dickens' point that wealth can corrupt one's personality. And the fact that Mrs. Clennam is a prisoner of her own mind is visually suggested by the confining imagery and the tomb-like darkness of her 'home.' Whenever the Clennam house appears on the screen, it is always first seen through the bars of its wrought iron gate, a metonym of the Marshalsea that visually codes the house as a prison. Furthermore, Mrs. Clennam's psychological state, which correlates with her fierce religion, is suggested by her tense facial expression as well as the sound of the monstrous dusty bible thudding on her lap. Once again, the themes of money, death, and imprisonment are combined in a fascinating manner.

It is also worth noting that in the film version, William Dorrit's breakdown occurs in a different context, namely at his daughter Fanny's (Amelda Brown) wedding-feast (rather than abroad and several weeks later). Also, we see agonizing shots of Old Dorrit slowly dying on the screen. That is to say, scenes that stress Fanny's burning desire to be part of society's *crème de la crème*[15] are juxtaposed with William Dorrit's relapse into his role as the 'Father' of the Marshalsea and his subsequent on-screen death. The juxtaposition of scenes that deal with materialism, imprisonment, and death, once again evokes the imprisoning and killing potential of wealth. The collapse is successfully enacted by Alec Guinness and carefully built up: before Old Dorrit's speech, we are presented with an extraordinary orchestration of surreal conversation (which we can hardly understand), weird looks, POV-cum-low-angle shots from Amy's perspective,[16] and peculiarly choreographed movements (Sinyard "Dickensian" 111).

Moreover, the film version repeatedly confronts us with posters that advertise a popular Bulwer-Lytton drama called "MONEY!." These posters are notably placed on the wall outside the Marshalsea gate, i.e., on the wall that separates the prison from the outside world. They suggest a link between the inside and the outside that correlates with money. For me, the major function of the prison in the film adaptation is to show how the envious pride and egotistical materialism of the outside world are reproduced within the walls of the Marshalsea. Also, since the novel's dark and malodorous nightmare city was sanitized and cleaned of most types of poverty in the film (apart from the Bleeding Heart Yard where Mrs. Plornish [Ruth Mitchell] puts her baby into a chest of drawers), it is primarily the institution of the debtors' prison which illustrates that extreme poverty can be damaging on the personality as well.

A connection between the prison and the world outside is also suggested by the fact that we are presented with the same variety of costumes and top hats on the crowded streets of London as we are inside the debtors' prison—the prisoners' costumes being slightly more shabby. Additionally, the film presents the prison as being like society by paralleling shots of the collegians in prison smoking, drinking, and playing cards with shots of Doyce, Arthur and Meagles (Roger Hammond), drinking and playing cards in Meagles' house. The film moreover suggests a link between the morality inside and outside prison through the visual similarity between William Dorrit and the snobbish Casby (Bill Fraser). While Casby continually urges Pancks to squeeze the poor inhabitants of the Bleeding Heart Yard—he repeatedly tells him that he is "paid to squeeze and must squeeze to pay" —, Old Dorrit receives tips inside prison, which are accentuated by the loud 'chink-chink-chink' of coins.

The Prison and the Novel's Narrative Structure

Let me turn to the novel's narrative structure and its relation to the prison as well as to prison novels and films of the twentieth century. *Little Dorrit* is an authorial novel and critics have traditionally seen a close connection between this type of narration and Bentham's *Panopticon*. More specifically, authorial narration was considered to be prison-bound because the position of the authorial narrator allegedly reproduces the position of the guard in Bentham's central watchtower. For example, Mark Seltzer thinks that the 'omniscient' narrator is an authoritarian guard-like tyrant and argues that

> [...] the most powerful tactic of supervision achieved by the traditional realist novel inheres in its dominant technique of narration—the style of 'omniscient narration' that grants the narrative voice an unlimited authority over the novel's 'world,' a world thoroughly known and thoroughly mastered by the panoptic 'eye' of the narration. (*Henry James* 54)

Similarly, D.A. Miller describes the Balzacian narrator's "infallible supervision" as follows:

> [...] this panoptic vision constitutes its own immunity from being seen in turn. [...] We are always situated inside the narrator's viewpoint, and even to speak of a 'narrator' at all

> is to misunderstand a technique that, never identified with a *person*, institutes a faceless and multilateral regard. (24)

Later on in *The Novel and the Police*, Miller extends his argument to writers like Flaubert, George Eliot, Trollope, and Zola. More specifically, he argues that their 'omniscient' narrators also correlate with a "faceless gaze" and police the worlds of their narratives by means of "panoptical narration" (ibid.). *Little Dorrit* clearly falsifies this argument about the link between authorial narration and the *Panopticon* or the prison in general because in this case, we are presented with an authorial narrator who is extremely critical of the prison.[17]

McKnight identifies a parallel between the sun's obtrusiveness and the narrator's perpetual 'gaze' at the beginning of *Little Dorrit* (111). She seems to follow the critical impetus mentioned above because she argues that this parallel implies the Panoptical dimensions of *Little Dorrit*'s world. This does not really make sense either because the *Panopticon* is nowhere present in the novel. The jail in Marseilles and the Marshalsea are not similar to Bentham's design. Rather, they are dark and filthy 'old' prisons in which surveillance does not play any role at all.[18] Also, unlike the Benthamite observer, the narrator of *Little Dorrit* does not always allow us to properly 'look' into the cells of the prison which are frequently shrouded by shadows. For instance, we learn that usually "the morning light was in no hurry to climb the prison wall [of the Marshalsea, J.A.] and look in at the snuggery windows" (97). Similarly, throughout the novel, the narrator is in no hurry to allow us to look into the novel's prisons.

Sean Grass makes a similar observation and even goes one step further by arguing that *Little Dorrit* "illustrates the failure of omniscience to account for the fundamental meanings of the cell" (118), i.e., the prisoners' private selves.[19] Grass conflates the sun's staring with the narrator's alleged 'gaze,' which is a fundamental mistake in narratological terms,[20] and argues that since the novel's prisoners frequently stand in the shadows, the private meanings of the cell also remain "hidden from the narrative stare" (120). As I have shown, this is not true either because the narrator does inform us about the internal states of

Tip, Amy, William Dorrit, and Arthur and uses metaphors of imprisonment to demonstrate how these prisoners experience the prison. Grass simply ignores such passages in order to demonstrate the alleged "failure of omniscience" (118) to narrate the prison. On the other hand, it is true that (like the camera in film) the authorial narrator in *Little Dorrit* has a tendency to concentrate on external details to visualize the inmates' internal states.

More specifically, in the first part of the novel ("Poverty"), the narrator simulates the inmates' interiority through external details (like their behavior or bodily position) and thus anticipates prison films, while in the second part ("Riches"), 'he' additionally allows them to deliver their own first-person narratives, thus foreshadowing the representation of internal states in prison novels of the twentieth century. But in contrast to Grass, I do not think that the shadows in the novel's prisons prevent the authorial narrator from presenting us with the prisoners' internal states. Grass persistently plays down the role of the authorial narrator and seems to believe that the novel's shadows have power over 'him' because they allegedly "baffle [...] the omniscient stare" (108). It is rather the case that the narrator has power over these shadows, and arranges them for us. The novel's shadows serve as 'visual' comments on the idea of a prison 'taint,' and as such anticipate the cinematic attempt to visualize internal states (like mental confinement) through settings or the *mise-en-scène* (like the shadows of bars on an actor's face). The authorial narrator does not fail to narrate the prison. Rather, 'he' concentrates on the visualization of interiority through external details, and in doing so, foreshadows prison films of the twentieth century. And in the novel's second part, the narrator allows the novel's prisoners to narrate their own first-person stories, thus pointing toward the many first-person prison novels of the twentieth century.

Grass draws a rather simplistic link between the prison and first-person narration. For him, the connection correlates with "the prison's power to *invent* the self, in a first-person account of crime and punishment that the prison demanded and controlled." He thus argues that "first-person narration, more than surveillance, is the means by which the novel reflects the prison's power" (220). In what follows, I provide close readings of the embedded first-person accounts in *Little Dorrit* to demonstrate that they are not per se prison-bound. Rather, they enable their narrators to express their feelings about the prison and simultaneously shed a critical light on the novel's various prisons.

In "Riches," the question of whether "a prisoner [can] forgive [...] his prison" (35) becomes more and more important, and the authorial narrator turns to embedded[21] first-person accounts that reveal some of the secrets of the novel's prisons. These narratives draw a rather bleak image. They suggest that, albeit for different reasons, all of the novel's first-person narrators depend on the prison and cannot live without it. To put this slightly differently, these narratives suggest that even such confessional narration will never free the prisoners (or former prisoners) from the prison they have internalized.

For example, the accounts of Amy and William Dorrit suggest that the prison creates split personalities who continuously oscillate between a hopeless self (that continues to depend upon the prison) and a hopeful self (that wants to overcome the prison). Amy's letter to Arthur allows her to explain the psychological wounds inflicted by the Marshalsea from an inside perspective. When Amy realizes that in contrast to Fanny, she does not manage to adapt to her father's 'new' fortunes, the letter continues: "I sometimes almost despair of ever being able to do so. [...] As soon as I begin to plan, and think, and try, all my planning, thinking, and trying go in old directions" (452). Later on, Amy tells Arthur about her split personality and states: "I am [...] not familiar enough with myself" (453). The prison continues to lurk within her. The Marshalsea has created two versions of Amy, and she does not manage to reconcile her two selves because she cannot adapt to the habits in the world outside.

We are presented with another embedded first-person account when William Dorrit relapses into his role as the 'Father of the Marshalsea' at a fashionable High Society dinner organized by the Merdles in Rome:

> Ladies and gentlemen, the duty—ha—devolves upon me of—hum—welcoming you to the Marshalsea. Welcome to the Marshalsea! The space is—ha—limited—limited—the parade might be wider; but you will find it apparently grow larger after a time—a time, ladies and gentlemen—and the air is, all things considered, very good [...]. Those who are habituated to the—ha—Marshalsea, are pleased to call me its father. I am accustomed to be complimented by strangers as the—ha—Father of the Marshalsea. Certainly, if years of residence may establish a claim to so—ha—honorable a title, I may accept the—hum—conferred distinction. My child, ladies and gentlemen. My daughter. Born here! [...] Bred here. Ladies and gentlemen, my daughter. Child of an unfortunate father, but—ha—always a gentleman. Poor, no doubt, but—hum—proud. (621)

This first-person account also demonstrates what the prison may do to its inmates. Psychologically speaking, William Dorrit is doomed to remain tied to the prison even though he has been released. Old Dorrit does not manage to reconcile his prison self and his hopeful self, and at this stage, slips back into his former prison identity.

Miss Wade's narrative of self-observation (635–43), which encapsulates the novel's preoccupation with neurotic repression, is another telling first-person account. Miss Wade's story suggests that the torturous and frustrating human relationships she experienced have turned her into a violent and hateful human being. She describes her development as follows:

> I have the misfortune of not being a fool. From a very early age I have detected what those about me thought they hid from me. If I could have been habitually imposed upon, instead of habitually discerning the truth, I might have lived as smoothly as most fools do. (635)

Miss Wade suspects everybody of lying to her and thinks that she has to protect herself by wielding power over other people. She even uses the disciplinary techniques of observation and domination to gain power over Tattycoram. For instance, when Miss Wade thinks that Tattycoram is again interested in the Meagleses (only because she looked in at the garden gate of their cottage), she insults her: "You are not worth the confidence I placed in you. You are not worth the favor I have shown you. You are no higher than a spaniel, and had better go back to the people who did worse than whip you" (633–34). Miss Wade seems to depend on the power she exercises over her 'prisoner' Tattycoram because for her, this guard-like position correlates with security and stability. From this perspective, Miss Wade clearly depends on the prison as well.

Tattycoram's account corroborates that Miss Wade is a power-driven control freak. Tattycoram puts it as follows: "[Miss Wade] has made me her dependant. And I know I am so; and I know she is overjoyed when she can bring it to my mind" (634). Interestingly, Tattycoram's first-person narrative additionally illustrates that she depends on the prison, too. Toward the end of the novel, and after having escaped Miss Wade's 'prison,' Tattycoram wishes to return to the 'prison' of the Meagleses. She explains her actions as follows:

> I am bad enough, but not as bad as I was indeed. I have had Miss Wade before me all this time, as if it was my own self grown ripe—turning everything the wrong way, and twisting all good into evil. I have had her before me all this time, finding no pleasure in anything but keeping me as miserable, suspicious, and tormenting as herself. (773)

Occasionally, the part of Tattycoram that wishes to overcome the prison dominates her behavior. In such instances, she realizes that she is imprisoned by other people and attempts to free herself. However, Tattycoram is ultimately so prison-bound that she ends up in prison again and again. In other words, she merely moves to and fro between Miss Wade's 'prison' and the 'prison' of the Meagleses. Perhaps she does so because for her, the state in which somebody wields power over her correlates with security and stability.

Finally, there is Mrs. Clennam's voluntary self-imprisonment. When Rigaud threatens to tell her story, she decides to inform us about her imprisonment in her room:

> I will tell it with my own lips, and will express myself throughout it. What! Have I suffered nothing in this room, no deprivation, no imprisonment, that I should condescend at last to contemplate myself in such a glass as *that*! (739)[22]

The story of Mrs. Clennam's imprisonment is a story laden with guilt and strange motives. Mrs. Clennam forced her husband to give her his son Arthur, whose mother was a poor singer he had truly loved. Mrs. Clennam then constructed a type of educational prison around Arthur and decided that he should work out his release in bondage and hardship. Her husband's uncle had left one thousand guineas to the youngest daughter Frederick Dorrit might have at the age of fifty, or his brother's youngest daughter, on her coming of age. Since Frederick was unmarried and childless, Amy Dorrit should have received the money which would have saved her and her family from incarceration in the Marshalsea. However, Mrs. Clennam withheld the money and is thus responsible for the fate of the Dorrits. Mrs. Clennam seems to depend on her self-imprisonment because she believes that it can serve as a recompense for the Dorrits' imprisonment. For her, "inexorable justice is done" (96), but with regard to the Dorrits and their suffering, this is simply not true.

For me, the function of the embedded first-person accounts mentioned above is not to continue the work of the prison. Rather, they accentuate the psychological scars of the prison and demonstrate how difficult it is to overcome the prison one has internalized. On the one hand, one might argue that the novel's first-person narratives reproduce the split personalities the prison has created. But on the other hand, this is done to critique the prison by illustrating the consequences of imprisonment. The novel as a whole sheds a critical light on its various prisons by presenting us with sympathetic inmates who suffer severly in prison. The novel's embedded narratives contribute to this general perspective. Characters who have been imprisoned will never be in a position to forgive or overcome their prison.

Little Dorrit presents us with two prison settings (the Marseilles jail and the Marshalsea debtors' prison), a wide variety of inmates

(Rigaud, Cavaletto, the Dorrits, and Arthur Clennam), a number of prison-like scenarios (the quarantine barracks and the convent of the Great Saint Bernard), a whole range of prison metaphors and many characters who are metaphorically imprisoned (like Miss Wade, Tattycoram, and Mrs. Clennam). Furthermore, the novel sheds a rather critical light on the prison. In particular, the incarceration of debtors is represented as being impolitic and unjust because incarcerated debtors cannot earn any money to pay their debts. Our disapproval of the prison system is heightened by the fact that we are primarily confronted with likeable inmates who suffer severely in prison. The novel also contains a wide range of metaphors of imprisonment that clearly accentuate the suffering of prisoners and falsify Grass' argument about the alleged "failure of omniscience to account for the fundamental meanings of the cell" (109). The narrator alludes to the internal states of the inmates by describing the prison as a cage, as hell, as a tomb, as a voyage on a ship, etc. Even the womb imagery in the novel stresses the prisoners' suffering because it accentuates the infantilization of the inmates (or their dependence on the prison). Also, even before the narrator turns to the embedded first-person accounts in the second part of the novel, we learn that the prison determines the psychological states of its inmates. Most of the inmates get so used to the prison that they cannot live without it.

Moreover, the literal imprisonment in the Marshalsea resembles the various forms of metaphorical imprisonment in the world outside. The novel draws an intimate connection between the prison and the world outside, which gradually turns into a critique of society and defines the whole world as a prison. A famous passage toward the end of the novel combines the various prison-like settings, prison metaphors, and metaphorically imprisoned characters into one image that describes the whole world as a prison:

> The last day of the appointed week touched the bars of the Marshalsea gate. Black, all night, since the gate had clashed upon Little Dorrit, its iron stripes were turned by the early-glowing sun into stripes of gold. Far aslant across the city, over its jumbled roofs, and through the open tracery of its

> church towers, struck the long bright rays, bars of the prison of this lower world. (729)

Little Dorrit suggests that the 'free' world is also dominated by the prison. Those who are not literally imprisoned cannot escape the prison because they devote their energies to wrong purposes. First, criminals like Merdle and the Barnacles dominate life in the world outside so that society appears to be a society of criminals (like the prison). Second, characters like Mrs. Clennam, Miss Wade, and Tattycoram are shown to be metaphorically imprisoned or mentally confined.

In this context, the selflessness of Little Dorrit's love for Arthur seems to provide some sort of redemption. However, Little Dorrit's hardworking generosity borders on self-destruction so that she continues to live in a kind of prison after her release. Additionally, since the novel's world is full of deceit, hypocrisy, and wrongdoing, it is very hard to believe in the redemptive power of love and the happiness of the marriage between Amy and Arthur. The novel's final sentence significantly implies descent or downfall: "They went quietly down into the roaring streets, inseparable and blessed; and as they passed along in sunshine and shade, the noisy and the eager, and the arrogant and the froward and the vain, fretted and chafed, and made their usual uproar" (787). One might speculate that sooner or later, their marriage will become a prison, like the marriage of Dombey and his wife in *Dombey and Son*.[23] *Little Dorrit* is a rather bleak prison novel. It constructs the prison as an all-embracing shadow which cannot easily, if ever, be overcome.

Edzard's film adaptation concentrates on the Marshalsea and its inmates, and primarily renders the prison experience and the prisoners' suffering through external details: the atmosphere of the prison setting, the *mise-en-scène*, and the behavior of characters allude to the prisoners' internal states. Furthermore, by focusing on two types of metaphorical imprisonment, this experimental film version approaches the prison theme from a particular angle. First, the film version accentuates society's egotistical materialism and the imprisoning potential of wealth. The film adaptation clearly ascertains who (or what) is responsible for most of the ills of the film's world. Second, Edzard's film version suggests that Amy and Arthur are trapped in their self-centered world views. Amy and Arthur may be anti-materialists who are not corrupted by money or greed. However, Amy is mentally confined by her naive or idealized world view, while Arthur is mentally confined by his melancholic self-centeredness which makes him oblivious to the feelings of others. Both characters live in a solipsist world that is based on false projections. Edzard's film adaptation thus alludes to the potential impossibility of grasping an external reality beyond one's own perception, and suggests that we are all mentally confined because we live in essential isolation.

"I Hope You Care to Be Recalled to Life?": Incarceration in *A Tale of Two Cities*

The Imprisonment of Dr. Manette

The first character who is incarcerated in Dickens' next novel *A Tale of Two Cities* is Dr. Manette, the father of Lucie Manette. Dr. Manette is one of the many victims of the tyrannical Marquis St Evrémonde and was imprisoned in the Bastille for eighteen years because he knew of a brutal crime which the younger brother of the Marquis had committed. After his release, Manette goes to live in the house of Ernest and Thérèse Defarge, the two major plotters of the French Revolution, and is then taken to England by Lucie and Mr. Lorry, the sixty-year old confidential clerk at Tellson's Bank.

Except during the storming of the Bastille, the novel's authorial narrator does not show us Manette's prison cell. Instead, we get to know Manette in a prison-like "dim and dark" (41) room above the wine shop of the Defarges. Later on, we learn that in Manette's cell,

> there was a small, heavily-grated, unglazed window high in the wall, with a stone screen before it, so that the sky could be only seen by stooping low and looking up. There was a small chimney, heavily barred across, a few feet within. There was a heap of old feathery wood ashes on the hearth. There was a

> stool, and table, and a straw bed. There were four blackened walls, and a rusted iron ring in one of them. (227)

This description is followed by Defarge's violent destruction of the furniture. This outbreak of violence is not so much a desperate attempt to get "a clear definition of the mystery called Manette" as Tom Lloyd has it (159). Rather, it foreshadows the cruelty with which the revolutionaries gain control over Manette and his identity.

Even though the prison experience is rendered retrospectively (and by means of external focalization), the novel manages to present the prison as the authorities' most powerful tool of controlling the prisoner's identity. When Lorry and Lucie visit the freed Manette in his room, Lorry asks the formerly "buried man" Manette, "I hope you care to be recalled to life?" Manette then answers "I can't say" (53). Throughout the novel, the Bastille is associated with death and thus reminiscent of a tomb.[24] For me, this means that the authorities managed to destroy or kill a part of Manette's personality. The former prisoner wishes to be locked in his room because, as Defarge puts it, "he has lived so long, locked up, that he would be frightened—rave—tear himself to pieces—die—come to I know not what harm—if his door was left open" (39).

Dickens' *Tale* accentuates that since the prison also affects the inmate's psychology, to be released does not solve all the prisoner's problems. Like the Dorrits in *Little Dorrit*, Manette remains tied to the prison even after his release. When Defarge asks him for his name, Manette answers: "One Hundred and Five, North Tower" (44). The prison deprived Manette of his former identity and even though he has been freed, he still considers himself to be a number. The ex-inmate does not fully exist as a person, and even appears to have become indistinguishable from his clothes: "He, and his old canvas frock, and his loose stockings, and all his poor tatters of clothes, had, in a long seclusion from direct light and air, faded down to such a dull uniformity of parchment-yellow, that it would have been hard to say which was which" (43). Manette's body is "withered and worn," and when he puts up his hand to shield his eyes from the incoming light, "the very bones [...] seemed transparent" (43). His voice is like the voice of a ghost: "it was like the last feeble echo of a sound made long ago"; "it was like a voice underground" (42).

Furthermore, the prisoner appears to have "lost the habit of associating place with sound" (43). Manette has been transformed into a docile body used to comply with orders: "In the submissive way of one long accustomed to obey under coercion, he ate and drank what they gave him to eat and drink" (51). When Lucie marries Darnay, Manette is under shock and relapses into the shoemaking he learned in prison because he knows that Darnay is the nephew of the tyrannical Marquis[25]: "The bench was turned towards the light, as it had been when he [Lorry] had seen the shoemaker at his work before [i.e., at the wine shop, J.A.], and his head was bent down, and he was very busy" (202).

The authorial narrator operates like a camera and uses external focalization to inform us about what the hellish Bastille did to the innocent Manette. At one point, Miss Pross states that Manette has internalized the prison but we learn very little about his thoughts and feelings. She merely points out that "his mind is walking up and down, walking up and down, in his old prison" (102). Generally speaking, the narrator prefers to simulate the psychological problems related to incarceration through external details. Nevertheless, I think that Grass once again exaggerates when he argues that *A Tale of Two Cities* "attests to the failure of omniscience" (137) in *Little Dorrit*. The narrator does not fail to narrate the prison. Rather, 'he' anticipates film by concentrating on the simulation of the former prisoner's interiority through details like Manette's appearance, his bodily constitution, the tone of his voice, the prisoner's facial expressions, and his actions. Even though Manette's unjust suffering and the internalization of the prison are rendered through external focalization, the depiction of Manette is "a powerful, and a plausible, rendering of the permanent damage to the personality which such an experience [of imprisonment, J.A.] may inflict" (Collins *Dickens* 137). At one point, the narrator moves to a quasi-close-up of Manette's face, and argues that it is difficult to learn something about a prisoner's mind by studying external features:

> No human intelligence could have read the mysteries of his mind, in the scared blank wonder of his face. Whether he knew what had happened, whether he recollected what they had said to him, whether he knew that he was free, were questions which no sagacity could have solved. (51)

A Tale of Two Cities does not show that the authorial narrator fails to narrate the prison. Rather, the novel expresses a certain need for a first-person account by Manette, which may help to understand the mysteries of the prisoner's mind.

In the novel's second book, Manette presents Lucie with such an account about "his old condition" (197), and tells her that in the Bastille, he imagined two daughters. One version of Lucie was "perfectly forgetful of me—rather, altogether ignorant of me, and unconscious of me" (196). The other version was sympathetic but unable to free him from his cell. The former prisoner argues that the second Lucie would take him "out to show me that the home of her married life was full of her loving remembrance of her lost father. My picture was in her room, and I was in her prayers. Her life was active, cheerful, useful; but my poor history pervaded it all" (197). The existence of two versions of Lucie clearly demonstrates what the prison did to Manette. As in *Little Dorrit*, the prison created two selves which Manette does not manage to reconcile, namely an imprisoned and hopeless self on the one hand, and a hopeful self (which ultimately does not manage to set him free) on the other. And these two selves have clearly fed into Manette's vision of two Lucies.

The novel's third book continues to depict the prison from an internal perspective by presenting us with Manette's testimony (331–45). This first-person document illustrates that the ultimate purpose of the prison experience is to gain control over the prisoner's identity construction. To begin with, Manette notes that he was policed by agents of the prison, and only in a position to work "at stolen intervals, under every difficulty." We also learn that he had "slowly and laboriously made a place of concealment for it [his testimony, J.A.]," namely "the wall of the chimney" (331). Furthermore, we are told that after a weary decade in prison, Manette's senses began to wither away ("my reason will not long remain unimpaired" [331]), and he argues that he experienced some kind of psychological death ("Hope has quite departed from my breast" [331]) in the Bastille, which he calls his "living grave" (344).

Later on, social authorities gain power over Manette's testimony and redefine his identity. First, the revolutionaries turn him into a celebrity. His long years of hopeless misery allow him a strong position so that he can save Charles Darnay, his accused son-in-law.[26] Manette's suffering enables him to experience a social rebirth under the reign of Terror: "His high personal popularity, and the clearness of his answers made a great impression; [...] as he showed that the Accused was his first friend on his release from his long imprisonment; [...] the Jury and the populace became one" (295). However, Darnay's second sentence[27] is ironically based on the evidence of Manette's testimony which the revolutionaries and Defarge found in Manette's cell in the Bastille. In this document, Manette denounces all Evrémondes: "I, Alexander Manette, unhappy prisoner, do this last night of the year 1767, in my unbearable agony, denounce to the times when all these things shall be answered for. I denounce them to Heaven and to earth" (344). The supposed utility of Manette's suffering is rendered pointless, and ends in disillusionment. When Manette requests his shoemaking tools, we do get a sense that he will remain tied to the prison until he dies. Manette's state of mind is again conveyed through external focalization. He shrinks "into the exact figure that Defarge had had in keeping" (356). The revolutionaries instrumentalize his testimony for their purpose. The political powers manage to transform the meaning of Manette's testimony and condemn Darnay to death by making the account say something that Manette no longer agrees with. At this stage, revolutionary France becomes Manette's metaphorical prison or living grave and, once again, hope departs from his breast so that his hopeful self is completely eradicated and he is dominated by his hopeless prison self.

Like the novel, Jack Conway's 1935 film *A Tale of Two Cities* visualizes Manette's (Henry B. Walthall) inner state by way of facial expressions and the atmosphere of his environment. The film's *mise-en-scène* suggests that Manette has become an object, a part of his room at the Defarges. The visual similarity between his tousled hair and his long white beard on the one hand, and the room's spider-webs on the other, invite us to see a link between the two. The character merges with the setting as his dark-gray tatters fade into the leaden darkness of the room. When Mr. Lorry (Claude Gillingwater) addresses him as "Dr. Manette," he lets his shoe drop. This suggests that he is surprised to be reminded of his former (pre-prison) identity. Later on, Lorry and Lucie (Elizabeth Allan) want to take him away, and he looks for his written testimony, which Defarge (Mitchell Lewis) refers to in terms of a "reminder of the horror" he had to endure. This scene accentuates Manette's lack of orientation (through external focalization). In this version of the *Tale*, he has certainly not realized that he is no longer imprisoned. In the movie, Manette loses control over the meaning of his testimony as well. Manette's return to the imbecile mode of consciousness after Charles is sentenced to death on the basis of his testimony is conveyed by Manette's vacant gaze.

Charles Darnay's Time in Prison

The second character who is incarcerated is Charles Darnay. The revolutionaries first send him to the prison of La Force and then to the Conciergerie because he is an aristocrat. Like Manette, he is completely innocent and did not commit any crime. In the novel, the prison of La Force is described as "a gloomy prison, dark and filthy, and with a horrible smell of foul sleep in it" (265). Like the Bastille, this prison is associated with a tomb that leads to an inner or psychological death. The narrator points out that the inmates "were changed by the death they had died in coming here" (265). The novel also comments on the consequences of imprisonment for Lucie, who is not allowed to visit Charles and desperately hopes that her husband might see her standing in front of the prison.

> In all weathers, in the snow and frost of winter, in the bitter winds of spring, in the hot sunshine of summer, in the rains of autumn, and again in the snow and frost of winter, Lucie passed two hours every day at this place [which her father

> pointed out to her, J.A.]; and every day, on leaving it, she kissed the prison wall. Her husband saw her (so she learned from her father) it might be once in five or six times: it might be twice or thrice running: it might be, not for a week or a fortnight together. (287–88)

Lucie's repetitive actions suggest that she is devoted to her husband but also that she has become prison-bound. Her behavior is reminiscent of the dull routine of prison life. This passage also alludes to the fact that the loss which the relatives of prisoners experience correlates with some sort of psychological (or spiritual) death.

In the film, Darnay (Donald Woods) rides to revolutionary France to rescue Gabelle (H.B. Warner), and his future imprisonment is visually accentuated as barriers close behind him that separate him more and more clearly from England. We see a barrier closing behind him as he passes beneath an immensely spacious sky. This scene is followed by a shot of a wooden door that is shut behind him, and the sky is gone completely. These scenes are clearly visual renderings of the following passage from the novel. When Darnay returns to France, we learn that

> […] not a mean village closed upon him, not a common barrier dropped across the road behind him, but he knew it to be another iron door in the series that was barred between him and England. The universal watchfulness so encompassed him, that if he had been taken in a net, or were being forwarded to his destination in a cage, he could not have felt his freedom more completely gone. (255)

While the novel familiarizes us with Darnay's feelings about his future imprisonment, the film visually reduces the cinematic space within which Darnay is allowed to move in order to allude to Darnay's emotions. After Darnay's conviction, the film visually conveys the loss of the inmate's individuality by means of a long shot of the prison's identical windows. These windows may imply that the prison deprives inmates of their individuality and reduces them to insignificant numbers. The *mise-en-scène* also codes Darnay's cell as a tomb. It is as dark as a grave and we only see his white face which appears to have lost contact with the rest of his body, thus visually alluding to the identity crisis of newly incarcerated inmates and wryly foreshadowing his possible guillotining. The film also comments on the effects of confinement for relatives when we are presented with a shot of Manette, Lucie and her daughter waving at the prison. Suddenly, we are presented with a white handkerchief waving back at them. One might read this metonymically as his reduction to an object.

A major difference between the novel and the film is that in the novel Darnay is released from the prison of La Force owing to the intervention of Dr. Manette and later on sent to the Conciergerie, whereas in the film he is immediately sentenced to be guillotined because Manette fails to persuade the Jury, a point which dramatizes Manette's disillusionment. In the film, he never experiences the social rebirth he goes through in the novel and immediately relapses into his former prison identity. Furthermore, in contrast to the film, the Charles of the novel is struck by the inmates' strange dignity when he arrives at the prison of La Force. This community of friendly prisoners was notably omitted in the cinematic version. For me, these kind inmates are significant because they occupy an important place between the enormous metaphorical prison of France and Darnay's solitary cell at the Conciergerie, where he is later on replaced by Carton[28]:

> In the instinctive association of prisoners with shameful crime and disgrace, the new comer recoiled from this company. But, the crowning unreality of his long unreal ride, was, their all at once rising to receive him, with every refinement of manner known to the time, and with all the engaging graces and courtesies of life. So strangely clouded were these refinements by the prison manners and gloom, so spectral did they become in the inappropriate squalor and misery through which they were seen, that Charles Darnay seemed to stand in a company of the dead. Ghosts all! (265)

The prisoners are interested in Darnay and "hope" that he will not be "in secret," i.e., solitary confinement. When Darnay is then taken away from them, they give him "good wishes and encouragement" (266).

From this community, Darnay is led "into a solitary cell. It struck cold and damp, but was not dark" (267). Darnay then begins to walk to and fro in his almost empty cell, counting its measurements: "Five paces by four and a half, five paces by four and a half, five paces by four and a half" (267). As Tom Lloyd has shown (155), the prison's solitary cell comes close to reducing Darnay to an 'it' like Manette. The initial shock upon arrival in prison causes Darnay to experience a severe identity crisis. His thoughts descend into a confused interior monologue in which scraps of his tenuously retained selfhood "toss [...] and roll [...] upwards from the depths of his mind" (267). Also, the repetitions in his interior monologue suggest that he is beginning to internalize the prison: "[...] Let us ride on again, for God's sake, through the illuminated villages with the people all awake! **** He made shoes, he made shoes, he made shoes. **** Five paces by four and a half" (267).

When Darnay is reincarcerated to be guillotined, he is sent to solitary confinement in a small cell of "the black prison of the Conciergerie" (360). We learn that "it was not easy to compose his mind to what it must bear." Also, "there was a hurry [...] in all his thoughts, a turbulent and heated working of his heart, that contended against resignation" (360). The narrator informs us that Darnay was "walking regularly to and fro with his arms folded on his breast," and adds that he was "a very different man from the prisoner who had walked to and fro at La Force" (363). The latter phrase might mean that Darnay is even more scared because he is about to be guillotined and knows that "no personal influence could possibly save him" (360); but it might also be a reference to the fact that identities are never stable and might change (as in the case of Manette).

Most critics who deal with the prisons in the novel (e.g., Collins "A Tale" and Grass) have overlooked the significance of the small community of benevolent prisoners at the prison of La Force. These friendly prisoners are diametrically opposed to France, which is dominated by public violence, and Carton, who retreats into some sort of privacy and dies a noble (but solitary) death. In the novel, both the revolutionaries and Carton ultimately fail. The revolutionaries strive for power and achieve nothing but tyranny and injustice, while the individualist Carton rejects power and even though he helps a seamstress at the end, remains completely lonely. The motto of his life is indeed "I care for no man on earth, and no man on earth cares for me" (89). In prison, Carton dictates Darnay a letter for Lucie which begins as follows:

> If you remember [...] the words that passed between us, long ago [he refers to the moment when he told her that he would give his life to keep a life she loves beside her, J.A.], you will readily comprehend this when you see it. You do remember them, I know. It is not in your nature to forget them. (365)

The meaning of Carton's love thus crucially depends upon Lucie's correct interpretation. One could argue that Carton loses control over the meaning of his identity because his letter might be misinterpreted by Lucie. If she forgets Carton's words, nobody may actually grasp the nobility of his death. In this case, Carton might indeed remain a "profound secret and mystery" (14) to her and to everyone else.[29] Carton's vision at the end, which he does not share with anyone, thus constitutes the one and only 'correct' (but unknown) version of his identity. "In the case of Carton's internalized grammar at the close, his repeated stress on private vision is delivered in first-person rather than second, inner-directed, unperformed, unconfirmed" (Stewart 170), i.e., without any results in the world of the novel.

In this context, the prison of La Force, which is located between the power-driven revolutionaries and the powerless Carton, is represented as the only space in France where relationships, friendship, and dignity are possible. The metaphorical incarceration in the world (as in the case of revolutionary France) and in the self (as in the case of Carton) render human relations and friendship impossible. In this sense, the revolution and Carton's private sacrifice are merged at the end of the novel. The prisoners of La Force are isolated from the aggression of revolutionary France, and in contrast to Carton, they form intense relationships unequaled in the world outside. The description of these prisoners as "ghosts" (265) or "apparitions" (266) may even suggest that they are weightless spirits—free from prosaic concerns. These prisoners do something which neither the power-driven revolutionaries nor the individualist Carton manage to achieve. Like a family, they express respect for, and share the narratives of, others.

The prison community at La Force clearly falsifies the argument that "in *A Tale of Two Cities* other people are primarily a threat and source of danger" (Gross 189). The novel idealizes this family-like community and presents it as a clear alternative to the violent macrocosm of revolutionary France where the attempt to achieve liberation leads to nothing but senseless massacres. The microcosmic world of Carton is also criticized because he withdraws from all interaction, and only manages to express his love for Lucie through his death. By contrast, the prisoners at La Force neither seek to dominate the self-construction of others (which is what the revolutionaries do), nor do they withdraw from interaction into a state of private intimacy (which is what Carton does). This small community perhaps also foreshadows the domestic bliss in which Biddy and Joe live at the end of *Great Expectations*. From this perspective, Dickens' *Tale* might argue that certain constraints and limitations are necessary preconditions for a happy life (even though he is also aware of the fact that marriages or love may quickly turn into prisons).

On the basis of two major changes, the film constructs Carton differently in comparison to the novel. The community of friendly prisoners at the prison of La Force was omitted and Darnay and Carton (Ronald Colman) do not resemble one another at all. While the novel invites us to sympathize with the family-like community of prisoners, the film invites us to identify with the non-conformist Carton. As Bialkowski (206) has shown, the movie also altered the role of Barsad in the treason trial. In the film, Barsad appears in a new scene before the trial boozing, bowling and boasting about his skills at concocting treason cases against others. Later on, Barsad is surprised to see Carton as a barrister at the trial but not because Carton looks like Darnay but because Barsad did not expect the slovenly Carton to be a barrister and had told him all about the blackmail. When Barsad then claims that he cannot distinguish

Carton and Darnay, we as viewers are quite surprised because they do not look like twins. The implication of this lack of resemblance is quite clear. In contrast to the novel, the film suggests that Darnay is not at all the man that Carton might have been. By contrast, in the novel, the process of doubling is clearly observable in the treatment of the main characters: Carton and Darnay are presented as doubles.[30]

Given the onscreen prominence of Carton in the film, the implication is that there is no way that Darnay could ever hope to be like Carton. In the film, Carton is a likeable and intelligent non-conformist who clearly dominates the scenes in which he appears together with the relatively affectionless Darnay. Carton is the film's most remarkable character. This is visually conveyed at the end of the movie when the camera moves from him to the guillotine, and then toward the sky, thus suggesting Carton's way to heaven.

The Rulers Who Run the Prison

Finally, I would like to say a few words about the Marquis and the revolutionaries because they are the rulers who are responsible for the prisons that destroy other people's lives. In the novel, the Marquis is a cruel, ignorant, and arrogant ruler who does not care about the peasants at all. At one point, the brother of the Marquis raped a young peasant woman, and Dr. Manette was called in to save her from dying. In his testimony, Manette describes the victim as follows:

> The patient was a woman of great beauty, and young; assuredly not much past twenty. Her hair was torn and ragged, and her arms were bound to her sides with sashes and handkerchiefs. I noticed that these bonds were all portions of a gentleman's dress. On one of them, which was a fringed scarf for a dress of ceremony, I saw the armorial bearing of a Noble, and the letter E [for Evrémonde, J.A.]. (333)

The heartless Marquis then comments on the brutalized peasant woman as follows: "'What strength there is in these common bodies!' he said, looking down at her with some curiosity" (340). He is obviously surprised that she is still alive after having been raped by his brother. Manette does not manage to save her and later on, writes "privately to [a] Minister" to "relieve [...] [his] mind" (342). However, the letter reaches the Marquis who then imprisons Manette because of "the knowledge" (344) he possesses. Also, at one point, a peasant child is killed by the Marquis' carriage and he wishes to leave the scene "with the air of a gentleman who had accidentally broken some common thing" (115). The Marquis objectifies the peasants and the prisoners. He even dismisses the poor as "dogs" and maintains "an unchanged front, except as to the spots on his nose" (117). His cruelty lies hidden behind the "fine mask" (126) of his face.

The revolutionaries are described as being much more openly brutal. Later on in the novel, when we are invited to 'watch' the revolutionaries sharpening their weapons at a grindstone, they are represented as uncivilized beasts or savages. Their faces are said to be "more horrible and cruel than the visages of the wildest savages in their most barbarous disguise." Also, they are described as being "all awry with howling, and all staring and glaring with beastly excitement and want of sleep" (272).

It is also worth noting that the heartless Marquis and the revolutionary Defarge objectify Manette in a very similar way. Defarge is not at all interested in Manette as a person but only as a victim of the *ancien régime* with special knowledge about the Marquis. The following conversation between Defarge and Lucie alludes to the fact that the objectification of people like Manette will continue under the new regime:

> 'I am afraid of it,' she answered, shuddering.
> 'Of it? What?'
> 'I mean of him. Of my father.' (40)

As Cockshut has shown (45), Lucie's discourse is 'contaminated' by Defarge's objectifying attitude toward the former prisoner. A further parallel consists in the fact that the Marquis and Defarge are extremely concerned with the individual's loyalty to the ruling powers and use the prison to gain control over their identities. More

to empathize with the innocent prisoners and to condemn the prison system.

Both the novel *A Tale of Two Cities* and Conway's 1935 film adaptation critique the prison by presenting us with innocent prisoners who suffer severly in prison, while the prisons are run by truly criminal and heartless rulers. Also, both the novel and the film code the prison as a tomb or grave that kills individuality and creates split personalities. In both versions, Dr. Manette is the most tragic prisoner because he has experienced some sort of psychological death during his confinement in the Bastille. While the Bastille has not quite managed to eradicate the hopeful part of his personality, the revolutionaries ultimately achieve this goal. Manette will remain tied to his prison after the revolutionaries have instrumentalized his account to sentence Darnay to death. The novel and the film present the conditions of imprisonment as well as the heartlessness of the rulers under the *ancien régime* as being very similar to the revolutionary Terror.[31] The underlying theory of history is expressed as follows: "crush humanity out of its shape once more, under similar hammers, and it will twist itself into the same tortured forms" (385). Since despite the restless movement of the French Revolution no progress seems to be made, one might relate *A Tale of Two Cities* to Friedrich Nietzsche, for whom history is an endless spectacle repeating the will to power. The ultimate purpose of the excessive violence in the two versions is the struggle for control: over society, over meanings, and especially over identity constructions.

However, it is also worth noting that in the novel, the prison is not only represented as a negative force. In the novel, Charles Darnay learns that the prison of La Force is the only place in France where true friendship is possible. The community of friendly prisoners at La Force sheds a critical light on both the violent revolutionaries and the individualist Carton. Both the revolutionaries and Carton are incapable of engaging in friendships. By omitting this community of benevolent prisoners, the film provides us with a much stronger statement against imprisonment than the novel and at the same time makes a hero out of Carton. While the novel idealizes the family-like community of friendly prisoners as an alternative to both the revolutionaries' violence and Carton's inward retreat, the film presents Ronald Colman as the movie's 'transcendental' star who escapes from worldly constraints and moves toward heaven at the end of the film.

Moreover, the novel anticipates both prison films and prison novels of the twentieth century. Dickens' *Tale* foreshadows prison films by narrating the prison through external focalization and by simulating the internalization of the prison through external details (like the *mise-en-scène*, facial expressions, and bodily positions). The novel also points toward the first-person prison novels of the twentieth century which concentrate on an imprisoned narrator and the way in which he internalizes the prison. The numerous embedded first-person accounts in the novel—the letter which leads to Manette's incarceration, Manette's testimony written in the Bastille, Manette's account concerning his past imprisonment, Darnay's interior monologue, the letters Darnay writes in the Conciergerie, the letter Carton dictates to Darnay in the Conciergerie, Carton's vision at the end—provide an important impetus for later first-person prison novels.

In this context, it is worth noting that Dickens produced the first-person novel *Great Expectations* immediately after *A Tale of Two Cities*. *Great Expectations* is closely linked to its predecessor because Pip's story continues the internalization of the prison that is already alluded to in the *Tale*. Dickens notably abandons the authorial mode of *Little Dorrit* and *A Tale of Two Cities* in favor of first-person narration, which allows him to explain the way in which the narrator internalizes the prison in greater detail. One might even argue that the last words of *A Tale of Two Cities* ("It is a far, far better thing that I do, than I have ever done; [...]" [390]) directly point toward *Great Expectations*, where Dickens presents us with a 'better' (or more comprehensive) rendering of the internalization of the prison than he does in his authorial novels. Like the embedded first-person narratives in *Little Dorrit* and *A Tale of Two Cities*, Pip's narrative suggests that it is difficult to leave the prison one has internalized. *Great Expectations* is prison-bound because it is a guilt-ridden confessional narrative that reproduces the processes of self-surveillance and self-discipline inspired by the prison.

The Internalization of the Prison in *Great Expectations*

Pip's Guilt Complex in the Novel

Great Expectations presents imprisonment as an essential condition of Victorian society: we are confronted with convicts, hulks, Newgate Prison, transportation to a penal colony,[32] prison-like settings, and metaphorical extensions of the prison theme. However, in contrast to *Little Dorrit*, the prison is not a dominant image casting long shadows on every part of the novel. Rather, the prison operates in the background as a garden or "fertile soil out of which things grow for the delight or the profit or the undoing of people who have never thought about this soil" (Cockshut 48). Also, imprisonment is less central in terms of setting. Rather, the prison dominates the psychological states of various characters. In other words, the novel focuses on the feeling of constraint, which is the psychological equivalent of actual constraint. People in the world outside prison have interiorized the prison, and this can most clearly be demonstrated by looking at Pip, the guilt-ridden first-person narrator himself.

At the beginning of the novel, the escaped convict Magwitch asks the young Pip to steal food, and after this criminal deed, Pip begins to feel guilty. Later on, the narrator feels responsible for the death of his bullying sister, who was killed by Orlick with Magwitch's leg-iron. Throughout the novel, Pip never manages to overcome his feelings of guilt. These emotions ultimately lead him to write an autobiography with the aim of justifying his deeds. However, Pip's confessional narrative is far from liberating. First, Pip does not realize that his initial 'crime' was actually a moral deed because he saved a starving convict, and he also does not see that he is innocent of his sister's death. Pip permanently tries to distance himself from any link with criminality or the prison. The narrating self is still an arrogant snob who has not learned very much from his story and still tries to distance himself from 'evil' prisoners and criminals. Second, in his confessional autobiography, the narrator accounts for his disordered identity and feelings of guilt and this is precisely what the political powers that run the prison desire: to gain access to identity constructions of prison inmates in order to wield power over them. Pip is indeed "encompassed by all this taint of prison and crime" (249) because he has internalized the discourse that disciplinary society promotes and goes through a process of self-policing and self-inspection that ties him closely to the prison.

The novel intertwines incarceration and the idea of hierarchical surveillance in the sense of Foucault. *Great Expectations* is actually the first novel of my corpus that can be related to Foucault's reading of Bentham in a meaningful way. In *Discipline and Punish*, Foucault argues that the *Panopticon*

> [...] must be understood as *a generalizable model* of functioning; *a way of defining power relations* in terms of the everyday life of men. [...] It is *the diagram of a mechanism* of power reduced to its ideal form; its functioning, abstracted from any obstacle, resistance or friction, must be represented as a pure architectural and optical system: it is in fact *a figure of political technology* that may and must be *detached from any specific use*. (Foucault *Discipline* 205; my emphasis, J.A.)

I am aware of the fact that Foucault relates his notion of 'panopticism' to disciplinary institutions like factories, schools, hospitals, etc. Nevertheless, I think that one can extend his notion of "a generalized surveillance" to society's gaze, i.e., to the way in which people observe and control one another. A society in which everyone observes everyone else comes close to Bentham's dream of "a network of mechanisms that would be everywhere and always alert, running through society without interruption in time and space" (ibid.).

For instance, when Pip goes to Satis House for the first time, he feels that he is "under close inspection" (91) by his relatives.[33] Also, at the "great festival" during which Pip is 'bound' as apprentice to

Joe, the narrator is exposed to social control and permanently looked at: "they wouldn't let me go to sleep, but whenever they saw me dropping off, woke me up and told me to enjoy myself" (113). Furthermore, in London,[34] the narrator has already internalized the idea of hierarchical surveillance and finds it difficult "to avoid the suspicion of being watched" (315) and in Jaggers' room, Pip thinks that "the distorted adjoining houses" look "as if they had twisted themselves to peep down at [him]" (162). Tambling even argues that Jaggers is "like the unseen watcher in the central tower of the Panopticon" ("Prison-Bound" 131) because he confers identities and controls destinies, while he himself resists classification. Indeed, when Jaggers informs Pip about his great expectations, he looks at Pip with a penetrating gaze, "as if he were expressly taking aim at [him] with his invisible gun" (87) and, later on, "as if he were determined to have a shot at [him]" (88). Pip also believes that Jaggers' clerk has got "the same air of knowing something to everybody else's disadvantage, as his master" (162). When Pip and his friend Herbert attempt to smuggle Magwitch out of the country, the narrator cannot "get rid of the notion of being watched" (349). Throughout the novel, people supervise one another with "depreciatory" eyes (105), keep "an eye" on others (136), refuse to remove their "stern" eyes from the observed (152), or take "searching" looks at one another (204). This gaze of social control clearly links society to the 'new' prison system where the inmates' bodies are perpetually observed.

The novel presents us with two escaped convicts, namely Magwitch and Compeyson.[35] At the beginning of the novel, the young Pip encounters both prisoners on the marshes. Later on, we learn that Magwitch and Compeyson were committed "on a charge of putting stolen notes in circulation" (323). Magwitch's fate illustrates that in comparison to rich people, the poor may be much more severely punished. Since Compeyson was extremely wealthy and could afford a lawyer, and also because he implicated Magwitch, he was sentenced to serve only seven years, while Magwitch received fourteen years in prison (324). When Pip sees Magwitch for the first time on the marshes, he is terrified:

> A fearful man, all in coarse grey, with a great iron on his leg. A man with no hat, and with broken shoes, and with an old rag tied round his head. A man who had been soaked in water, and smothered in mud, and lamed by stones, and cut by flints, and stung by nettles, and torn by briars; who limped and shivered, and glared and growled; and whose teeth chattered in his head as he seized me by the chin. (24)

Pip's meeting with Magwitch begins with a forced self-declaration of identity: "'Tell us your name!' said the man. 'Quick!' 'Pip, sir.' 'Once more,' said the man staring at me. 'Give it mouth!' 'Pip. Pip, sir'" (24). From this moment on, Pip's identity is tied to the nexus of Magwitch, criminality and the prison—a taint Pip desperately wishes to shake off. Magwitch demands that Pip obtain food and a file for him. Pip steals the required items from his sister and her husband Joe and feels guilty because he has committed a crime. Pip projects his fear of reprisal onto the cattle and believes that they shout: "A boy with Somebody-else's pork-pie! Stop him!" Also, "the cattle came upon [him] with like suddenness, staring out of their eyes, and steaming out of their nostrils" (36). By perceiving the cattle as staring judges (or perhaps as his sister), the young Pip begins to internalize the hierarchical surveillance to which disciplinary society exposes its citizens and constructs his identity in accordance with it.

When we learn that Pip's sister was killed, Pip immediately thinks that he "must have had some hand in the attack" (125). Pip believes that the leg-iron with which she was killed was "my convict's iron—the iron I had seen and heard him filing at, on the marshes [...]" (126). Pip feels guilty because he supplied the file that released the leg-iron from Magwitch's feet. Later on, we learn that it was Orlick who attacked Pip's sister. He magnifies Pip's sense of guilt by suggesting that Pip committed the crime: "I tell you it was your doing—I tell you it was done through you. [...] It warn't Old Orlick as did it; it was you" (389). Throughout the novel, the narrator desperately tries to silence his feelings of guilt and all potential links with criminality. Paradoxically, since his confessional autobiography reproduces the disciplinary discourse of Victorian society, this attempt to silence his 'deviant' self brings him ever closer to the prison. In other words, the more he tries to silence his feelings of guilt, the guiltier he feels.

Even though the narrator clearly feels guilty for having stolen the pantry items for Magwitch, he simultaneously develops a strange liking for the prisoner whom he frequently refers to as "my convict" (53). Duncan argues that the expression "conveys an affectionate and proprietary attitude toward the escaped felon" (104). There are various instances which suggest some kind of union between Pip and the criminal: the "damp cold seemed riveted" to Pip's feet like "the iron was riveted" to Magwitch's leg (36); Pip's sister speculates that he is interested in prisoners and went to take a look at the hulks (40); Pip flees from the Christmas dinner table into the arms of a soldier holding out handcuffs (47); etc. When Magwitch is caught, he conceals Pip's involvement and confesses that he stole food "from the blacksmith's" (55) on his own. From this moment on, Pip wishes to continue this concealment, while the prisoner Magwitch draws him closer and closer to the nexus of criminality and imprisonment. The bond between Magwitch and Pip becomes more and more intense because Pip's wealth grows out of Magwitch's work in the penal colony.[36] In other words, the penal colony is the garden in which Pip's riches grow.[37] In this context, it is also worth noting that Magwitch gradually develops into the novel's moral center: his crimes resulted from necessity rather than greed; also, he is honest and cares for Pip. Pip's initial 'crime' was actually a morally sound deed because he prevented another human being from starving. But throughout his narrative, Pip feels guilty of having committed a 'crime.' By contrast, Joe seems to have a much more balanced view on Pip's 'criminal' deed when he tells Magwitch: "We don't know what you have done, but we wouldn't have you starved to death for it" (56).

The interesting thing about the relationship between Magwitch and the first-person narrator is the way in which Pip's attitude changes from identification to ignorance once he has become a gentleman and assumes Miss Havisham to be his benefactor. When Pip sees Magwitch again in a coach in London (216–20), he conceals the fact that he knows the prisoner and does not even disclose his identity. As

Cockshut argues, the incident of Pip traveling in the same stagecoach might suggest the idea of "all in the same boat" (48) and could thus be an allusion to Pip's own metaphorical imprisonment.

In the course of the novel, Pip becomes more and more obsessed with his snobbishness and his great expectations concerning the rich and beautiful Estella. In other words, Pip begins to feel superior to other characters. The psychological function of his snobbishness is to hide Pip's link with the criminal Magwitch and to confront Pip's fear that he is essentially inferior to others. Thus, by excluding Magwitch (as well as his own 'deviant' self) from his life he acts like a prison which also excludes criminals from the lives of 'normal' law-abiding citizens. In other words, by the time Pip passes "into the interior of the jail" (246), i.e., Newgate Prison in London, the jail has already passed into him.[38] The gentleman Pip manically tries to distance himself from any association with the 'disgusting' nexus of Magwitch, crime, and the prison. The following passage describes his thoughts after his visit to Newgate:

> I consumed the whole time in thinking how strange it was that I should be encompassed by all this taint of prison and crime; that, in my childhood out on our lonely marshes on a winter evening I should have first encountered it; that, it should have reappeared on two occasions, starting out like a stain that was faded but not gone; that it should in this new way pervade my fortune and advancement. (249)

Pip even wishes not to have entered the 'soiling' prison before he meets his beloved Estella because he does not want to have

> […] Newgate in my breath and on my clothes. I beat the prison dust off my feet as I sauntered to and fro, and I shook it out of my dress, and I exhaled its air from my lungs. So contaminated did I feel, remembering what was coming, that the coach came quickly after all, and I was not yet free from the soiling consciousness of Mr. Wemmick's conservatory, when I saw her face at the coach window and her hand waving at me. (249–50)

The chapter ends with the following question: "What *was* the nameless shadow which again in that one instant had passed?" (250). For me, this nameless shadow is the prison taint which Pip desperately wishes to shake off.

As a snobbish gentleman, Pip does not only conceal the fact that he knows Magwitch. He also treats Joe and Biddy in a patronizing manner because he considers the two to be too common for him. He fails to appreciate Joe in London and ignores Biddy's quiet wisdom and implied criticism of his behavior (150–51). At the end of the novel, he wishes to marry her—perhaps because he realizes that he cannot get any other woman and considers the sisterly Biddy to be an easy option. Unfortunately, he arrives on the day of her wedding to Joe. Since his congratulations ("Dear Biddy, [...] you have the best husband in the world" [434]) and the subsequent confession ("I was ungenerous and unjust" [435]) involve an extremely quick change of mind, I am not convinced of Pip's sincerity. Rather, Pip attempts to disguise his true intentions regarding Biddy, and this process adds another aspect of guilt he has to hide. This hypothesis is corroborated by the following textual evidence. First, when he returns to the forge, Pip has "some hopeful notion of seeing her [Biddy] busily engaged in her daily duties" (433) and when he sees Joe and Biddy arm in arm, the first thing he notes is that she looks quite attractive ("so fresh and pleasant" [434]). Second, Pip faints when Biddy announces: "It's my wedding-day, [...] and I am married to Joe" (434). Arguably, people faint when they are in a state of shock and not when they are extremely happy. Pip wanted to 'have' Biddy and then realized that he will never get her. Third, the narrating self at this point desperately stresses that he is not a liar, which perhaps suggests that he still feels guilty of being one. Also, earlier on, the older Pip says about the lies he once told his family about Estella: "I beg to observe that I think of myself with amazement when I recall the lies I told on this occasion" (80). Since we are presented with certain inconsistencies concerning Pip's attitude toward Biddy at the end (433–35), one might feel that Pip is a self-deceiving narrator, i.e., a narrator who is deceived about his own psychological state.

Once Pip realizes that his rise in life is 'contaminated' because it was financed by a convict, the narrator describes his feelings of loathing as follows: "The abhorrence in which I held the man, the dread I had of him, the repugnance with which I shrank from him, could not have been exceeded if he had been some terrible beast" (298).[39] At this stage, Pip refers to Magwitch's riches in terms of "his gold and silver chains" (300). A situation of perceived lack of freedom is here presented as metaphorical restraint in the image of chains, a metonym of the hulks. Pip feels bound to Magwitch and even wishes to escape (like a prisoner): "Once, I actually did start out of my bed in the night, and begin to dress myself in my worst clothes, hurriedly intending to leave him [Magwitch, J.A.] there with everything else I possessed, and enlist for India as a private soldier" (312). This attitude does not change. Even the older Pip, the narrating self, still attempts to distance himself from 'evil' prisoners.

Throughout the novel, the threat of the prison haunts Pip. For example, when Pip is "bound" (112) as Joe's apprentice before the magistrates he is treated like a potential prisoner: in the Town Hall, Pip is "pushed over" like a felon by Pumblechook; the audience mistakes him for a criminal—they speculate "What's he done?" and others say "He's a young 'un, too, but looks bad, don't he?" (112)—and finally, a well-meaning philanthropist hands Pip a pamphlet on which it says "TO BE READ IN MY CELL" (112). Pip learns that he is "liable to imprisonment" (113) if he plays at cards, drinks strong liquors, keeps late hours or bad company, or indulges in other vagaries. At a later stage, Pip experiences his work as apprentice as well as his social position in terms of imprisonment. His life as a blacksmith, which he refers to as his 'time,' is reduced to monotonous repetitions, and the narrator "goes through a stage of purely iterative existence" (Brooks 487).[40] Pip feels dejected and constrained, and wishes to transcend his status:

> I remember that at a later period of my 'time,' I used to stand about the churchyard on Sunday evenings when night was falling, comparing my own perspective with the windy marsh view, and making out some likeness between them by thinking

> how flat and low both were, and how on both there came an unknown way and a dark mist and then the sea. (114)

Other characters might be classified as prisoners of their own minds as well. For example, one might argue that the blacksmith Joe Gargery, who cannot read, is imprisoned by his social position or, more specifically, his lack of education. He is clearly confined with regard to his chances to develop or climb the social ladder. To begin with, in a conversation with Miss Havisham and Pip, he does not dare to address the educated lady and talks to Pip instead (108). At one point, Pip argues that Joe "is rather backward in some things. For instance, [...] in his learning and his manners" (150). When Joe visits the gentleman Pip in London, he calls him "Sir" and behaves with stiff attempts at polite behavior (210–15). Joe considers himself to be in the wrong place, and prefers to hide his 'anomalous' personality at the marshes: "I'm wrong out of the forge, the kitchen or off th' meshes. You won't find half as much fault in me if you think of me in my forge dress, with my hammer in my hand, or even my pipe" (215).[41]

Other psychological states are described in terms of imprisonment, too. For instance, Miss Havisham is imprisoned by her past and/or her broken heart. When she was jilted on her wedding day, she decided to confine herself to the prison-like and timeless limbo world of Satis House. She stopped all the clocks—which evokes the irrelevance of time in prison—the bride-cake still sits on the table, and she still wears her wedding dress. This is her way of showing others that life and time ended for her with the destruction of her innocent and romantic hopes. Like Mrs. Clennam in *Little Dorrit*, Miss Havisham lives in a state of voluntary self-imprisonment, attempting to conceal her lacerated feelings in the darkness of her house. In the course of his first meeting with Miss Havisham, Pip describes Satis House as a dungeon or tomb:

> [...] Miss Havisham's house [...] was of *old brick*, and *dismal*, and had a great many *iron bars* to it. Some of the lower windows had been *walled up*; of those that remained, all the lower were *rustily barred*. There was a court-yard in front,

> and that was *barred*; so, we [Pip and Pumblechook, J.A.] had to wait, after ringing the bell, until some one should come to open it. (68; my emphasis, J.A.)

Like a prison, the house has got "high enclosing wall[s]" (69) and the passages are "all dark" (70); it has "an airless smell" and is infested with "mice" and "black-beetles" (94). The hideous condition of Satis House speaks of her psychological and moral deterioration over the years of her self-imposed confinement. At one point, Pip has to walk Miss Havisham around the room in circles, which evokes the circularity of prison routine.[42] Furthermore, Pip describes the old lady as a mummy or corpse:

> I saw that the bride within the bridal dress had withered like the dress, and like the flowers, and had no brightness of her sunken eyes. I saw that the dress had been put upon the rounded figure of a young woman, and that the figure upon which it now hung loose, had shrunk to skin and bone. Once, I had been taken to see some ghastly wax-work at the Fair, representing I know not what impossible personage lying in state. Once, I had been taken to one of our old marsh churches to see a skeleton in the ashes of a rich dress, that had been dug out of a vault under the church pavement. Now wax-work and skeleton seemed to have dark eyes that moved and looked at me. (71)[43]

Additionally, the broken-hearted and vengeful Miss Havisham wishes to force Pip into loving Estella to wreak revenge on men: "Love her, love her, love her! How does she use you?" (228). She wishes to imprison Pip by love, which she defines as follows: "It is blind devotion, unquestioning self-humiliation, utter submission, trust and belief against yourself and against the whole world, giving up your whole heart and soul to the smiter—as I did" (229). In other words, for her, the behavior of somebody who is in love is similar to the behavior of a prisoner. Later on, in a conversation with Pip, Miss Havisham feels remorse when she realizes what she has done to Estella and in a sense manages to overcome her 'imprisonment': "I stole her heart away and put ice in its place" (366).

Finally, Estella is imprisoned by Miss Havisham's education in the prison-like Satis House. Miss Havisham never really cared about Estella and merely abused her beautiful *protégée* for her purpose: "I bred her and educated her, to be loved. I developed her into what she is, that she might be loved" (228–29). After having been brought up by the egotistical Miss Havisham, Estella's capacities for emotions are empty and disused (like Satis House), and she will presumably never be able to develop any positive feelings for another human being. She is beautiful like a flower; yet incapable of emotions. When Pip hopelessly declares his love for Estella, she calmly says that for her, love is a signifier without signified:

> It seems [...] that there are sentiments, fancies—I don't know what to call them—which I am not able to comprehend. When you say you love me, I know what you mean, as a form of words; but nothing more. You address nothing in my breast, you touch nothing there. (333)

In a sense, Estella will remain emotionally unreachable—"like a star" (72). For instance, when Miss Havisham thinks that Estella is tired of her and passionately reproaches her charge for being distant and cold, Estella expresses "a self-possessed indifference to the wild heat of the other, that was almost cruel" (284). This cruel type of self-possession or ignorance to emotions (like love or fury), is a type of (psychological) prison as well.

The novel *Great Expectations* also defines the prison as garden, greenhouse, or fertile soil. The soil image is rather ambivalent because it is inextricably linked with the cycle of life and death. Soil evokes associations with both life and death. On the one hand, fertile soil may have a positive connotation because beautiful things can grow on it. On the other hand, soil can be perceived as being dirty, possibly disgusting,[44] and, at the end of our lives, we are usually buried in, and ultimately become, soil. At one point, Newgate is depicted as a "greenhouse" (247) or "conservatory" (250) in which Wemmick tends his prisoners like flowers: "Wemmick walked among the prisoners much as a gardener might walk among his plants" (246). When he talks to the inmates who are about to be executed, he acts "as if he were taking particular notice of the advance they had made, since last observed, towards coming out in full blow at their trial" (ibid.). One might argue that the greenhouse image primarily evokes positive associations because nice flowers may grow there. Fludernik ("Prison Metaphors" 165; fn 23) argues that the passage correlates with a perversion of the nice garden image that inverts traditional imagery. In other words, for her, death is here ironically figured as fulfilment and hell as paradise. In contrast to her, I argue that negative aspects of the treatment of flowers in a greenhouse are mapped onto the prison. In conservatories, flowers or plants are grown with scientific detachment and with the ultimate goal of being plucked. Hence, greenhouses are linked to the icy treatment of living things, which was a typical feature of Victorian prisons, i.e., the 'new' prison system.[45] I attribute the depiction of Newgate as a conservatory or greenhouse to Wemmick's quasi-scientific detachment and, more importantly, to Pip's ignorance or distant attitude toward the prisoners.

Yet another metaphor in the novel links the prison with gardening. When Pip visits Pumblechook's shop where the latter works as a corn-chandler, he perceives the drawers, tiers and paper-packets as jails:

> It appeared to me that he [Mr. Pumblechook, J.A.] must be a very happy man indeed, to have so many little drawers in his shop; and I wondered when I peeped into one or two on the lower tiers, and saw the tied-up brown paper packets inside, whether the flower-seeds and bulbs ever wanted of a fine day to break out of those *jails* and bloom. (67; my emphasis, J.A.)

In this case, an element of the outside world, namely the shop's drawers and tiers are described as prisons. The metaphor which defines prisoners as flowers is thus reversed and the flower-seeds are presented as prisoners. The link between prisons and greenhouses as well as the connection between Pumblechook's seed shop and the prison create a whole mosaic of images. Both the prison and the world may be seen as soil, garden or greenhouse, where people are grown like flowers only to be plucked, while some flowers (like the death-row prisoners at Newgate or Magwitch) will be picked earlier than others. Furthermore, these garden metaphors define both the prison and life in the outside world as an inextricable mixture of growing and dying, of pleasure and pain. The cycle of life and death may even be mirrored in the rather circular structure of the novel. This circularity, which is also reflected in the structure of the name of Pip, evokes repetitive prison routines, where the same things happen again and again. At the end of the novel, Pip is again on the marshes, i.e., precisely where he was at the beginning of the novel, and has not really learned anything. Peter Brooks points out that "'Pip' sounded like a beginning, a seed. But of course, when you reach the end of the name 'Pip,' you can return backward, and it is just the same: a repetitive text without variation or point of fixity" (500).

The Prison and Interiority in the Film

At this point, I turn to an analysis of psychological constraints in David Lean's 1946 film *Great Expectations*. The film differs from the novel in a variety of ways. First, Orlick was omitted so that Pip's sister (Freda Jackson) is not killed by him and dies of natural causes instead. Second, in comparison with the novel, Biddy (Eileen Erskine) is much older so that there is no suggestion of a possible love relationship between Pip and Biddy. Since Pip's darker side and his wish to get Biddy remained trapped in the novel's pages, the Pip of the movie is less guilt-ridden than the Pip of the novel. Generally speaking, the older Pip, the film's voice-over narrator (John Mills), is wiser than the younger versions of Pip (Anthony Wagner and John Mills) we see on the screen. In contrast to the novel's narrating self, the older Pip of the film version seems to have overcome his arrogance and snobbishness, and he also does not need to manically distance himself from prisoners and criminals.[46] For instance, when Joe (Bernard Miles) visits Pip in London, the voice-over self-critically informs us:

> As I watched Joe this Tuesday morning, dressed grotesquely in a new suit, let me confess that if I could have kept him

> away by paying money, I certainly would have paid money. In trying to become a gentleman I had succeeded in becoming a snob!

The voice-over clearly presents the fact that he developed into a snob as an unattractive element of his past. Thus, the narrating Pip must have recognized and outgrown the moral failures of that time. Later on, when Pip visits Joe and Biddy on the marshes but stays at the snobbish Blue Boar, the voice-over tells us that he is aware of the self-deception he was dominated by when he was younger: "All other swindlers upon earth are nothing to the self-swindlers. And with such pretences did I cheat myself. Surely, a curious thing."

Apart from voice-over commentaries, the film uses camera angles to illustrate Pip's moral progress and change of mind. For instance, when Pip watches an execution scene in the yard of Newgate Prison from one of the windows in Jaggers' (Francis L. Sullivan) office, we are presented with a high-angle shot filmed from Pip's point of view. The distance between the scene and the camera (and/or Pip) suggests the emotional distance and superiority Pip feels with regard to the criminals in the yard. On the other hand, the camera's slow movement from a medium close-up of Pip, who is framed by the window, to a close-up of Pip without the window frame suggests that he is in the process of questioning his emotional detachment and the confines of his snobbishness. His social conscience begins to emerge. Finally, when Magwitch (Finlay Currie) is sentenced to "be hanged by the neck"[47] with a number of other felons—who are young and old, adults and children, men and women—we are presented with a cut from Pip in medium close-up to a medium shot of these prisoners. The camera pans along the criminals' faces. This eye-level pan, which suggests Pip's perspective *vis-à-vis* the convicts, accentuates that Pip views himself as being on the same level with (and in a sense equal to) these criminals. The camera angles thus clearly underline and stress Pip's moral progress.

The film comments on the mental confinement of Estella, Miss Havisham, Pip, and Joe as follows: it suggests a link between the prison and the psychological mindset of these characters by means of their behavior and facial expressions, through the *mise-en-scène* or by juxtaposing them with metonyms of the prison (like bars or barred gates).

Pip first sees Estella (Jean Simmons) through the barred gate of Satis House. The fact that the gate's shadow falls on her beautiful face suggests the idea of a prison taint.[48] Later on, when she watches the rather hilarious box fight between Pip and the young Herbert Pocket (John Forest), she is juxtaposed with the bars of a window, which again alludes to the mental confinement of this emotionless *femme fatale*. Furthermore, Estella's expressionless and powdered face, which is reminiscent of the Marquis in Conway's film *A Tale of Two Cities*, links her to the bricks of the prison-like Satis House, thus defining her as being stone cold. However, in contrast to the novel (and with the help of Pip), the mature Estella manages to overcome her mental confinement and, at the end of the film, begins a love relationship with Pip.

Miss Havisham's (Martita Hunt) entrapment in a static, neurotic world is conveyed through the dark and dusty rooms of Satis House where time has stopped. She tells Pip that she "has never seen the sun since [Pip] was born." And later on, she states: "I know nothing of days of the week, nothing of weeks in the year." As in the novel, the gloomy long corridors and passageways effectively rework her psychological set-up, i.e., the mental confinement caused by her broken heart. Also, as in the case of Manette in Conway's *Tale*, the similarity between the spider webs in Satis House and Miss Havisham's hairstyle invites us to see a link between the setting and the character. In the film, her moral rottenness is conveyed by extreme close-ups of black-beetles and rats emerging from the rotting wedding cake where they take on strange proportions.

Before Pip enters the prison-like Satis House, he looks up at an imposing clock tower. In other words, we are presented with a POV-shot, which is at the same time a low-angle shot that conveys connotations of power and control. With his entry into Satis House, which swallows him like a crypt, Pip begins to be confined by his unhappy love for Estella. When he leaves the gloomy setting after his first visit we see him crying in misery and humiliation behind the barred gate—a juxtaposition which suggests that he is imprisoned by his sadness. The beginning of the film already accentuates Pip's lowly position in a prison-like world by presenting us with a panoramic shot of a small and isolated figure which is dominated by an oppressive and lowering sky, foreboding gallows, and creaking trees. Also, a close-up of the hinges of the gate to his sister's house alludes to the fact that Pip feels confined by his life on the marshes. In the house, the young Pip is seated in a chair that is much too large for him, while frightening adult faces loom above him and tell him to "be grateful." Later on, before his first visit to Satis House, we are presented with a close-up of Pip's sister washing him. In this shot, her tense facial expression stresses her cruelty and obsession. After the washing, she drags him along by the hair and forces him into a clean shirt: he is treated like a prisoner. Also, when Pip works as Joe's apprentice, he and Joe are merely represented as shadows between which Jaggers intervenes. The suggestion of this synecdoche is quite obvious. The work at the forge imprisons them, and reduces them to mere shadows.

Later on, the film also conveys the fact that Pip is confined by his great expectations through visual details. For instance, when he arrives in London, Pip looks up at the looming towers around St. Paul's Cathedral which is reminiscent of his looking up at the imposing clock tower of the prison-like Satis House. Also, Jaggers' office is full of objects that suggest death and define London as a tomb. More specifically, we see a hangman's noose and pistols as well as a death-mask of a former client. The significance of this metaphor becomes clearer later on. We learn that city people are socially or emotionally dead when the paralysed Pip stumbles through the crowded streets of London after Magwitch's death, and nobody cares about or even looks at him. When Pip is led to his new lodgings by Wemmick (Ivor Barnard), he is juxtaposed with the bars of a banister, which suggests his confinement in the city of London. The fact that Pip does not actually fit into city life is also highlighted by his learning to dance with a chair. When Magwitch all of a sudden turns up in London and discloses the fact that he is Pip's unknown benefactor, he looms over Pip (like the trees, towers and adult faces before) and his shadow falls on Pip's face. This shot visually alludes to Pip's being bound to Magwitch. The fact that Pip does not feel comfortable in his situation, is also suggested by the fact that he immediately leaves the chair he sat on.

Finally, I wish to comment on Joe's mental confinement. The first shot of the disoriented Joe in London is taken through the bars of Pip's window, which alludes to some sort of imprisonment. Joe is extremely clumsy in dealing with his top hat, and does not know where to place it. Later on, his hat flies about Pip's and Herbert's flat while an embarrassed Joe chases it. When Herbert Pocket (Alec Guinness) asks Joe whether he would prefer tea or coffee, he answers: "I'll take whichever is most agreeable to you." As in the novel, Joe is limited with regard to his social skills and hence in a sense confined to the forge.

Two Views on Mental Confinement

The film differs from the novel in a variety of ways. For instance, the Pip of the film has definitely developed in the course of the narrative. In contrast to the narrating self of the novel, the film's voice-over narrator has managed to overcome his feelings of guilt. This development also correlates with the film's decidedly happy ending. When Pip and Estella float hand in hand from the sepulchral Satis House in the film's final shot, the movie's title is superimposed so that its hopeful sentiment is stressed. Pip and Estella are shown to have great expectations concerning their future relationship. Before this happy ending, the film primarily alludes to the mental confinement of characters by juxtaposing them with metonyms of the prison (such as bars, gates, and shadows). Nevertheless, the prison can be overcome in the film version.

The novel is bleaker in comparison with the film and suggests that most forms of mental confinement cannot be overcome. Interestingly, the various psychological states of imprisonment interact with the novel's metaphor of imprisonment that defines the prison as garden. Pip's riches grow out of Magwitch's work at the penal colony called Botany Bay, where he is literally imprisoned. At the same time these riches imprison Pip at a psychological level because they turn him into a snobbish and arrogant gentleman and tie him to Magwitch. The beautiful 'flower' Estella grows out of Miss Havisham's treatment at the prison-like Satis House. Estella is imprisoned by her lack of feelings, while Miss Havisham is imprisoned by her broken heart. Furthermore, Wemmick treats the inmates of Newgate Prison in a detached manner like flowers in a greenhouse, and inhabits a prison-like house which he refers to in terms of his "Castle" (201). For me, the Castle's existence clearly echoes the prison's presence in Wemmick's thinking. Additionally, the hierarchical surveillance in the world outside prison aligns the novel to the way of seeing which is inscribed in the Benthamite *Panopticon*. Ultimately, the prison in the novel appears to be universal and inescapable. Most characters are closely linked to actual prisons, forms of mental confinement or both at the same time.

We also learn that even after having finished his confessional story, the older Pip must still be a snobbish and arrogant gentleman. In the following passage, Pip looks back "at that time," and we can deduce that he has actually learned nothing from his own story:

> At that time, jails were much neglected, and the period of exaggerated reaction consequent on all public wrong-doing—and which is always its heaviest and longest punishment—was still far off. So, felons were not lodged and fed better than soldiers (to say nothing of paupers), and seldom set fire to their prisons with the excusable object of improving the flavour of their soup. (246)

One might read this ambiguous passage as an expression of a general liberal-conservative consensus, "wanting prisons as simply neither too hard nor too easy" (Tambling "Prison-Bound" 128). Indeed, Collins attributes the attitudes toward prisons that are expressed to Dickens (*Dickens* 17; 73) and argues that the author here ironically refers to the "great riots at Chatham Convict Prison" in 1861, "which had been provoked mainly by a sudden reduction in the prison diet" (20).[49] In contrast to Collins and Paroissien (*Companion* 272), I attribute the opinions in the passage to Pip rather than Dickens, i.e., to the (fictional) narrator as opposed to the (real) author. On the one hand, the narrator notes that prisons were "much neglected" at that time, and (quite arrogantly) argues that he understands prisoners who "set fire" to prison in order to improve the bad quality of prison food (because for him, such behavior is at least "excusable"). On the other hand, since the narrator makes fun of "exaggerated" reactions to public wrong-doings like tough prison conditions, he seems to believe that penal places should never turn into penal palaces. Also, he wishes to place prisoners below soldiers and paupers, and argues that convicts should be punished by being provided with food and cells that are worse than the food and accommodation of soldiers and paupers. One should perhaps keep in mind that, following my interpretation, these attitudes are the opinions of the narrating self (as opposed to the experiencing self). Thus, even the older and allegedly wiser Pip continues the stigmatization of prisoners and criminals, and does not see that he still reproduces the dominance discourse inspired by the carceral network.

If the guilt-ridden narrator had realized that he is not a criminal, his attitude toward prisoners might have changed and he would perhaps not have written this confessional autobiography which follows his desire to silence his feelings of guilt.[50] Pip has not managed to overcome his feelings of guilt. Even at the end of the novel, the narrator continues to live as a divided self: a guilt-ridden Pip on the one hand, and a Pip who wishes to silence these feelings on the other. Pip's divided self is of course reminiscent of the split that the prisons in *Little Dorrit* and *A Tale of Two Cities* initiate in the Dorrits or Manette. In these two novels, the former inmates do not manage to reconcile their former prison identities (or hopeless selves) and their hopeful selves. The novel *Great Expectations* also suggests that since Pip's feelings of guilt cannot easily be overcome, Pip will remain a prisoner of his own mind until he dies. And this once again sheds a critical light on the prison.

The consecutive novels *Little Dorrit, A Tale of Two Cities*, and *Great Expectations* are connected by the way in which they narrate the prison. First of all, it is worth noting that in the course of these novels, the descriptions of the prison settings become less and less detailed, while the representation of internal states becomes more and more elaborate. The detailed renderings of the Marseilles jail and the Marshalsea in *Little Dorrit* develop into an empty center at the beginning of *A Tale of Two Cities*. Even though the story is clearly about the Bastille and the question of what it did to Manette, the prison setting is at first not described at all. It is only later on that the narrator tells us what his cell looked like and that we are presented with detailed descriptions of the prison at La Force and the Conciergerie. This movement away from external details is continued in *Great Expectations*. We learn next to nothing about the hulks or the architecture of Newgate, and the penal colony in Australia is not described at all. Dickens' narrators seem to gradually realize that one has to peer beneath surfaces to grasp the functioning of the prison. At the same time, the representation of internal states becomes more and more dominant and reaches its peak in *Great Expectations*. In this novel, we are no longer confronted with descriptions of prisons at all. The prison operates in the background and within the characters; it has been internalized. Even though Pip was never imprisoned, he reproduces the process of self-surveillance inspired by the prison. Pip attempts to liberate himself from his feelings of guilt by distancing himself from any link with criminality and/or prisons but ultimately fails. Paradoxically, his confessional autobiography ties him closer and closer to the prison. *Great Expectations* serves as an important link between Dickens and first-person prison novels of the twentieth century because Pip's autobiography foreshadows the representation of the inmate's internal states in first-person narratives of the twentieth century. The authorial novels *Little Dorrit* and *A Tale of Two Cities*, on the other hand, foreshadow the way in which films narrate the prison. In their selections and arrangements, the narrators present us with detailed representations of surfaces and they simulate internal states through external details.

In his mature fiction, Dickens renders the experience of imprisonment through the unjust suffering of many inmates. Dickens clearly condemns the prison by highlighting how severly his sympathetic prisoners may suffer in the dark dungeons he confronts us with. It is also worth noting that Dickens focuses on 'negative' metaphors of imprisonment which accentuate the prisoners' plight as well. In the following chapter, I will show that most prison novels and films of the twentieth century concentrate on one innocent identificatory figure who is usually set apart from the rest of the prison population, while the 'other' inmates are normally presented as 'real' criminals. In contrast to Dickens' mature fiction, such narratives critique the imprisonment of our prisoner-hero but tacitly accept the incarceration of the other inmates. In Chapter VI, I will additionally show that twentieth-century prison narratives use both 'positive' and 'negative' metaphors of imprisonment. This binary arrangement serves to illustrate that certain forms of imprisonment are not too bad after all. More specifically, the two sets of metaphors accentuate the distinction between reformative penal styles, which most prison narratives of the twentieth century approve of, and punitive or discipline-based institutions, which they critique.

ENDNOTES

1. I am, of course, aware of the fact that the authorial narrator "does not *see* the story; 'he' produces it. What the narrative focalizes on on the story level is therefore the result of *selection* and not the result of *perception*" (Fludernik *Towards* 345). However, it is worth noting that *what* Dickens' authorial narrator in *Little Dorrit* (and also in *A Tale of Two Cities*) selects and arranges for us, i.e., the detailed descriptions of settings and external features, is reminiscent of a camera eye because of the general focus on exteriority rather than interiority.
2. The prison is here defined as a cage for rats or beasts. The juxtaposition of rats and inmates is also used in prison films to suggest that the prison staff view the inmates as vermin and treat them like animals. Examples of such juxtapositions can be found in the films *Birdman of Alcatraz* (1962), *Sleepers*, and *The Shawshank Redemption*.
3. Amy Dorrit, the 'Child of the Marshalsea,' is selflessly devoted to her father, for whom she works and cares incessantly.
4. At one point, Rigaud refers to the prison in Marseilles as "the old infernal hole" (135).
5. At the begining of the novel, William Dorrit is incarcerated for debt. Later on, the money he owes is miraculously found again and the Dorrits are released. Then Arthur, who unwisely invested money in Merdle's enterprises, is ruined and in turn imprisoned in the Marshalsea.
6. Little Dorrit's mother died when Amy was eight years old.
7. Similarly, the suspicions of other people (like the landlady) may have turned Rigaud into a criminal.
8. According to Manfred Jahn, focalization in film relates to "the ways and means of presenting information from somebody's point of view. Focalization can be determined by answering the question *Whose point of view orients the current segment (track, channel) of filmic information?* Or: *Whose perception serves as the current source of information?* Perception is here used as quite a general term which includes actual as well as imaginary perception (such as visions, dreams, memories) and other states of consciousness" (F4.3). With regard to external focalization, the camera allows us to look *at* the characters from the outside, whereas with regard to internal focalization, the camera simulates a character's gaze (e.g., through POV-shots or memory sequences).

9. 'Free indirect discourse' denotes a third-person rendering of a character's thoughts that stays close to the character's own oral syntax and diction except that tenses are shifted to the current narrative tense and pronouns are adjusted.
10. The film adaptation can also be said to animate William Dorrit's welcome to new inmates of the Marshalsea ("The space is [...] limited [...]; but you will find it apparently grow larger after a time [...]" [621]).
11. The narrator informs us that since the social stratification in prison is like society's, it is impossible to differentiate between prisoners and non-prisoners: Arthur, "the unaccustomed visitor from outside, naturally assumed everybody here to be prisoners [...]. Whether they were or not, did not appear [...]" (95). The way in which Frederick and William Dorrit are said to walk up and down the prison yard, might also lead to false conclusions concerning their status: "Frederick the free, was so humbled, bowed, withered, and faded; William the bond, was so courtly, condescending, and benevolently conscious of a position; that in this regard only, if no other, the brothers were a spectacle to wonder at" (219).
12. The first thing Arthur notices when he visits his mother is his former room and the closet where he used to be locked up as a child: "There was the old cellaret with nothing in it, lined with lead, like a sort of coffin in compartments; there was the old dark closet, also with nothing in it, of which he had been many a time the sole contents, in days of punishment, when he had regarded it as the veritable entrance to that bourne to which the tract had found him galloping" (45). The structure of the Clennam house clearly mirrors the architecture of the Marshalsea (68). At the end of the novel, Mrs. Clennam's house literally becomes Rigaud's tomb because he dies in its collapse. The question of whether this involves poetic justice—as Collins (*Dickens* 250) claims—remains unclear.
13. I disagree with Smith's argument that the film's soundtrack is "an assortment of often undifferentiated noises which contribute little to the film's atmosphere" (*Dickens* 146). Smith appears to be completely unaware of the metaphorical potential of the interplay between sound and images.
14. Originally, Dickens had intended to title his novel *Nobody's Fault* with an ironic reference to the irresponsible Circumlocution Office.
15. By contrast, the sensitive non-materialist Amy witnesses her father's death and cries at the side of his bed, whereas the social-climbing Fanny decides to remain at her party. Afterwards, in a line Dickens never wrote, she hypocritically announces: "I don't know how I shall

ever recover from this shock. Not having been with poor papa till the last grieves me more than I can say."

16. Such shots effectively convey the idea that Little Dorrit was "overshadowed by a large pair of black whiskers and a large white cravat" (619).
17. Bender even sees a putative link between structural attributes of the penitentiary and free indirect discourse. For him, "the penitentiary habilitates, in its own technical practices, devices parallel to those of free indirect discourse. The mode of literary production and the social institution present collateral images of one another" (*Imagining* 203). This alleged parallel is particularly bizarre because in actual prisons, prison officers can only gain external knowledge about the inmates.
18. The effects of imprisonment as they are depicted in the case of Arthur (721) are the only instance with regard to which the 'new' prison system seeps into *Little Dorrit*. These effects appear to be based on the "torturing anxieties and horrible despair" (Dickens "Philadelphia" 101) which Dickens observed in prisoners at two 'new' prisons in Pennsylvania which followed the 'separate' system.
19. Grass never defines the term 'private self' in his book. Here is the definition that I use: while the term 'social self' refers to the way in which others perceive an inmate and construct his identity, the term 'private self' refers to the way in which the prisoner himself perceives and constructs his identity (see Frey 46–55).
20. Grass argues that the "novel establishes the stare as the basis for its narration" (118), and repeatedly speaks of "the omniscient stare" (121; 123). The authorial narrator does not 'stare'; 'he' arranges the sun and the shadows.
21. In narrative theory, an embedded narrative or story-within-the-story is called a hypodiegetic narrative. According to Genette (*Narrative* 228–34; *Revisited* Ch. 14), an extradiegetic narrator (who can be homodiegetic or heterodiegetic) presents us with an intradiegetic narrative (the frame narrative), and characters at the intradiegetic level may become intradiegetic narrators who present us with their own story, and these stories are located at the hypodiegetic level. Genette had initially suggested the term 'metanarrative' but Bal ("Notes" 48–50) suggested the term 'hyponarrative' in order to avoid confusing the term with 'metafiction,' which refers to fiction *about* fiction.
22. Mrs. Clennam's state of psychological imprisonment is also stressed when the narrator informs us that "[s]he stood at the window, bewildered, looking down into this prison as it were out of her own different prison" (753).

23. At one point, Dombey realizes that he and his wife are an "ill-assorted couple, unhappy in themselves and in each other, bound together by no tie but the manacle that joined their fettered hands" (618). That love may become a prison is also illustrated in *Little Dorrit*. In John Chivery's imagination, his love for Amy becomes a prison in which he wishes to keep his beloved under lock and key: "Say things prospered, and they were united. She, the Child of the Marshalsea; he, the lock-keeper. There was a fitness in that. [...] Then, being all in all to one another, there was even an appropriate grace in the lock. With the world shut out (except that part of it which would be shut in); with its troubles and disturbances only known to them by hearsay, as they would be described by the pilgrims tarrying with them on their way to the Insolent Shrine; with the Arbour above, and the Lodge below; they would glide down the stream of time, in pastoral domestic happiness" (211).
24. Originally Dickens wanted to call the novel *Buried Alive*.
25. Manette's fears are of course unjustified: the French aristocrat Charles Evrémonde had detested the tyranny of his uncle and attempted to free himself from the associations of his family name and the power of the old order. In 1775, he therefore emigrated to England and began to teach French under the name of 'Charles Darnay.' In England, Barsad and his accomplice, Roger Cly, then accuse him of treason, alleging that he smuggled confidential documents to the French. During the cross-examination, Barsad is unable to distinguish Darnay from Sidney Carton, an English barrister who looks almost exactly like Darnay. When the jury returns from its deliberation, Barsad and Cly have fled and Darnay is declared innocent. In the course of the trial, both Darnay and Carton fall in love with the beautiful Lucie Manette but Carton decides not to disturb the deep feelings between Darnay and Lucie.
26. During the course of the French Revolution, the Marquis is killed and Darnay inherits his title. The Defarges then manage to lure him to France with a letter from Gabelle, a former servant of the St Evrémonde family. The revolutionaries send Darnay to the prison of La Force because he is an aristocrat.
27. After his release, Madame Defarge's relentless hatred of the aristocracy causes Charles to be sent before the Tribunal again, which this time consigns him to the Conciergerie and sentences him to be guillotined.
28. The crook Barsad allows Carton access to Darnay's trial and, after this, to his prison cell. Carton takes Darnay's place and is executed instead of him.

29. Darnay's story about an anonymous prisoner in the Tower of London, who hid some personal writing under the (almost undecipherable) sign D.I.G., which turned out to be the imperative 'dig!' (105), demonstrates that identity may not necessarily be preserved in the memories of others (Lloyd "Language" 155–56).
30. It is not only that they look like twins. The novel constructs further similarities. For instance, when Darnay is imprisoned, it is Carton who strikes Lorry as having the wasted air of a prisoner: "Taking note of the wasted air which clouded the naturally handsome features, and having the expression of prisoners' faces fresh in his mind, he was strongly reminded of that expression" (322). Also, when Carton exchanges positions with Darnay in his solitary cell, the desperate prisoner suddenly appears to be endowed with a strength of both "will and action" that "appeared quite supernatural" (364) so that we do get a sense that Carton dies to save his mirror-image.
31. The title *A Tale of Two Cities* might thus not only refer to Paris and London but also to Paris before and after the French Revolution. In this case the title would involve irony because upon closer inspection, the 'two' cities turn out to be rather similar.
32. It is perhaps worth noting that the penal colony in Australia is mentioned but never explicitly described. This 'absence' might reflect the distance between such types of punishment and 'normal' citizens like Pip. Also, one could argue that this 'absence' mirrors the 'normal' citizen's ignorance toward "the pursuit of profit, the building of empire, and [...] social *apartheid*" that "produced modern Australia" (Said 524).
33. At Satis House, the rich Miss Havisham attempts to make Pip love the beautiful Estella, who is in her charge. Miss Havisham, whose husband-to-be did not turn up at their wedding, has turned Estella into a *femme fatale* to wreak revenge on men. Pip falls in love with Estella, and becomes ashamed of his humble origins.
34. At one point, the lawyer Jaggers informs Pip that he has got 'great expectations.' Pip becomes a gentleman and moves to London thanks to an unknown benefactor, whom he assumes to be Miss Havisham. However, one night Pip learns that it was Magwitch, the convict whom he had once aided on the marshes, who financed his advancement. Magwitch has returned to England from a penal colony in Australia in violation of his sentence of transportation to see the gentleman he has created.
35. Toward the end of the novel we learn that the crook Compeyson is responsible for Miss Havisham's psychological state because he "is the man who professed to be Miss Havisham's lover" (325).

36. Magwitch tells Pip that he worked as "a sheep-farmer, stock-breeder, other trades besides, away in the new world" and that he lived "in a solitary hut" (296–98). "Botany Bay" (307) was a well-known Australian penal colony where convicts had to work extremely hard and suffered from inadequate supply of food. Convicts were expected to grow their own food on public farms, and ex-convicts were supposed to become a self-sufficient peasantry. Paroissien quotes James Ives, Keeper of Horsemonger Lane Gaol, Southwark, as having said: "I know that every one that ever I have heard of or known would do anything in the world rather than go to Botany Bay, or return there again" (Paroissien *Companion* 320).
37. It was literally impossible to create a gentleman in London because the convicts of Botany Bay did not receive any money. Paroissien states that this was so because "it [i.e., money, J.A.] could buy no comforts there" (*Companion* 320). The name of 'Mag-witch,' which might be a blend of the lexemes 'magic' (or 'magician') and 'witch,' perhaps suggests that the whole thing was done by magic.
38. This is of course reminiscent of the Dorrits and Manette. The major difference between *Little Dorrit* and *A Tale of Two Cities* on the one hand and *Great Expectations* on the other is that Pip becomes mentally confined without having ever been a prisoner.
39. Pip's classification of Magwitch as a beast reflects his general attitude toward criminals and convicts. However, he is mistaken because one might consider Magwitch to be the moral center of the novel. Pip's classification is reminiscent of the authorial narrator in *Little Dorrit* who initially describes Cavaletto and Rigaud as vermin.
40. Magwitch also went through a stage of purely iterative existence. Once he has returned from Australia, he alludes to the circuit of delinquency and tells Pip: "In jail and out of jail, in jail and out of jail, in jail and out of jail. There you've got it. That's *my* life pretty much" (319).
41. On the other hand, one might argue that like Magwitch, Joe represents some sort of moral center because he is honest and rather fond of Pip. When Pip is ill after the ruin of his 'great expectations,' Joe gently tends him and pays his debts. Pip thinks that there is "a simple dignity in him" (215).
42. On the one hand, the inmates of Victorian prisons actually had to walk around the prison yard in circles (see e.g., Mayhew and Binny). On the other hand, this circularity mirrors Miss Havisham's psychological state and life style, and perhaps also the circular structure of the novel.
43. The word 'waxwork' provides another link between Satis House and the prison because it recurs when Pip stands before Newgate Prison

for the very first time: "While I looked about me here, an exceedingly dirty and partially drunk minister of justice asked me if I would like to step in and hear a trial or so: informing me that he could give me a front place for half-a-crown, whence I should command a full view of the Lord Chief Justice in his wigs and robes—mentioning that awful personage like waxwork, and presently offering him at the reduced price of eighteenpence" (163). As Cockshut argues, in both cases Pip thinks of himself as "a detached spectator," while he is actually "about to be deeply involved" (47).

44. For example, Pip beats "the prison dust off [his] feet" and feels contaminated by "the soiling consciousness of Mr. Wemmick's conservatory" (249–50). Similarly, Jaggers obsessively uses "scented soap" (202) to wash off the prison's literal (and perhaps also metaphorical) dirt.
45. One only has to think of the medical and scientific prison committee that Du Cane appointed (McConville "Victorian" 147).
46. Since Pip never feels guilty of having murdered his sister, the guilt complex in the film is rather harmless. Pip's only 'crimes' are that he steals pantry items for Magwitch and fails to appreciate Joe in London. His cruelty to Biddy also did not survive on the screen.
47. The courtroom scene suggests the emotional distance of the judicial system by the fact that the judge is only metonymically represented in terms of his voice. Like some distant god, he coldly passes a sentence on to the prisoners. In this scene, the judge is unseen like the character of Jaggers in the novel.
48. Such shots were anticipated by the shadows on the Dorrit family in the novel *Little Dorrit*: "the shadow of the Marshalsea wall was a real darkening influence, and could be seen on the Dorrit family at any stage of the sun's course" (250).
49. See also Paroissien (*Companion* 272) who argues that "Dickens shared the view that the correction of earlier public wrong-doing had prompted a period of 'exaggerated reaction.'"
50. Booth argues that the narrating Pip is "a generous man whose heart is where the reader's is supposed to be" (*Rhetoric* 176). Similarly, Baston claims that Pip achieves a "final position of moral balance" (323), and Tharaud thinks that Pip's autobiography is "morally mature" and "emotionally honest" (102). Giddings et al. consider the novel to be a *Bildungsroman*, with regard to which the central character has learnt something about the world and himself (54). I obviously disagree with these arguments because I do not necessarily see a significant development in Pip.

Chapter Four

The Experience of Imprisonment in Prison Narratives of the Twentieth Century

Critical Counter-Discourse or Pro-Prison Propaganda?

Fictional prison narratives fulfil a moral function because they comment on the reasons why people are sent to prison and on the treatment they receive behind bars. Since a connection exists between sympathy for prisoners and contempt for the prison system (as well as between dislike of inmates and an approval of prison as an institution), it is of primary importance to provide a close reading of the representation of the prison population in fictional prison narratives.

Our identificatory figures in twentieth-century prison narratives are often prisoner-heroes who are wrongfully imprisoned.

For example, the film *The Shawshank Redemption* plays upon a retroactive establishment of Andy Dufresne's (Tim Robbins) innocence. More specifically, the 'innocent' city banker is convicted for murdering his wife and her lover and descends into the hell of the Shawshank State Prison, where he is exploited and raped. In the movie *Down by Law*, the disc jockey Zack (Tom Waits) and the pimp Jack (John Lurie) are both set up and then exposed to the monotonous and boring life at the Orleans Parish Prison. Sometimes our identificatory figures undergo cruel punishments for what are only apparent transgressions or accidents. For instance, the four boys in the novel *Sleepers* and its 1996 film version are sent to the Wilkinson Home for Boys in New York because following a stupid prank, they accidentally killed a man with a hot dog vendor's cart.[1] Some prison narratives focus on the social causes of crime, thus pointing out that certain criminal acts may be motivated by poverty or other types of social pressure. For example, the major protagonist of the prison autobiography *I Am a Fugitive from a Georgia Chain Gang!* and its 1932 film adaptation steals a few dollars because he is hungry and is then sentenced to serve time in a hellish chain gang.[2] Similarly, in the film *The Loneliness of the Long-Distance Runner* (1964), Colin (Tom Courtenay) is sent to borstal for robbing a bakery. The film 'explains' the crime as follows: Colin accuses his mother (Avis Bunnage) of not having waited to get a new boyfriend (Raymond Dyer) until his dead father was cold in his grave. She then hits him and throws him out of the house. As an afterthought, she hurls the order not to return without some money.

At first glance, one might feel that this almost essential erasure of criminality on the part of the prisoner-heroes correlates with an attempt to construct a fictional counter-discourse to society's strategies of stigmatising prison inmates. However, upon closer inspection, one realizes that the innocent hero is frequently constructed as an exception within the prison world and that he is in fact diametrically opposed to the 'other' prisoners. More specifically, he is normally surrounded by a group of guilty or 'real' criminals who 'belong where they are.' Hence, most prison narratives of the twentieth century question the legitimacy of the central protagonist's incarceration but tacitly accept imprisonment when it comes to the other prisoners who are usually represented as the 'real' criminals.

For instance, at first one may feel that the film *The Shawshank Redemption* condemns the prison system because the prison world is upside down. The Shawshank State Prison houses innocent inmates like Andy and is run by sadist criminals like Warden Norton (Bob Gunton) and Captain Hadley (Clancy Brown).[3] However, the movie also represents the prison as a societal necessity because wicked murderers like Elmo Blatch exist. This devilish criminal, who committed the crime for which Andy is incarcerated, confronts us with the fact that prisons are not only instruments of injustice. The representation of the villainous Blatch, who is once shown laughing insanely with stereotypically bad teeth, demonstrates that prison films may also stigmatize criminals and justify the existence of prisons. More specifically, the movie opposes Warden Norton's 'old' and brutal prison regime, which it critiques, with a more progressive apparatus, which it agrees with because ultimately we need prisons to confine wicked criminals like Elmo Blatch and most of the other prisoners (and perhaps also the sadist Captain Hadley). *The Shawshank Redemption* thus participates in a discourse of subtle pro-prison propaganda that tries to persuade its recipients of the existence of evil criminals and the necessity of well-run or rehabilitative prisons. Furthermore, the film encourages self-satisfaction and contentment. By means of the contrast between the traditional and the more progressive prison, as well as by setting the movie in the remote past of the late forties, this film of the 1990s implies that prisons today are not as bad as they used to be. Viewers are drawn into believing that penal reform has already taken place and that today's prisons are run by well-meaning individuals.

It is also worth noting that most prison narratives of the twentieth century argue in favor of imprisoning the guilty as long as our innocent identificatory figures can manage to break out of prison. For example, in *I Am a Fugitive from a Georgia Chain Gang!*, the first-person narrator Burns, with whom we are supposed to identify and who twice manages to escape from the chain gang, persistently distances himself from his fellow inmates whom he perceives as 'real' criminals. Already in custody, Burns is eager to stress that he is "*not* a criminal" and complains about being "locked up in the new State Street Police Headquarters with *the riff-raff of the underworld*" (107; my emphasis, J.A.), thus at least implicitly arguing that they belong where they are. Similarly, the film *Down by Law* focuses almost exclusively on the sympathetic inmates Zack, Jack, and Bob, who ultimately escape from prison. We only see the other prisoners in the course of a dolly shot at the beginning of the prison sequence. The camera moves slowly and smoothly past a row of barred cells and then stops at a medium shot of Zack, who will be joined by Jack, and later on by Bob. After the medium shot, we are presented with "a 30-minute sequence during which the camera never leaves the confines of the cell" (Jarvis 224). The other prisoners are reduced to off-screen murmurings so that we do get a sense that their imprisonment does not really matter. Indeed, the examples listed above verify Wilson's ("Inside" 79) and O'Sullivan's ("Representations" 321) argument that in prison films, escape and/or redemption is usually reserved for exceptional individuals, while the mass of ordinary prisoners deserve what they get.

Sillitoe's novella "The Loneliness of the Long-Distance Runner" is another prison narrative that contains both a 'liberal' (or critical) and a 'conservative' reading of the prison. The first-person narrator Smith is a young working-class man who is sent to borstal for robbing a bakery. The governor of the institution, who believes that the inmates are redeemable through athletic discipline, quickly discovers that the new inmate is an excellent long-distance runner, and wants him to win a cross-country race so that he can put one more feather on his career cap. On the day of the race, the trainee arrives at the finishing line far in front of the other competitors but deliberately stops short of the tape and refuses to win the cup. One might sympathize with Smith who tries to point out that the hypocritical borstal governor does not actually care about the inmates and merely attempts to exploit their talents for personal gain. From this perspective, the novella may be read as an argument in favor of defiant individualism and against the borstal's hypocritical demands of conformism.

On the other hand, it is worth noting that the narrator is a wicked juvenile delinquent who is simply on the prowl for another bit of thievery when he commits the crime of robbing a bakery: "if our [i.e., his and his friend Mike's] eyes worn't glued to the ground looking for lost wallets and watches they was swivelling around house windows and shop doors in case we saw something easy and worth nipping into" (24). The narrator is an alienated and socially hostile individual who has spent time in "Remand Homes," and had been convicted before he was sent to borstal (16; 21–23). By the time of narration, he has been released and completed a new and more substantial theft:

> I'm out now and the heat's switched on again, but the rats haven't got me for the last big thing I pulled. I counted six hundred and twenty-eight pounds and am still living off it because I did the job all on my own, and after it I had the peace to write all this, and it'll be money enough to keep me going until I finish my plans for doing an even bigger snatch, something up my sleeve I wouldn't tell to a living soul. (54)

At the end of the story, Smith is still a hardened criminal. He is planning "an even bigger snatch," the details of which he "wouldn't tell to a living soul" (54). Thus, Smith can rightly be considered to be an "incorrigible thief and thug" (Leonardi 58) or an "unrepentant ne'er-do-well" (Slack 3). From this perspective, the primary function of the intimacy between the roguish narrator and the reader might be to make us feel and fear the narrator's criminal impulses and dangerous attitude to society. The novella may be read as a warning by a criminal to law-abiding citizens. It seems to suggest that since people like Smith exist, we definitely need ways to protect society from these hoodlums. Also, since the narrator's rehabilitation in borstal did not work out, the novella might argue in favor of reformed borstals that are run by well-meaning individuals rather than selfish hypocrites like the governor.

It is not only the case that in fictional narratives our sympathies for the prisoners influence our perception of the prison. The representation of the prison system also impacts on our perception of the inmates. The harsh treatment of prisoners by diabolic wardens or prison officers evokes sympathy for the prisoners (usually regardless of whether they are guilty or not). The film *A Clockwork Orange* (1971) presents us with such a constellation. In this movie, Alex (Malcolm McDowell) is the leader of a gang called the droogs, and delights in gratuitous acts of violence. When peer pressure drives him from assault, rape, and robbery to murder, he is caught and sent to prison. And from the moment he is knocked over the eyes with a milk bottle by one of his 'droogs' and abandoned to the police, he becomes a suffering victim with whom we are invited to sympathize. Once Alex is caught, he is beaten, cursed at, spat on and ultimately exposed to the Ludovico Technique[4] so that our hostility is quickly directed toward everyone but him.

> Against the corporate violence of institutions, Alex's [...] violence takes on another redeeming feature. The *mise-en-scène* in the second part takes account of the changed rapport of forces. For whereas Kubrick stylizes the violent behaviour of his hero by a strategy that substitutes, disperses and masks consequences, his victimization at the hands of society is undistanced, in fact, calculated to yield a maximum of 'realism' and verisimilitude and to spare the spectator nothing of Alex's emotional agonies and physical suffering. (Elsässer 187)

The film argues that the perfect rehabilitation, which the Ludovico treatment achieves, is not desirable because it implies the complete destruction of individual willpower. The movie ends with Alex lying on his hospital bed fantasizing about a life of more sex and violence. Rafter argues that the film's ending shows us "the confirmed delinquent's delight in violence" (3). For me, the message of the film is slightly more specific. I think that it argues that Alex's criminal violence correlates with individuality, autonomy, spontaneity, and perhaps even art,[5] and as such should not be disciplined by conformist forces like the prison or the Ludovico Medical Facility.

The ending of the film differs from the ending of the novel. In the novel, Alex decides to found a family and is suddenly happy to conform with society's norms ("Perhaps I was getting too old for the sort of jeezny I had been leading, brothers. I was eighteen now, just gone" [236]). The question "what's it going to be then eh?," which is repeated fourteen times in the novel and might function as some sort of *leitmotif*, is now answered: "That's what it's going to be then my brothers, as I come to the end of this tale" (239). The novel thus argues that rehabilitation and reform are possible but they must be a matter of personal choice and cannot be imposed by the state. In this context, the prison chaplain raises the novel's most important questions: "What does God want? Does God want goodness or the choice of goodness? Is a man who chooses the bad perhaps in some ways better than a man who has the good imposed upon him?" (131).

Robert F. Stroud in the novel *Birdman of Alcatraz* and its 1962 film version is another example of a criminal who is exposed to an unjust treatment in prison. Stroud killed a man (22) and later on a guard in prison (43), but becomes a sensitive ornithologist who clearly shows signs of rehabilitation. Ultimately, the prisoner turns out to be more humane than the prison staff at Leavenworth and Alcatraz. By constructing Stroud as a scientist and sympathetic individual, Gaddis' novel and its film version clearly wish to counter processes of dehumanization and depersonalization, i.e., the idea that Alcatraz houses the 'worst of the worst.' Additionally, the two narratives question the penal practice of merely exposing prisoners to deadening routines and abstract rules and regulations, and support reformative prisons in which inmates are given an occupation like bird-breeding that allows them to develop their personality.[6]

Most prison narratives of the twentieth century critique and legitimate the prison at the same time. More specifically, they tend to condemn 'traditional' prisons based on discipline but simultaneously legitimate rehabilitative incarceration.[7] Therefore, the following statement by Bell Hooks about films in general also applies to prison novels and films. According to Hooks, a "film may have incredibly revolutionary standpoints merged with conservative ones. This mingling of standpoints is often what makes it hard for audiences to critically 'read' the overall filmic narrative" (3). The elements of twentieth-century prison narratives are normally always the same. We are confronted with an innocent prisoner-hero who suffers under a brutal system. The fate of this unique character is then represented as being illegitimate. The mass of ordinary prisoners, on the other hand, are depicted as 'real' criminals who have to be imprisoned (but not necessarily under the awful circumstances we are presented with). Most twentieth-century prison narratives only invite us to sympathize with the innocent prisoner-hero but they do not allow us to empathize with the 'deviant' rest of the prison population. Generally speaking, the representations of prison in such fictional narratives "actively contribute towards legitimizing prison as a form of punishment" (O'Sullivan "Representations" 321). I would only add that they tend to legitimize reformative incarceration rather than the prison system per se.

NARRATING PRISONERS AND PRISON SETTINGS IN NOVELS AND FILMS

The Prison Population in Fictional Prison Narratives

In opposition to demographics within the British and the US correctional system, both prison novels and films focus almost exclusively on white and heterosexual inmates.[8] More specifically, our identificatory figures in prison narratives are almost always Caucasian. This is true of both prison films and prison novels. For instance, Stroud in the novel *Birdman of Alcatraz* as well as the narrators of *I Am a Fugitive from a Georgia Chain Gang!*, "The Loneliness of the Long-Distance Runner," *A Clockwork Orange*, and *Sleepers* are all white. Surprisingly, even Red, the narrator of "Rita Hayworth and Shawshank Redemption" is white—even though he was transformed into an African American in the film *The Shawshank Redemption*. In King's novella, Red is white because we learn that as a kid, he had "a big mop of carroty hair" (55).

Furthermore, the colored inmates that exist are usually relegated to the general prison population who are represented as 'real' criminals. Occasionally, colored characters appear in prison narratives and offer assistance to our identificatory figure but their story always serves as the subplot of a much more important white master narrative. Film examples are the colored inmates Sebastian (Everett Brown) in *I Am a Fugitive from a Chain Gang!*; English (Paul Benjamin) in *Escape from Alcatraz*; Angel (Alrick Riley) in *Scum*; Coombes (Yaphet Kotto) in *Brubaker* (1980)[9]; Rizzo (Eugene Byrd) in *Sleepers*; and Red (Morgan Freeman) in *The Shawshank Redemption*. Their primary function is to increase our admiration for white heroes who are clearly at the center of interest. Examples of such prisoner-heroes are James Allen (Paul Muni) in *I Am a Fugitive from a Chain Gang!*; Frank Morris (Clint Eastwood) in *Escape from Alcatraz*; Carlin (Ray Winstone) in *Scum*; Brubaker (Robert Redford) in *Brubaker*; the four white boys in *Sleepers*; and Andy Dufresne in *The Shawshank Redemption*. It is also worth noting that the colored inmates are always clearly guilty, while the white prisoner-heroes are typically wrongfully convicted.

Some narratives like Burns' autobiography *I Am a Fugitive from a Georgia Chain Gang!* are even openly racist. The narrator concentrates on his own suffering, and makes very few comments about the role of race in prison. Also, Burns habitually refers to African Americans as 'niggers' (63; 156–57), and when he protests against Georgia's violations of its own penal regulations, he complains that contrary to the law, "whites and Negroes worked side by side" (176). The film adaptation also

> [...] pushes African Americans into the background of a segregated prison yard. [...] All of the principal and supporting actors are white, and the most striking images of the film show James Allen chained to a dozen white men, sitting uncomfortably on their cots or gulping down meals of grease, fried dough, pig fat and sorghum. (Lewis 236)

The film clearly distorts the historical reality of the southern chain gangs because in them, African Americans made up more than

75 percent of the inmates (Rotman 176). Prison narratives of the twentieth century are narratives about the victimization of white[10] and heterosexual men—and they are usually rescued from their victimization at the end.

In this respect, the film *Wilde* is exceptional because we are presented with a bisexual identificatory figure who leaves the prison as a broken man. Nevertheless, I wish to note that like most prison narratives of the twentieth century, the film presents us with an extremely one-sided perspective. First of all, the bleak prison sequence focuses exclusively on the fate of the poor genius Oscar Wilde (Stephen Fry) and ignores the rest of the prison population. Second, the film plays down the fact that it was the writer himself who initiated the trials that led to his conviction. In 1895, the historical Wilde received a card by the Marquess of Queensberry, the father of Wilde's lover Lord Alfred Douglas ("Bosie"), on which it said "To Oscar Wilde posing Somdomite [*sic*!]." Wilde then brought the Marquess before the court on a libel charge.[11] The trial ironically led to two subsequent trials in which Wilde was found guilty for having violated the Criminal Law Amendment Act of 1885, i.e., for having committed acts of 'gross indecency.' The writer was then sent to the prisons at Pentonville, Wandsworth, and Reading.

The movie represents Wilde as a gay martyr *avant la lettre*, while the other Victorians "are largely portrayed as hypocritical moral police who destroyed a man of genius" (Waldrep 50). The film represents the Victorian prison as an instrument of a hypocritical society. At the same time, however, the movie limits its critique to this particular late nineteenth-century context and fails to even mention that the Labouchère amendment, under which Wilde was convicted for 'gross indecency' in 1895, was actually in effect until 1967.

Most twentieth-century prison narratives concentrate on one identificatory figure who is in some way distinguished from the 'other' prisoners. The film *Wilde* presents us with a bisexual prison newcomer, but most other prison narratives of the twentieth century focus on the fate of wrongfully convicted members of the white and heterosexual middle class. These prisoner-heroes are normally set apart from the 'rest' of the prison population who are depicted as 'real' criminals.

Prison Settings in Novels and Films

In contrast to Dickens' novels *Little Dorrit* and *A Tale of Two Cities*, in which the prison settings conform with the 'old' prison system, the prisons we see in most prison novels and films of the twentieth century comply with the 'new' penitentiary system, and are bright and clean. For example, Alex in the novel *A Clockwork Orange* points out that a new inmate tried "to like shake the bars, creeching" (120), and he also mentions the "electric light" that is usually "switched on all over the zoo" (125). Similarly, the narrator of *Sleepers* points out that he was

> [...] placed in a private twelve-foot cell that came equipped with a cot and a spring mattress, a toilet with no lid, and a sink with only a cold water faucet. The iron door leading into the room had three bars across the center and a slide panel at its base. Above the sink was a small window, its glass entwined with wire, which offered a view of what seemed to me to be an always colorless sky. (177)

At one point, he also mentions the "fluorescent lights" (203–4) in the library.

The prison settings in most prison films are bright and clean as well. For example, when Stroud (Burt Lancaster) arrives at Alcatraz prison in *Birdman of Alcatraz*, we witness the following conversation between the prisoner and Warden Shoemaker (Karl Malden):

> SHOEMAKER: "It's modern, well-heated, and clean."
> STROUD: "First thing I noticed. Almost antiseptic."
> SHOEMAKER: "Yeah, you'll not find cockroaches here. We have linoleum on all the floors of the cells."

Furthermore, as a general tendency, the prisons we see on the screen are much more concrete and detailed in comparison with prison settings in novels. For example, we only learn about the borstal in "The Loneliness of the Long-Distance Runner" that it is located in Essex, houses three hundred inmates, and that it has a stone floor (8–9). In the film adaptation, on the other hand, the borstal is concretized and we can see its many details: towers, rooms, the governor's office, the dining hall, the yard, and the 'hole.' Similarly, in the novel *Sleepers*, the narrator informs us that "the Wilkinson Home for Boys held 375 youthful offenders, housed in five separate units spread across seven well-tended acres. It had two large gyms, a football field, a quarter-mile oval track, and one chapel suitable for all religions" (176). The film, on the other hand, which was filmed at "a facility for the mentally disabled near Newtown, Connecticut" (Turner 40), gives us a much more detailed sense of the reform school's architecture.

Occasionally, prison novels also present us with very detailed descriptions of prison settings. For instance, the narrator of *Birdman of Alcatraz* depicts Stroud's cell as follows:

> Behind the enormous stone facade of Leavenworth, past the great cell blocks, the Isolation Building huddled alone. On the first floor, the rear half of the structure held eighteen segregation cells, nine on each side. It was a prison within a prison. Stroud's cell was twelve feet long and six feet wide, and the thick plaster walls were painted gray. At the rear was a small barred window. The door was of heavy steel bars covered by wire netting. There was a second door of solid wood which could be swung upon the steel door, shutting out light and air. In the cell stood a lavatory, washbasin and a narrow bed. From the high ceiling dangled a twenty-five-watt bulb. (69)

In "Rita Hayworth and Shawshank Redemption," the first-person narrator Red also gives us a rather detailed rendering of the Shawshank State Prison:

> Our yard is big, much bigger than most. It's a perfect square, ninety yards on a side. The north side is the outer wall, with a guardtower at either end. The guards up there are armed with binoculars and riot guns. The main gate is in that north side. The truck loading-bays are on the south side of the yard. There

> are five of them. Shawshank is a busy place during the work-week—deliveries in, deliveries out. We have the license plate-factory, and a big industrial laundry that does all the prison wetwash, plus that of Kittery Receiving Hospital and the Eliot Sanatorium. There's also a big automotive garage where mechanic inmates fix prison, state, and municipal vehicles—not to mention the private cars of the screws, the administration officers ... and, on more than one occasion, those of the parole board. (24)

A novelist may present us with very detailed descriptions of prison settings but he or she can never simulate the density and complex architecture of the prison in the way a filmmaker can. The filmmaker must visualize and concretize prison settings beyond the material the novel provides. Thus, when we see the prison in the film *The Shawshank Redemption*, we are presented with an even more detailed rendering of an actual prison, namely the Ohio State Reformatory, a century-old prison located in the town of Mansfield, which was closed in the 1980s. When we first see the gothic prison in the film, the camera, mounted on a helicopter, climbs from a low-angle shot of its facade to a bird's-eye view of the yard, picking out hundreds of inmates. The shot then "pans sideways as the camera looms down over a roof-top to reveal the bus [which contains the newcomers, J.A.] turning into the entrance" (Probst 66). Later on, we are confronted with detailed renderings of the prison's observation bridges and towers, and when the camera moves into the prison we are presented with conspicuous shots of tiers of landings, barred cells, the mess hall, the laundry, the warden's office, etc.

One advantage of the medium film is that it can present us with detailed and sometimes also relatively accurate architectural portrayals of prisons. If prison films employ actual inmates, they may also confront us with comparatively precise images of prisoners. However, our identificatory figures in prison films are usually part of a 'star system' so that we are confronted with prisoners who look like the superstars Paul Muni, Burt Lancaster, Paul Newman, Malcolm McDowell, Steve McQueen (in *Papillon* [1973]), Clint Eastwood,

Robert Redford, or Tim Robbins. These heroic figures, with whom we are supposed to identify, clearly misrepresent or distort the realities of penal practise. The novel, on the other hand, cannot show the external features of prison settings and inmates with the sovereign conviction in which films may accomplish this task. As far as prison settings are concerned, the novel's lack of concreteness is perhaps a disadvantage, whereas with regard to the representation of inmates, the novel's power of ambiguity, non-commitment, or vagueness may be an advantage because the visualization of inmates by readers is not influenced by any star system. Since rationales for action cannot be photographed, films do not usually provide us with access to a character's internal life in the way fictional literature can. In other words, prison films correlate with the observation of the prisoner's body (from a hypothetical third-person perspective), whereas prison novels of the twentieth century typically allow us access to the prisoner's mind so that we can acquire internal knowledge about prisoners. The following comparison of Sillitoe's novella "The Loneliness of the Long-Distance Runner" and its film adaptation corroborates this point.

The Representation of Minds and Bodies in "The Loneliness of the Long-Distance Runner" and its Film Version

In contrast to the borstal staff who cannot gain access to the inmate's interiority we as readers are well aware throughout Sillitoe's novella that the narrator is planning to lose the cross-country race against a sister borstal institution. The first-person narrative situation creates a certain intimacy and emotional closeness between Smith and the reader. Smith's confessional narrative offers us inside views into the life of a criminal we would normally never get. The novella allows us to see Smith's "take" on how he refuses to "play ball" with the governor and the borstal staff by pretending to go along with the physical training program, while in secret he is planning his own counter-subterfuge.

At the beginning of the novella, the governor says to Smith: "Good show. I know you'll get us that cup." Smith then goes on to describe his reactions: "And I swear under my breath: 'Like boggery, I will.' No, I won't get them that cup, even though the stupid tash-twitching bastard has all his hopes in me" (13). Throughout the novella, we can witness the narrator's secret thoughts about not intending to win the race. A few pages earlier, Smith explicitly comments on the fact that the borstal staff do not have any access to the inmates' interiority: "They can spy on us all day to see if we're pulling our puddings and if we're working good or doing our 'athletics' but they can't make an X-Ray of our guts to find out what we're telling ourselves" (10). Later on, the governor suggests that Smith "might take up running in a sort of professional way when he gets out." The inmate once again gives him the desired answer while we as readers learn that he has got something different in mind: "A line of potbellied pop-eyes gleamed at me and a row of goldfish mouths opened and wiggled gold teeth at me, so I gave them the answer they wanted because I'd hold my trump card until later. 'It'd suit me fine, sir,' I said. 'Good lad. Good show. Right spirit. Splendid'" (39–40). Throughout the novella, the borstal staff can only inspect the inmate's body and acquire external knowledge about the narrator. And Smith is aware of the fact that they will never be able to penetrate his mind or learn anything about his internal processes.

In the film adaptation *The Loneliness of the Long-Distance Runner*, on the other hand, we do not learn anything about Colin's intentions of not winning the cross-country race until Colin actually stops before the tape. If one disregards the flashback or memory sequences that inform us about Colin's life before he came to borstal, the film clearly focuses on the inmate's body (as opposed to his mind). The movie (perhaps deliberately) puts its viewers into a position that is reminiscent of the position of the borstal staff because we watch the inmates' bodies from a third-person perspective. Also, in comparison with the novella, the film stresses the near-continuous surveillance to which the inmates' bodies are exposed in even greater detail. For example, in the course of the induction process, the new inmates have to line up before the governor who believes in the use of physical training for rehabilitation purposes. The head administrator nicely informs the new inmates about his philosophy of *mens sana in corpere sano*:

> You are here for us to try and make something of you, to turn you into industrious and honest citizens. [...] We like to run things smoothly here of course both for you and for us. The sooner we have your co-operation the sooner you'll be out of here. If you play ball with us we play ball with you. We want you to work hard and play hard. Good athletics, sports, inter-house competition. We believe in all that.

In another significant scene, the governor stands on one of the borstal's imposing towers and uses binoculars to watch the inmates play soccer. The head administrator observes the trainees' bodies in order to find out how fast they can run. At this stage, he finds Colin to be an impressive runner and tells the new housemaster that this inmate "can run" and that "he might be useful to us" because he may run in the race against Ranleigh school, an elite local public (i.e., private) school. Later on, the governor enters the shower room and congratulates the naked Colin for scoring an impressive goal, which accentuates the lack of privacy in prison. Throughout the film, the inmates are treated as bodies. They are regularly counted during their meals, and they are even observed by officers during their sleep. At one point in the night, we are presented with a POV-shot taken from the perspective of a prison officer who uses a torch to make sure that nobody has escaped.

In a second step, the movie shows us that this almost permanent observation does not allow us access to the inmates' minds. Up until the contest, Colin has been a model prisoner so that both the governor and we as viewers think that he is being rehabilitated. When Colin's friend Mike (James Bolam) becomes an inmate of HM Borstal Ruxton Towers, the other trainees inform him about Smith's running in the cross-country race. The stunned Mike asks Colin: "Whose bloody side are you on all of a sudden?" The inmate Stacey replies: "He's the governor's blue-eyed boy now."[12] At this point, we also think that Colin is actually on the side of the governor. In other words, we do not find out that Colin will lose until the end of the race, when the inmate deliberately pauses near the finish. Colin arrives at the finishing line far in front of the other competitors and deliberately stops short of the tape, while the raving crowd chants "run, run, run!" Colin stares intensely at the governor as his rivals cross the line ahead of him. In the course of this sequence, shots alternate between Colin's triumphant face and the governor's expression of impotent rage, while the intercutting suggests eye contact between the two as their moral standards finally clash.

This climactic scene is diametrically opposed to the novella, where Smith's intent to subvert the governor's trophy-winning hopes is revealed almost from the start, so that the actual running race is almost anticlimactic. Also, cinema audiences are presumably as surprised as the governor when Colin refuses to make the final moves to win the cup. By not making the final move in the race, Colin invites us and the governor to understand an essential truth about prison. However long one may train and control Smith's body and his behavior in long-distance races, physical training and athletics will never suffice to control his interiority or subdue his independent feelings. The cathartic effect of Colin's stopping before the finish is also closely connected to the fact that in contrast to the novella, the film explains Colin's crime of robbing the bakery which sent him to borstal. The attempt to rehabilitate people like Colin is pointless. He does not have to be rehabilitated because his crime was caused by his (working-class) family background and not by criminal impulses that might be disciplined.

In contrast to prison films (like *The Loneliness of the Long-Distance Runner*), prison novels of the twentieth century typically focus on inmate interiority, and familiarize us with the thoughts, feelings, and motivations of inmates or former inmates. For example, the first-person narrative situation in "Rita Hayworth and Shawshank Redemption" also allows its narrator Red to illustrate how the prison affected him psychologically. More specifically, the simultaneous necessity and lack of hope in prison has turned Red into some sort of schizophrenic who is unable to distinguish between illusion and reality.

Inmate Interiority in "Rita Hayworth and Shawshank Redemption"

Like Sillitoe's novella, King's "Rita Hayworth and Shawshank Redemption" focuses on the internal life of a formerly imprisoned narrator. Also, it presents us with the narrator Red's perception of the innocent city banker Andy Dufresne. In contrast to Hampe who merely notes that the novella is full of "magical events" (20) but does not explain them, I demonstrate that the hopeful and optimist Andy was actually invented by the first-person narrator because the imprisoned Red needed somebody to believe in. In other words, he created the ambiguous and mystical figure of Andy as some sort of role model.

To begin with, Red tells us that the innocent Andy remains untouched by the bleakness of the prison, and walks through the prison like a mysterious visiting saint. The narrator admits that he is "describing someone who's more legend than man [...]. To us long-timers who knew Andy over a space of years, there was an element of fantasy to him, a sense almost of myth-magic" (37). Additionally, Red argues that Andy wore

> [...] his freedom like an invisible coat [...]. He *never really developed a prison mentality*. His eyes *never* got that dull look. He *never* developed the walk that men get when the day is over and they are going back to their cells for another endless night—that flat-footed, hump-shouldered walk. Andy walked with his shoulders squared and *his step was always light*. (75; my emphasis, J.A.)

Red (and the other inmates) seem to idealize Andy perhaps to cover up their own weaknesses and feelings of impotence. In this context, it is worth noting that at one point Red agrees with the statement that "if enough people *want* you to remember something, that can be a pretty powerful persuader" (19). Furthermore, Red stresses that his stories about Andy are partly based on vicarious experience and that he occasionally altered the information he was given:

> You may have noticed how much of what I've told you *is hearsay*—someone saw something and told me and I told you. Well, in some cases, *I've simplified it even more than it really was*, and have actually repeated fourth- or fifth-hand information. (37; my emphasis, J.A.)

Moreover, Red's 'report' of Andy's escape involves numerous "educated guesses" (104) and two unresolved contradictions. According to Red, Andy, who persistently worked on the hole in his cell through which he escapes at the end, remained in prison until 1975 even though he had already broken into the shaft in 1967 and could have escaped (103). Red first comes up with an absolutely ridiculous explanation and is aware of its silliness: "One possibility is that the crawlspace itself was clogged with crap and he had to clear it out. But that wouldn't account for all the time" (104). Red's second assumption that "maybe Andy got scared" (104) is not very convincing either because up until this point, Andy has been extremely courageous. For instance, Andy constantly worked on the hole in his cell even though he faced "regular weekly inspection[s]" or the danger "of being surprised by an unscheduled inspection in the middle of the night while he had his poster unstuck" (100–1).

Earlier on, Red speculates that Andy paid the guards to have the rapist Bogs Diamond beaten up: "I'm not saying it was Andy Dufresne, but I do know that he brought in five hundred dollars when he came [...]" (33). For some reason, however, the rapists, without Bogs, are soon after Andy again: "There was a little hiatus, and then it began again, although not so hard nor so often" (34). Why do these rapists not get the message after Bogs was beaten up? Why does Andy not have another rapist taken care of? An obvious solution to these contradictions is to question the narrator's reliability. Since Red's narrative involves two unresolved contradictions (namely the eight years between 1967 and 1975 in the course of which Andy remained in prison and the 'return' of the prison rapists) and numerous speculative assumptions, Red can be seen as an unreliable narrator.[13]

There is definitely something wrong with the narrator's story. Maybe Red and the other inmates simply wanted to shed a better light on Andy in order to create a powerful figure they could believe in. Another possibility is that Andy is completely invented and represents something like joy, optimism or hope. Red may have made up the hopeful Andy, who carries "a kind of inner light" (48) with him, in order to survive the bleak prison conditions. This may have initiated some sort of schizophrenia so that in Red's memory, fact and fiction merge and can no longer be distinguished. At one point, we do get a sense that Andy is actually only an aspect of Red's personality rather than a different character:

> *Well, you weren't writing about yourself,* I hear someone in the peanut-gallery saying. *You were writing about Andy Dufresne. You're nothing but a minor character in your own story.* But you know, that's just not so. It's all about me. Every damned word of it. Andy was the part of me they could never lock up, the part of me that will rejoice when the gates finally open for me and I walk out in my cheap suit with my twenty dollars of mad-money in my pocket. That part of me will rejoice no matter how old and broken and scared the rest of me is. (106; original emphasis, J.A.)[14]

Andy is presumably nothing but the sum of the projections of the narrator's dreams, wishes and desires. Since the novella restricts itself to the perspective of the first-person narrator, we never learn whether Andy exists independently of the narrator's discourse. Andy appears to exist only discursively.

Red's first-person account offers us insights into what the prison can do to its inmates. The simultaneous necessity and lack of hope in prison can drive prisoners to the verge of madness and, as in the case of Red, even turn them into schizophrenics. The novella, which allows us access to the narrator's thoughts and feelings, provides a fairly strong statement against prisons. At the end of the narrative, Red is released from prison but remains tied to its ignominy and his fantasies about Andy. Like the first-person narrators in *Little Dorrit* and *A Tale of Two Cities*, Red is torn between a hopeless prison self (that continues to depend upon the prison) and a hopeful self (that wants to overcome the prison and led him to invent Andy). At the end, Red is left to finish the story in terms of his own hopes for the future and free himself from the prison he has internalized. However, the "conclusion is uncertain" (113).

One advantage of first-person prison novels is that they can present us with detailed accounts of inmate interiority. More specifically, novels like "Rita Hayworth and Shawshank Redemption" offer us rather elaborate inside views of the narrator's mind. Such narratives allow their narrators to illustrate in great detail what the prison has done to them. Cases like King's novella corroborate my hypothesis that first-person narratives are not per se tied up with a certain pro-prison ideology. First-person narratives can highlight the psychological scars of the prison, and they may shed a rather critical light on the prison. Prison films, on the other hand, usually confront us with extremely detailed images of the prison architecture and frequently even use real prison locations. However, they can never present us with the thoughts or ruminations of imprisoned characters in the way fictional literature can. Prison films correlate with the observation of bodies from a third-person perspective and are thus reminiscent of literary third-person neutral narratives. That is to say,

> a scenario of things evolving as if by themselves can be observed, but since no narrator persona is at hand [...], one then has the typical 'camera-eye' effect of the mechanical shutter which registers incoming stimuli but does not interpret them, leaving it to the viewer of the film to make sense of the data transmitted. (Fludernik *Towards* 175)

Interestingly, Hale draws a parallel between the way in which prison films narrate the prison and the idea of panoptic vision. More specifically, he points out that

> [...] few prison films are built around secrecy. As if we were visitors to Bentham's Panopticon, an invited audience in the zoo of punishment everything is disclosed. [...] The dark cell becomes a camera obscura revealing the glass and iron transparency of the Inspection House. (62)

However, the observation of bodies from a third-person perspective does of course not reproduce Bentham's *Panopticon* and is not in itself bound up with a certain ideology. Prison films allow us visual access to a forbidden realm, namely the secretive and mysterious world of the prison. But they do not necessarily invite us to enjoy the punishments we see. Rather, they may occasionally also shed a critical light on the prison. For instance, the film *The Loneliness of the Long-Distance Runner* uses the neutral observation of bodies to critique the prison by highlighting that the surveillance in borstal does not effect the inmate's spirit. On the other hand, many prison films do indeed justify the existence of the prison—but not because they are third-person neutral narratives. Rather, they construct a split between the 'normal' bodies of law-abiding citizens and the 'deviant' bodies of vicious criminals. Furthermore, most films use the star system to differentiate between one innocent identificatory figure and the rest of the prison population. The star system creates an 'us' and 'them' divide which suggests that the innocent and good-looking representatives of cool masculinity do not belong into prison, whereas the 'depraved' rest of the prison population are rightfully incarcerated.

After these general remarks about the representation of the prison population and prison settings in twentieth-century narratives, I turn to a more specific analysis of the way in which such novels and films narrate individual segments of the prison experience. First, these elements widen the gap between our 'poor' prisoner-hero and the 'deviant' rest of the prison population. Second, most twentieth-century prison narratives ignore less sensational segements of the prison experience and instead focus on elements that correlate with processes of symbolic 'feminization.' These processes serve to amplify our sympathies for the 'poor' identificatory figure who has to defend his 'untainted' masculinity.

THE PRISON AS A TESTING GROUND FOR MASCULINITY: THE PROCESS OF BECOMING AN INSIDER

The first important aspect of the prison experience is the induction process. In the course of this process, the newcomers are dehumanized and transformed into numbered objects. Also, they typically experience some sort of entry shock as their former identities are eradicated. Prison novels of the twentieth century typically represent this identity crisis by describing related feelings and emotions, and focus on internal processes. Prison films, by contrast, render this transformation of individuals into prisoners and the newcomers' initial shock from an external (or hypothetical third-person) perspective. In a sense, viewers can observe the slipping away of the new inmates' identities. On the visual level, the prison uniform is the most striking difference between a criminal and a free citizen. Shabby prison uniforms suggest a dereliction of the new inmates' self-image. For example, the prisoners in *The Shawshank Redemption* wear outworn jeans jackets, blue jeans, and shabby gray or light blue prison shirts, and even the teenagers at the reform school in the film *Sleepers* have to wear dark, gray uniforms, thus highlighting their depression. Additionally, prison films employ differing colors or styles of music to mark the passage from freedom to incarceration. The initial shock is also conveyed through facial expressions and submissive bodily positions, which are 'indirect' visualizations of the newcomers' internal states.

In prison novels, the new inmates typically attempt to handle their identity crisis upon arrival by distancing themselves from the other prisoners, whom they represent as the 'real' criminals. For instance, in the novel *A Clockwork Orange*, Alex argues that his identity was altered in prison. He points out that he became a number in the course of the transformation from outsider into insider:

> So here I was now, two years just to the day of being kicked and clanged into Staja 84 F, dressed in the heighth of prison fashion, which was a one-piece suit of a very filthy like cal colour, and the number sewn on the groody part just above the old tick-tocker [heart, J.A.] and on the back as well, so that going and coming *I was 6655321 and not your little droog* [mate, J.A.] *Alex* not no longer. (108; my emphasis, J.A.)

Alex then immediately distances himself from the "vonny leering like criminals" and "real perverts" who are "ready to dribble all over a luscious young malchick like your story-teller" (108). The narrator tries to uphold his 'untainted' heterosexual identity to stress his difference from the 'real' criminals and perverts. In prison, Alex has to share his cell with five of the most violent prisoners, whom he describes as "a terrible grahzny lot really" (119). Also, Alex notes that Zophar, one of his cellmates, speaks "this very old-time real criminal's slang" (118). Later on, a new and homosexual inmate sneaks to Alex's bunk and begins to caress the narrator ("I woke up to find this horrible plenny [bloke, J.A.] actually lying with me on my bunk, which was on the bottom of the three-tier and also very narrow, and he was govoreeting [speaking, J.A.] dirty like love-slovos [words, J.A.] and stroke stroke stroking away" [121]). In order to uphold his 'untainted' masculine identity, Alex beats the inmate to death.

In *I Am a Fugitive from a Georgia Chain Gang!*, the narrator Burns commits a petty crime and is then sentenced to serve ten years on a Georgia Chain Gang. Burns manages to escape but is caught and imprisoned again. In a manner which is reminiscent of the dichotomies in colonialist discourse, Burns points out that

> [...] the majority of the prisoners were unable to read and write and were typical 'hill billies,' never having been more than fifty miles away from their scenes of birth. Thus they lack knowledge of the outside world and its common decencies and saw no hardship in not washing their hands or faces or cleaning their teeth before the morning meal. (175)

Burns constructs himself as the educated and decent "exception" to the chain gang's wilderness who is "accustomed to the simple refinements of civilization" (176) and associates himself with "the better class of Georgians" who "were in favor of [his] parole" (189). Such arrogant identity constructions presumably serve to cover up Burns' own inferiority complex about ending up in prison.

In *Sleepers*, the narrator Shakes and three friends are sentenced to serve time at the Wilkinson Home for Boys. Shakes describes his feelings of panic, fear, and impotence as well as his attempts to escape these imprisoning emotions upon arrival as follows:

> I had been in my cell for less than an hour when the panic set in. To fight it, I closed my eyes and thought of home, of the neighborhood, of the streets where I played and of the people

> I knew. [...] It doesn't take very long to know how tough a person you are or how strong you can be. I knew from my first day at Wilkinson that I was neither tough nor strong. It takes only a moment for the fear to find its way, to seep through the carefully constructed armor. Once it does it, it finds a permanent place. It is as true for a hardened criminal as it is for a young boy. (171–72)

Even though Shakes explicitly links hardened criminals and young boys in the final sentence quoted above, he goes on to radically distance himself and his three friends from the 'truly vicious criminals' who belong where they are. He tells us that "it was not a group of innocent young boys at Wilkinson," and feels that

> [...] most, if not all the inmates belonged there. Our population was composed of the toughest kids from the poorest and most dangerous areas of the state, a number of them riding out their second and third conviction. All were violent offenders. Few seemed sorry about what they had done or appeared on the brink of rehabilitation. [...] My friends and I fell uncomfortably in the middle. We were there on assault charges, caused neither by drunkenness nor anger. We were there because of pure stupidity. (183–84)

Shakes does not only construct himself and his friends as being different from (and superior to) the tough, poor, dangerous, and violent offenders. By depicting the other inmates as incorrigible violent and brutal offenders, he even implicitly sanctions the existence of the reform school.

What about the process of becoming an insider in films? In the movie *Sleepers*, the boys' journey to the reform school is represented from an external perspective and accompanied by lugubrious synthesizer sounds which contrast sharply with the rather happy (and well-known) musical score of the first (pre-prison) part of the film.[15] The gloomy sounds create feelings of fear and anxiety of the unknown prison world on the part of spectators and foreshadow the horror of rape and torture the boys have to endure at the reform school. Additionally, the film uses contrasting colors to mark the difference between the hellish prison and the paradise-like world outside. The cinematographer Michael Ballhaus said that he and the director Barry Levinson wanted the first part of the film, which is set outside prison, to "have a *warm look* because the kids are growing up there and they're safe." They used "long lenses" to make the neighborhood "kind of *pretty and exciting*" and "filters" to get the "softness" of the colors. Interestingly, for the second part, which is set at the Wilkinson Home for Boys, they "wanted a *cool, dark look*—not friendly and warm. There's not one yellow or warm scene inside the school. It's all *bluish and contrasty*" (qtd. in Turner 36–38; my emphasis, J.A.).[16]

The journey to prison and the process of becoming an insider are of course interesting visual experiences. Thus, most prison movies open with shots of a wrongfully convicted newcomer who is taken to prison by bus, van, train or boat to undergo the dehumanizing induction process. Like the new inmate, who is supposed to serve as our identificatory figure, cinema audiences usually have limited knowledge of life behind bars. Goffman examines the prison as one of numerous 'total' institutions, whose "encompassing or total character is symbolized by the barrier to social intercourse with the outside and to departure that is often built right into the physical plant, such as locked doors, high walls, barbed wire, cliffs, water, forests, or moors" (4). At the beginning of prison films, the extra-textual viewers are introduced to the alien prison world like our intra-textual prisoner-hero and simultaneously linked with the fate of this newcomer. In the course of the journey to prison, the camera tends to concentrate on close-ups of the newcomers' faces, which allude to the characters' interior states. The close-ups of the new inmates' facial expressions invite us to identify with the protagonist and his plight of being locked up.

The film *The Shawshank Redemption* starts with shots of the innocent city banker Andy on the night of the murder and continues during his trial. When the judge passes a double life sentence on Andy, we are presented with a loud rendering of the rapping of the judge's gavel on the table. This sound, which is combined with a black screen, is reminiscent of the slamming of a heavy iron door or gate and might accentuate that Andy loses all his hopes. At this stage, he knows that he will have to spend the rest of his life behind bars. After the trial sequence, Andy is taken to prison in a gray bus. In the course of this journey, the camera moves to a close-up of Andy's scared face. Later on, Andy's facial expression and his insecure bodily position tell us that he must be terrified when he walks into the prison while being surrounded by shouting spectators who shake the fence of the arrival area. Before Andy enters the prison, he looks up at the imposing gray prison tower above the door. That is to say, we are presented with a POV-shot of the prison building which is at the same time a low-angle shot that conveys connotations of power, strength, and control. Like the audience, Andy does not know what to expect and feels overwhelmed and dominated by the prison institution. The first shot inside prison is an image of the new inmates' chained feet. This cinematic synecdoche may suggest that the newcomers will no longer 'fully' exist. Their former identities are about to be taken apart, and they will be transformed into prisoners.

The film then visually illustrates the transformation of Andy into prisoner #37927. All remnants of his former identity are taken away. Andy's naked body is hosed down in a steel cage with high pressure water spray. After that, the inmate's body is covered with white delousing powder. As part of the degrading induction process, the newcomers are given prison uniforms and a bible, and are marched exposed and naked to their individual cells. Additionally, by means of a bird's-eye view of the identically-looking prisoners in the exercise yard, the film accentuates the loss of the inmates' identity (and individuality) as well as their sense of insignificance in prison. Since the great distance between the scene and the camera gives the inmates an ant-like appearance, this shot can be said to comment on the prisoners' reification. It is also worth noting that the prison in the film is "laden with morose colors and foreboding shades of gray" which set the tone for Andy's "feeling of despair and isolation." The cinematographer Deakins said that "the whole approach [...] was a sort of cool, gray light and cool, gray exteriors" (qtd. in Probst 63).

In the course of the induction process, the new inmates are questioned, and everything they say is meticulously documented in files and note-books. For example, when Alex arrives at HM Prison Parkmoor in the film *A Clockwork Orange*, a prison officer hands over the committal forms to the Chief Officer, and we witness the following mechanical conversation:

> CHIEF OFFICER: "Name?"
> ALEX: "Alexander DeLarge."
> CHIEF OFFICER: "You are now in HM Prison Parkmoor and from this moment you'll address all prison officers as 'sir'! Name?"
> ALEX: "Alexander DeLarge, sir."
> CHIEF OFFICER: "Sentence?"
> ALEX: "Fourteen years, sir."
> CHIEF OFFICER: "Crime?"
> ALEX: "Murder, sir."

Alex is then asked to empty his pockets, and the Chief Officer places the inmate's "valuable property" into a white paper bag, while the individual items are meticulously registered by another officer. Alex has to undress and hand over his clothes to a prison officer who places them in a box, again meticulously naming and registering the individual items. Step by step, Alex's former identity is stripped off and taken apart. At the same time, the Chief Officer interviews Alex about his bodily constitution, which places the new inmate in a field of surveillance and situates him in a network of written documentation:

> Brown hair isn't it? [...] Blue eyes? [...] Do you wear eye glasses or contact lenses? [...] Have you been receiving medical treatment for any serious illness? [...] Have you ever had any mental illness? [...] Do you wear false teeth or any false limbs? [...] Have you ever had any attacks of fainting or dizziness? [...] Are you an epileptic? [...] Are you now or have you ever been a homosexual?

The newcomer then has to bend over so that the Chief Guard can inspect Alex's buttocks with a torch.[17] Alex's body remains bent over and the Chief Guard asks him: "Any venereal diseases? Rats? Lice?"

As Luckett has shown (324), the film also conveys the transformation of the artistic individualisist Alex into a prisoner through the contrast between fancy and colorful clothes and drab conformist suits or uniforms. The purple outfit Alex wears in the record store (where he picks up two girls and sleeps with them) is an elaborate peacock-style costume and the only one that represents his individual liking, i.e., his 'true' individuality. By contrast, Alex's cheap and unfashionable navy suit articulates his loss of control and is worn during some of his worst moments: as he checks in and out of prison; when he is humiliated to prove the success of the Ludovico experiment; and during his period of depression and degradation after leaving prison.

Moreover, in both *A Clockwork Orange* and *The Shawshank Redemption*, the prison is immediately established as a testing ground for our hero's masculinity which is threatened by the prison conditions but also by rapists, homosexuals, and other 'deviant' men like prison officers who carry long batons and handcuffs. For instance, before Andy enters the prison in *The Shawshank Redemption*, an old inmate shouts "Hey bitch, come over here." Then the voice-over narrator informs us that "the first night's the toughest, no doubt about it. [...] Most new fish come close to madness the first night. Somebody always breaks down crying. It happens every time. The only question is, who's it gonna be?" Andy successfully passes this first test of his masculinity because he does not break down crying but later on, his manliness is again threatened by the sadist Captain Hadley and the rapist Bogs and his 'sisters.'[18] Most prison narratives of the twentieth century code rapists as homosexuals because they normally constitute the one and only form of homosexuality in the prison context. In *A Clockwork Orange*, Alex's masculinity is threatened by a couple of stereotypical effeminate 'faggots' who throw kisses at him during a prison church service. Also, already during the course of the induction process, the gay Chief Officer stares avariciously at the naked Alex and his sexual organs.

Both prison novels and films of the twentieth century construct the prison as an alien and exotic space that tests the masculinity of our central protagonist. However, they render the induction process in radically different ways. Prison novels dramatize the acuteness of the newcomer's situation by describing his fear of losing his former identity from 'within.' They allow us access to the processes of identity construction newcomers usually go through. Following a dramatic shock, the new inmate tries to distance himself from the other prisoners whom he perceives in terms of radical Otherness. Prison films, by contrast, illustrate the prison's hold on the inmate's body from an external perspective. They mainly use external features like facial expressions or bodily positions, bird's-eye views of the prison yard, or low-angle shots of imposing prison towers to simulate the newcomer's identity crisis. The transition from outside to inside is frequently accentuated by bleak colors and lugubrious music. Since the induction process is an interesting visual experience, prison novels of the twentieth century do not usually thematize its details. Instead, they concentrate on related feelings and emotions. The audiovisual medium, on the other hand, can forcefully render the induction process in the course of which we see how humans are transformed into objects amenable to study and manipulation. The new prisoners are stripped; their bodies are then washed, deloused, searched, examined, and pushed into uniforms.

THE MONOTONOUS ROUTINE CYCLE OF TRADITIONAL DISCIPLINARY PRISONS

Another important element of the prison experience is the dull routine cycle of prison life. In fictional prison narratives, the repetitive prison routine is linked to traditional or disciplinary forms of imprisonment which are critiqued because they do not allow for the rehabilitation of the inmate. These non-reformative prisons are shown to transform the linear progress of time into some sort of circularity, which renders development impossible. Novels and films use segments of inmates performing the same tasks or speed-ups[19] to simulate the passing of time. The narrators of prison novels use rhetorical figures that involve repetition, while prison films use images of circularity or organize the screen space in such a way that we get a sense of how the regularity of prison routines affects the prisoners. More specifically, prison films sometimes use synecdoches and represent bodily parts of a prisoner to suggest that the monotony in prison causes the prisoners to fall apart and experience a serious identity crisis.

The narrator of *I Am a Fugitive from a Georgia Chain Gang!* stresses the uniformity of life in prison by stating that "each day was an exact duplicate of the one preceding it" (56). Later on, he uses various parallelisms and two similes to illustrate both the repetitive nature and the mechanical precision of the soul-breaking physical labor at the chain gang in Georgia:

> We began in mechanical unison and kept at it in rhythmical cadence until sundown—fifteen and a half hours of steady toil—as regular as the ticking of a clock. In the chain gangs, human labor had been synchronized like the goose step was in the German Army. When using pickaxes, all picks hit the ground at the same time, all are raised and steadied for the next blow with uncanny mechanical precision. So it was with all work, shoveling, hammering, drilling. The convict bodies and muscles move in time and in unison as one man. The tempo and speed is regulated by the chanting of Negro [sic!] bondage songs, led by a toil-hardened Negro of years of servitude as follows: 'A long steel rail,' croons the leader. 'Ump!' grunt all the rest in chorus as pickaxes come down. 'An' a short cross tie,' croons the leader. 'Ump!' grunt all the rest in chorus as pickaxes come up. 'It rings lik' sil-vah,' croons the leader. 'Ump!' goes the chorus as the picks come down. 'It shin's lik' go-old,' croons the leader. 'Ump!' and all the picks come up. (143–44)

The narrator also employs a third simile ("as one man") which highlights that the prisoners lose their individual features and are transformed into "bodies and muscles," i.e., into an insignificant part of a homogenous entity of hard-working convicts.

In the 1932 film adaptation, the mechanical nature of James Allen's life on a chain gang is twice illustrated by means of a combination of two shots which remain superimposed in the course of the sequence.

More specifically, a shot picturing calendar leaves which are falling down is superimposed on a close-up of the inmates' hands using sledgehammers to break rocks in the quarries. Furthermore, one does get the impression that the falling down of the leaves is caused by the prisoners' hammers. For the audience, this cinematic technique reduces a day of story time to a few seconds of discourse time. It is also worth noting that the prisoners are only represented by means of their hands. This cinematic synecdoche suggests that the prisoners do not exist as individuals or human beings. Rather, they are only perceived as pure work force and reduced to insignificant elements of the communal machine.

The prison sequence in *Wilde* presents us with two shots of the prisoners working on the treadwheel. The second image of the inmates' Sisyphean task is preceded by a close-up of the machine's cogwheels. This shot then dissolves into another shot of the prisoners working on the treadwheel. This superimposition involves a cinematic metaphor that invites us to see the hard-working prisoners *as* turning cogwheels. The film thus suggests that the inmates have lost their former identities—Wilde became number C.3.3—and have been transformed into insignificant wheels of the prison machinery.

While the strict prison routine in nineteenth- and early twentieth-century prisons (like the chain gangs) correlates with extremely hard work and does not allow the inmate to take minor decisions for himself, the routine in prisons of the later twentieth century correlates with boredom and lack of occupation. At one point in the novella "Rita Hayworth and Shawshank Redemption," the imprisoned narrator Red informs us that "prison time is slow time, sometimes you'd swear it's stop-time, but it passes. It passes" (54). In this case, one could argue that the anti-climactic chain 'prison time—slow time—stop-time' communicates the prisoner's impression that behind prison walls, time does not move on progressively but gradually comes to a rest. At the end of the quotation's first sentence, we learn that despite this impression, time "passes." One can relate the repetition of the phrase "it passes" in the sentence that follows to the repetition of the same content in a new unit, which relates to the repetition of the same routine on a new day.

In the film *The Shawshank Redemption*, the deadening sameness of the days in prison is accentuated by means of shots of the inmates performing the same tasks. For instance, we are frequently presented with shots of the inmates at work, in the mess hall, in the prison yard, or alone in their cells. Furthermore, we witness three meetings between the inmate Red and the parole board. The questions and answers we are presented with in the course of the first two sessions are almost identical and suggest circularity. Each time, a member of the parole board asks Red: "You feel you've been rehabilitated?" After Red has served twenty years of his life sentence, he answers: "Oh yes, sir. Absolutely sir. I mean I learnt my lesson. I can honestly say I'm a changed man. I'm no longer a danger to society. That's God's honest truth." Ten years later, i.e., after thirty years of his life sentence, Red answers: "Oh yes, sir. Without a doubt. And I can honestly say I'm a changed man. No danger to society here. God's honest truth. Absolutely rehabilitated." After both meetings, we are presented with a close-up of a big rubber stamp slamming down to print the word "REJECTED." Red is released once he actually regrets the crime he committed. In this meeting, Red says:

> Rehabilitated? Well now, let me see. You know, I don't have any idea what that means. I know what you *think* it means. To me, it's just a made-up word, a politician's word so that young fellas like yourself can wear a suit and a tie and have a job. What do you really want to know? Am I sorry for what I did? There's not a day goes by I don't feel regret. And not because I'm in here or because you think I should. I look back on the way I was then. A young, stupid kid who committed that terrible crime. I want to talk to him. I want to try and talk some sense to him. Tell him the way things are. But I can't. That kid's long gone. This old man is all that's left. I gotta live with that. Rehabilitated? That's just a bullshit word. So you go on and stamp your forms, sonny, and stop wasting my time. Because to tell you the truth, I don't give a shit.

Andy enables Red to confront himself and to break out of the repetitiveness of the futile parole board hearings of Norton's regime. In contrast to Warden Norton, Andy improves the educational facilities in prison and tries to teach the prisoners the importance of hope. Red's statement above is one aspect of "the film's transition from institutional critique to valorisation of rehabilitative penal styles" (Jarvis 197). The film suggests that the inmates themselves have to make an effort and confront themselves with their criminal deeds. And they need reformative prisons that allow them to do so.

In the novel *A Clockwork Orange*, the imprisoned narrator Alex complains about having to "itty [walk, J.A.] round and round and round the yard for like exercise" (108). In the 1971 film version, the circularity of the daily pattern in prison is visually simulated by depicting the inmates of HM Prison Parkmoor walking around in circles in the prison yard. For instance, before the sequence in which the Minister of the Interior (Anthony Sharp) visits the prison, we are presented with two shots of the prisoners whose bodily movements are stipulated by a white circle on the ground of the exercise yard. Shots of inmates walking around in circles in the prison yard occur in many prison films, e.g., in *Now Barabbas was a Robber* (1949), *Caged*, and *Birdman of Alcatraz*. On the one hand, this circular movement is one part of the boring prison routine. On the other hand, it may be seen as a symbol of the workings of non-rehabilitative prisons. Since the inmates are never allowed to break out of the prison's inflexible time-tables, their personalities are preserved because they are not allowed to develop, and consequently, the prisoners do not manage to transcend the circuit of delinquency.

Some convicts, like Stroud in the film *Birdman of Alcatraz* are sentenced to solitary confinement. In comparison with the inmates of the 'normal' prison population, this type of imprisonment involves even more monotony and less sensory stimulation. Thomas Gaddis' (Edmond O'Brien) voice-over narration informs us that

> [...] being in solitary is like being on rails. A man pushes your food through the door. You eat alone. Once a week you get

> a shower. You walk in the bullpen. Once a month an inmate comes and cuts your hair. You read. You pace your cell. Once a week you get clean laundry. You pace your cell. The routine's always the same. [...] You sit and listen to your heartbeat and you hear your life ticking away. The thing that swells in your head until you lose your mind is you know absolutely for sure what's coming next.

The film combines O'Brien's voice-over with shots of parts of Stroud's body that are linked together by means of dissolves. More specifically, we see a close-up of Stroud's face which dissolves into a close shot of the inmate's feet as he paces his cell. This shot is in turn superimposed and gradually replaced by a close-up of Stroud's hands playing with a string and then followed by a shot of the lonely convict in the bull pen. This shot then dissolves into another close-up of Stroud's feet and a shot of the prisoner in the snow-covered bull pen. This is followed by a close-up of Stroud's hands moving a spoon through his food and a shot of the inmate sitting down on the floor of the bull pen. At the end of the sequence, the last two shots together with an extreme close-up of Stroud's eyes remain superimposed so that viewers may get the impression of being within the prisoner's head. The end of the sequence may be an external allusion to the way in which prisoners internalize the prison.

This sequence highlights the idleness of life in solitary confinement where nothing happens at all. On the visual level, the dissolves reduce a year of story time[20] to a few minutes of discourse time. Interestingly, the images on the screen do not conform with the words of O'Brien's voice-over so that boredom on the part of viewers may be avoided. Since Stroud's bodily parts (his head, his feet, his hands, and his eyes) were all filmed separately and thus involve synecdoche, we do not conceive of his body as a seat of organic identity. Rather, we are confronted with a series of fragmented parts that in themselves seem to have no identity or essential being. Since Stroud is in a way falling apart, one might interpret this fragmentation of Stroud as an allusion to the inmate's identity crisis.

The film *Wilde* also uses dissolves to simulate the monotony and routine of prison life. More specifically, a shot of Wilde's hands ordering his metal dishes smoothly fades into a shot of the inmate's feet stumbling on the treadwheel. We are then confronted with a close-up of Wilde's pale face and we see that he is about to fall unconscious. Finally, the prisoner collapses on the floor of his cell. Such synecdoches, i.e., repeated exclusions of all but parts of the figure, allude to the prisoner's identity crisis. In contrast to the film *Birdman of Alcatraz*, where Stroud's identity crisis is clearly a consequence of his boredom, the shots in *Wilde* suggest that the inmate's crisis is not exclusively related to the daily routine conveyed by the smooth dissolves, but also to the combination of extremely hard labor with the prison's dietary. We frequently see Wilde eating something from his metal pot but are never presented with a single shot in which the food he was given is actually shown on the screen. Thus, we get a sense that he actually eats 'nothing.' For me, this visual absence of food is an excellent illustration of the the fact that in most Victorian prisons, food was virtually non-existent because the issued progressive dietary constituted deliberate malnourishment.

Both prison novels and films use segments of inmates performing the same tasks or speed-ups to simulate the monotonous routine cycles in prison. Additionally, they creatively combine circularity, repetition, and synecdoche to illustrate how repetitive routines may destroy the personality of inmates and cause them to fall apart. The segments and tropes in this section generate a contrast between disciplinary prison regimes, which expose inmates to boring routines, and rehabilitative prisons in which inmates are given a chance to develop. The representation of these routines thus primarily serves to critique disciplinary prison institutions. However, since these routines and monotony or boredom do not constitute proper and interesting threats to the masculinity of the major protagonist, twentieth-century prison narratives tend to mention these features in passing and quickly move on to proper threats like prison violence, rape, and time in the 'hole.'

Prison Violence and 'Homosexual' Rape as Forms of Symbolic 'Feminization'

Outbreaks of violence between prison officers and their charges as well as among inmates constitute important elements of the prison experience in the twentieth century. 'Homosexual' rape is a particular type of inmate-on-inmate violence that follows from the relatively free association of prisoners in twentieth-century institutions. In this section, I deal with the representation of prison violence and rape in novels and films. Two aspects are noteworthy. First, the major function of violence and rape is to intensify our sympathy for our prisoner-heroes. Second, the representations correlate with a threat to the hero's masculinity, which has to be defended against the symbolic 'feminization' in prison.

In Burns' *I Am a Fugitive from a Georgia Chain Gang!*, prisoners who are unaccustomed to the chain gang's regime of hard labor are frequently whipped by the guards. The following description of one of these whippings illustrates that the prison threatens the inmates' masculinity by placing them in submissive positions:

> Strong hands grabbed hold of him, pulled down his pants, baring his buttocks, and then laid him face downward on one of the benches. He was held down so that he could not move. A leather strap six feet long, three inches wide, one-quarter inch thick was brought forth. [...] And with a terrific crash, the heavy strap came down on bare flesh with all the strength of the wielder behind it. The convict let out a yell—pleaded for mercy—promised to work—promised anything, but the strap rose again and descended with a sickening crash, the force of which temporarily shut off the pleadings of the convict. And so it went—one, two, three, four, five, six, seven, eight, nine, ten. Ten licks and the convict, half fainting or perhaps unconscious, was stood up on his feet—blood running down his legs, and one of the guards carried or led him back into the sleeping quarters. (54)

It is also worth noting that after this horrifying incidence, which is depicted like a symbolic rape, the first-person narrator, who was notably not whipped, quickly notes that *he* is the true sufferer, and pushes himself back into the center of interest. He complains about "the agonized groans" of the prisoners "who had been beaten," and informs us that "fear and despair clutched [his] weary heart" (55).

The film adaptation differs slightly from the autobiography because the major protagonist James Allen is whipped as well but the message remains the same. We are supposed to identify with him and his plight. It is also worth noting that Allen is punished because he is true to himself and his ideals, i.e., because he behaves like a 'real man,' and not because he did not work properly. At the end of Allen's first day at the chain gang, the warden (David Landau) enters the sleeping quarters carrying a huge leather strap. Two guards single out a convict named Ackerman (Jack LaRue) and the inmate Red (James Bell) who fainted during work because he felt sick (this was presumably caused by the unpalatable food the prisoners are given). When Allen calls the warden a "skunk," the warden turns on him and ejaculates: "You're next!" The actual lashings take place off-screen, which perhaps heightens our horror because we have to imagine them. According to Campbell, "the shadow of the strap moves up and down the wall, as the crash of leather and (in Ackerman's case) excruciating yells of pain are heard" (18). Allen follows Ackerman who staggers back into the room, his bare back full of stripes. Our prisoner-hero receives sixteen blows but in contrast to Ackerman does not yell at all. Hence, Allen remains a 'true' man because he emerges unbroken from this 'test' of his masculinity.

The prison in the film *The Shawshank Redemption* also puts the newcomers' masculinity on trial. More specifically, the hardened cons take 'horse-bets' on who of the new inmates will break down crying during his first night. The inmate Heywood (Bill Sadler) puts his money on "the chubby fat ass," who drags his weight in terror, whereas the voice-over narrator Red decides in favor of Andy, whom he refers to in terms of "that tall drink of water with a silver spoon up his ass." While the new inmate "Fat Ass" proves to be too unmanly to survive prison, Andy passes the first test of his manliness because during the whole night, he "never made a sound." During the night, the inmate Heywood in the cell next to "Fat Ass" whispers: "I know a couple of old bull queers who'd just love to make your acquaintance, especially that big white mushy white butt of yours." The newcomer breaks down and cries "God, I don't belong here. I wanna go home. I want my mama." The sadist Captain Hadley pulls the newcomer from his cell and beats him to death with his night-stick. The violence establishes the prison as a hellish testing-ground for masculinity, and our sympathies are directed toward Andy who looks like a wimp (or a "tall drink of water") but turns out to be a 'real' man.

The prison's rapists, who are called the 'sisters,' constitute the next threat to Andy's manliness. In the mess hall, Bogs Diamond, one of the prison's 'sisters,' gives Andy a salacious glance, and then approaches him in the communal shower room. Later on, Bogs and two other 'sisters' corner Andy in the laundry storage room, and proceed to gang-rape him. The camera pulls back from the rape scene and moves around a corner. Red's voice-over narration sets in when the camera begins to pull back:

> I wish I could tell you that Andy fought a good fight and the 'sisters' let him be. I wish I could tell you that. But prison is no fairy-tale world. He never said who did it. But we all knew. Things went on like that for a while. Prison life consists of routine, and then more routine. Every so often, Andy would show up with fresh bruises. The 'sisters' kept at him. Sometimes he was able to fight 'em off, sometimes not. And that's how it went for Andy. That was his routine.

Phil Hardy points out that even though since the 1930s, "little has changed in the iconography [...] of the prison movie, [...] there has been an increasing concentration on homosexuality (rape in the showers)" (270). That is to say, 'homosexual' attacks were rarely (if ever) hinted at in early prison films. However, they do appear as an element in many post-1960s movies. One might relate this increasing concentration on 'homosexual' rapes in prison films to the more liberal spirit within the British Board of Film Censorship and the revision of the Hollywood Production Code in the 1960s. On the other hand, it is worth noting that we never see rapes on the screen because the camera always pulls back from the scene, which might have to do with the general ideological perspective of these movies. According to Rafter, most heroes in prison films "demonstrate that the old-fashioned tough-guy ideal is intact and available, even (or perhaps especially) in prison" (124). More specifically, the sexual submission or 'objectification' of Andy is alluded to but ultimately serves to heighten our sympathies for Andy who restores his manliness at the end of the film. In the words of Tony Magistrale,

> Andy is a man [...], who understands that the world will strip such a man of his essence if he is not vigilant and self-protective. Injustice follows Andy inside the prison; his intelligence and good looks are exploited by convicts and prison authorities alike when he is subjected to sexual assault and the [metaphorical, J.A.] rape of his financial acumen by Warden Norton [...] and his guards. But Andy is never relegated to victim status. (126)

Indeed, Andy finally fools everyone (including us as viewers), secretly tunnels his way out of the prison, thus overcoming the symbolic 'feminization' in prison and successfully restoring his masculinity.

Prison narratives of the twentieth century misrepresent prison violence because they tend to focus almost exclusively on acts of brutality between guards and inmates, and ignore the frequent fights and tussles between prisoners. As a general tendency, twentieth-century prison narratives also misrepresent homosexuality in prison because both novels and films fail to recognize consensual sex and homoerotic relations between inmates, and instead focus on 'homosexual' rapes which constitute a threat to the masculinity of our major protagonist. In terms of ideological underpinnings, it is also important to note that the rapists are not only coded as homosexuals (because they constitute the only form of homosexuality in these narratives) who threaten the masculine identity of our hero but in a second step also as 'real' criminals (like colored inmates). Examples of such criminal 'homosexuals' are the 'sisters' in *The Shawshank*

Redemption, Wolf in *Escape from Alcatraz*, Banks (John Blundell) and his gang in *Scum*, as well as the homosexuals in the novel *A Clockwork Orange* and its film adaptation. Generally speaking, the (almost obligatory) scenes of violence and rape in twentieth-century prison narratives are supposed to make captivity appear like hell and increase our sympathy for our suffering identificatory figure. Prison violence and rapes pose an additional threat to the hero's manliness because they exacerbate the enforced passivity (or 'feminization') in prison.

The Prisoner as 'Abject'—The Madness of the 'Hole'

Having to spend time in the 'hole' is another aspect of the prison experience in discipline-based institutions that heightens our feelings of empathy for the central protagonist. Also, since the dark 'hole' is used as a form of punishment for misbehaving convicts, it serves the purpose of a prison-within-the-prison. This architectural arrangement of prisons *en abyme* evokes a recursive structure of punishment, and correlates with an intensification of the prison's regime of injustice. Furthermore, Jarvis argues that "the hole is a fecund symbol [...], connoting not only grave and womb but also the rectum" (175). Indeed, one might see the 'hole' as the place of the 'abject.' The 'hole' contains those who are rejected by society and in a second step also excluded from the general prison population. The 'hole' may also symbolize the dark abyss of the human psyche. As we move deeper and deeper into the most hidden spots of the prison, we simultaneously move deeper and deeper into the darkest sides of the human soul. The 'hole' might symbolize the holes of despair into which the inmates are plunged or the prison officers' dark psychological subconsciousness which is dominated by sadistic drives.

Prison films usually render the dramatic identity crisis inmates experience in the 'hole' by means of external features. For example, in the movies *Birdman of Alcatraz* and *The Shawshank Redemption*, the inmates are shown huddling in dark and painful corners of the 'hole,' and they have to shield their eyes from the blinding light when the door is finally opened again. Thus, we do get a sense that the prisoners are 'washed out' by the full front lighting.[21] Also, in both films, shots of the inmates are juxtaposed with shots of rats. First, the juxtaposition of prisoners and rats illustrates that the prison staff view the inmates as vermin and treat them accordingly. Second, in both films the prison warden arrives immediately after we have seen the rat on the screen. Hence, one can also argue that these films define the wardens as vermin because they expose the inmates to the ravages of the 'hole.'[22]

In contrast to films, first-person novels offer us inside views of the suffering inmate in the 'hole.' In the novel *Sleepers*, the narrator Shakes is thrown into 'the hole' of the Wilkinson Home for Boys because the inmates won a game of touch football against the guards. This is even more unjust than the initial incarceration of Shakes and his three friends. They were sent to the reform school because they accidentally killed a man. Now they are thrown into the 'hole' for no reason at all. In the 'hole,' Shakes experiences a complete loss of orientation and a severe identity crisis, which correlates with what Julia Kristeva calls the 'abject' or abjection. According to Kristeva, the 'abject' deconstructs the distinction between object and subject, and threatens to draw us into an abyss where "meaning collapses" (2). More specifically, the 'abject' refers to ways in which we may react (e.g., through horror or vomit) to a threatened breakdown in meaning caused by the loss of the distinction between 'self' and 'other.' For Kristeva, primary examples of objects that may cause such a reaction are corpses, open wounds, excrement, sewage, and so forth. Indeed, in his depiction of the situation in the 'hole,' Shakes gradually erases the boundary between subject and object, inside and outside. The description of his cell merges with the rendering of his own inner state so that we do get a sense that he internalizes the 'hole':

> There was no bed in the hole. There was no toilet. There was no noise. There was no food. There was no water and there was no fresh air. There was only darkness and large, hungry

> rats. In the hole there was only madness. […] I spent my first day in the hole sleepless, moving my legs from side to side, hoping to keep the rats away from my cuts, knowing that sooner or later I would have to give in and close my eyes and they would make their move. My hours were filled with terror. Any noise, even the slight wine of a floorboard, sent fear through my body. […] I could not distinguish morning from night, dawn from dusk, each passing moment awash in a darkness that promised no rescue. The guards had not brought in any food or water, and the stench of dried urine and feces was overwhelming. […] I had been there only a matter of hours when I began to think about death. It was what I most wished for, the only thing worth praying to any God willing to listen. […] I had lost any sense of time, any grasp of place, my mind wandering back and forth on the cloudy road between delusion and nightmare. Rats crawled up and down my back and legs, feasting on my cuts and scabs, nestling in the holes in my clothes. […] I felt the open hydrants of Hell's Kitchen on my body, the cool spray of water stripping away summer heat. […] Left for dead in that hole of despair, I sought refuge in the safest spot my mind could wander—the streets of Hell's Kitchen. (212–15)

In order to stress the drastic bareness of his cell, Shakes uses the anaphoric phrase "there was no." The phrase "there was only," which is related to darkness, rats, and, finally, madness, provides some sort of anticlimax that notably ends with the narrator's psychological state, thus merging inside and outside. Shakes also links his feelings of "terror," "fear," and disorientation to external matters, namely to the rats, noise in the 'hole,' and the lack of food. Finally, the narrator seeks refuge by evoking scenes from his 'lost' childhood, and ultimately loses his orientation. At the end of this sequence, he is no longer in a position to distinguish between illusion and reality. When the rats crawl up and down his back and legs, and eat into his open wounds, he seems to have given in to the madness of the 'hole.' The distinction between inside and outside is also undermined by the urine and feces in this scenario. They are externalizations of something that used to be internal. These excretions then become a part of the 'hole' so that the cell absorbs the inmate, and the distinction between subject and object, which is crucial for the establishment of identity, becomes erased.

In a particularly degrading episode in the 'hole,' which also involves excrement (and does not occur in the film), the narrator literally internalizes something that is external. At one point, the guard Nokes opens the door of the inmate's dark cell. In the words of the narrator, "the sharp light that filtered in sent the rats scurrying into corners and forced me to shield my eyes" (213). Nokes brings him a bucket of dry oatmeal:

> I heard a zipper slide down, watched him spread his legs and listened as he peed into the bowl of food. 'There,' he said when he had finished. 'That's better. That should help it go down easier. ' [...] The minute I heard the lock turn and the bolt shut down I rushed for the bowl and ate my first meal in the hole. (214)

This segment also plays with the boundary between exteriority and interiority. To begin with, it is a peculiarity of food that it cannot easily be classified as subject or object. The act of eating is the absorbing of an aspect of the external world into the interior world; food is an object which becomes a part of the subject. Hence, by eating prison food, prisoners always internalize something which is associated with the prison institution. Since the narrator additionally incorporates Nokes' urine, which is an externalization of Nokes' body, Shakes also internalizes an aspect of the sadist Nokes. From the perspective of Nokes, the 'hole' might symbolize his perverse and deviant desires, which he can safely hide and conceal by closing the door of the 'hole.' Shakes' account also draws a parallel between Nokes and the rats. Nokes is like a rat because both Nokes and the rats 'enter' the first-person narrator. While the rats feast on the narrator's scabs and cuts, Shakes is forced to literally incorporate Nokes' urine so that various aspects of the reform school find their way into the narrator, who is then completely absorbed by the detention center. And the narrator's identity crisis consists precisely in this collapse of the distinction between self and other. In Kristeva's words, he finds himself "on the edge of non-existence and hallucination" (2).

By informing us of the dramatic identity crisis he experiences in prison, Shakes' first-person account tells us what the 'hole' did to him, namely erase the distinction between subject and object. Also, Shakes' identity crisis is a more dramatic version of the identity crisis we witness in "Rita Hayworth and Shawshank Redemption," where Red suffers from a split between a hopeful self that wants to overcome the prison and a hopeless prison self that continues to depend upon the prison. In the case of Shakes, the hopeful self appears to be completely eradicated so that he is completely dominated by the prison.

As far as the cinematic version of the degrading sequence in the 'hole' is concerned, the spatial coordinates of the cell and Shakes' (Joe Perrino) identity crisis have to be rendered in the showing mode. To begin with, the description of Shakes' bare cell is conveyed by means of two overhead shots, i.e., by means of two shots taken from above the 'hole.' Interestingly, Blandford et al. point out that such camera positions "are often used to imply fate or entrapment" (171). On the one hand, the two overhead shots illustrate the bareness of Shakes' cell. On the other hand, they convey the fact that the 'hole' is so small that there is hardly enough room for the inmate to move. The camera is positioned above Shakes to depict the cramped space in which he finds himself. The first of these overhead shots presents us with the inmate using his hands to inspect the size of his cell. Since the inmate has to use his hands for this inspection, we can infer that in contrast to us—we are provided with dim lighting—Shakes does not see anything in the cell. Later on in the sequence, we are confronted with another overhead shot of Shakes lying in the fetal position on the cell's wet floor together with a rat. Since there is not even a pail in the floor to relieve himself, much less a toilet or a washbasin, we can infer that, as in the written version, the prisoner is lying in his own excrement. It is also worth noting that in the 'hole,' Shakes is juxtaposed with sewage pipes. The juxtaposition of the prisoner with both sewage pipes and excrement visually codes Shakes as an 'abject.'

With regard to the rendering of Shakes' identity crisis and loss of orientation, the editing of the sequence in the 'hole' is very interesting because we are confronted with a rather confused representation of events that belong to three different temporal levels, namely (1) the 'now' of the younger Shakes who has to spend time in the 'hole,' (2) the touch football game at the Wilkinson Home for Boys, and (3) Shakes' 'lost' childhood.[23] The actual chronological order of the events would conform with the following formalization: AB (= childhood)—CDEFGH (= football game)—IJKLMNOPQ (= time in the 'hole').[24] In the film, the first two of these temporal levels are represented as flashback or memory sequences, and the events occur in the following order: ICJDKEFLGMHNOAPBQ. The film oscillates between exteriority and interiority because the first time-level is rendered through external shots of Shakes in his cell, while the other two time-levels are rendered as enacted mindscreens that represent Shakes' memory.

We are first presented with an external slow-motion shot of Nokes (Kevin Bacon) throwing the badly wounded Shakes into the 'hole' of the reformatory, which is followed by another external shot of the inmate inspecting his cell (I). The sequence in 'the hole' is intercut with black-and-white shots of the rather violent touch football game against the guards. Michael Ballhaus, the cinematographer of *Sleepers*, said that Barry Levison, the director of the film,

> was struggling with how to present the football game. Finally he said: 'I think it's best to do it as a flashback from the point of view of the boy in the cell, with him remembering what happened.' [...] We shot it handheld in black-and-white, which added a lot of drive to the story. (qtd. in Turner 42)

After the shots referred to above, the internal (black-and-white) sequence sets in, and we witness Shakes' memory about the boys determining that the African-American inmate Rizzo is the toughest touch football player (C). This is followed by an (external) shot of Shakes in his dark cell (J). Then, in the course of the flashback, we see Michael (Brad Renfro) persuading Rizzo to play the touch football game against the guards (D), which is followed by an external close-up of Shakes' wounded face in the 'hole' (K). The flashback sequence continues with Michael trying to persuade Rizzo (E), and the game finally begins (F). Then, we are presented with yet another external shot of Shakes in his cell (L), which is followed by another memory sequence in which the boys win the game and begin to chant Rizzo's name (G). We are then presented with an external shot of Shakes in the 'hole' as he whispers Rizzo's name (M) like the inmates in his memory. The film begins to deconstruct the distinction between the internal and the external sequence in the 'hole.' As the flashback sequence continues, Michael approaches Nokes and says, "Hey Nokes! Good game!" (H). This is followed by a longer (external) sequence of Shakes lying on the floor of his cell together with a rat (N), in the course of which the voice-over section sets in, which is accompanied by non-diegetic instrumental string music. Then, once again, we see the prisoner sitting in his dark cell (O).

At this point, the film goes even further back in the inmate's memory when a projected image of his 'lost' childhood (Shakes and his friends cavorting in a gushing stream of water) (A) is reflected onto actor Joe Perrino's hand. This image is then followed by another shot of Shakes in 'the hole' (P), a full-screen rendering of the projected sequence from his childhood (B), and a final shot of Shakes in the 'hole' (Q). Referring to the touch football game, the older Shakes states in his voice-over that

> for once we had a victory. But it didn't last. It couldn't last. And all I wanted to do was die. I was not alone in the 'hole.' I knew my friends were down in the depths with me. Each in his own cell, each in his own pain, suffering his own demons. Rizzo was there, too. I had lost any sense of time.

The confused representation of the actual chronology of 'events' in combination with the voice-over is a brilliant cinematic representation of the younger Shakes' feelings of disorientation. Without being able to depict Shakes' thoughts and feelings in the manner of the novel, the film oscillates between a description of exteriority (i.e., the external shots of Shakes in his cell) and interiority (i.e., Shakes' memory).

Also, the confused representation of the three temporal levels can be seen as a powerful visual correlative of the following statement by the novel's first-person narrator: "I had lost any sense of time, any grasp of place, my mind wandering back and forth on the cloudy road between delusion and nightmare" (214). Furthermore, by projecting an image of Shakes' 'lost' childhood onto the hand of Shakes in the cell, the film cuts across the distinction between inside and outside because we literally see a part of Shakes' memory, i.e., a part of his interiority, on the outside, i.e., in his cell. The use of the projected image informs us that Shakes is no longer in a position to discriminate between inside and outside. In other words, we can account for the above mentioned disruptions of ordinary human experience by attributing them to an experience of liminality. In the 'hole,' Shakes goes through some sort of shock or trauma which leads to his emotional disintegration.

Since the 'hole' is the most secluded and isolated place in prison where the prison officers can be alone with inmates, the prison-within-the-prison sometimes drives guards to the most sadistic treatment of the inmates. Being sent to the 'hole' correlates with a descent into the depths of human depravity. The 'hole' in fictional prison narratives symbolizes the dark abyss of the human psyche. On the one hand, the darkness of this small cell symbolizes the psychological state of the inmates who experience dramatic identity crises and are plunged into holes of despair that correlate with Kristeva's 'abjection.' On the other hand, the 'hole' also symbolizes the sadistic desires of the prison staff. Furthermore, the prison-within-the-prison evokes a recursive structure of punishment. The overall injustice of the prison system is repeated and intensified in the 'hole.' Most importantly, the sequences in the 'hole' are used to enhance our pity for prisoner heroes like Andy Dufresne or Robert F. Stroud who suffer from the enforced passivity in prison and have to regain their masculinity.

THE GUARDS OR THE 'OTHER' PRISONERS

Most fictional prison narratives of the twentieth century contain representations of prison officers. Interestingly, they are not only depicted as inhumane warders but also as victims of the prison system. One might therefore refer to them in terms of the 'other' prisoners. The situation of the guards in such prison narratives serves as an additional argument in favor of reformative incarceration or rehabilitative prisons. In them, the guards are not affected by the boring prison routines, have more responsibilities and hence do not begin to degrade the inmates.

For example, the novel *Birdman of Alcatraz* contains various references to the situation of the prison officers on Alcatraz island, and depicts their situation as being similar to that of the prisoners. The narrator points out that "despite their careful training," the guards were "worked upon by the same influences" as the inmates (207). Later on, the narrator suggests that as in the case of inmates, the stressful situation in prison turns some of the guards into violent creatures:

> Surrounded by routine, and physically separated from the mainland, wearing their lives away against the fearful sum of menace and hatred of three hundred suffering, desperate men, some guards grew no less savage than their charges. (213)

Finally, the narrator argues that the guards internalize the prison which in a sense turns them into prisoners as well. More specifically, he points out that the 'rock'

> [. . .] ate into the vitals of the keepers and the kept alike, unnerving their decency, making survival contingent upon ruthless force, steep routine, and counting [...] The guards become prisoners themselves, and everyone counting, the prisoners counting the hours and the guards counting the prisoners and the wardens counting the counts. (247–48)

The confrontation between Stroud and the guard Bull Ransom (Neville Brand) in the film *Birdman of Alcatraz* also suggests a certain similarity between guards and inmates. In the course of this confrontation, Ransom complains that Stroud perceives him only as a uniform and not as a human being with emotions: "I may be just a uniform to you but you've got no pattern on feelings. I'm a man—the same as you—and I wanna be treated like one." This scene demonstrates that the guards are also at the mercy of the prisoners who can either respect them as human beings or reduce them to their function as prison officers. When Stroud's wife-to-be Stella Johnson (Betty Field) visits Stroud at Leavenworth, Ransom ends the conversation by shouting "Time's up!" In the shot that follows the officer moves between the inmate and his visitor, thus accentuating the power that the institution exercises over the inmate. Furthermore, Ransom's head remains off-screen so that at this point, he is indeed "just a uniform," i.e., a dehumanized representative of the prison institution who does not 'fully' exist as a person.

Later on in the film, when Warden Shoemaker and Stroud meet at Alcatraz, we witness the following conversation:

> STROUD: "Coming over on the launch I saw some children playing."
> SHOEMAKER: "They belong to the guards and all the other personnel. We all live on the rock, too."
> STROUD: "Interesting, isn't it? [...] Do the children enjoy living here?"
> SHOEMAKER: "Well, I don't suppose any of us truly enjoy living on this island. It wasn't designed for pleasure."

Stroud here comments on the fact that like the inmates, prison officers have to spend a considerable amount of time in prison. In this case, the prison staff even have to live on a remote island together with the inmates.

Foucault refers to prison guards in terms of "supervisors" who are "perpetually supervised" and points out that although the "pyramidal organization" of the "hierarchized surveillance […] gives it a 'head,' it is the apparatus as a whole that produces 'power' and distributes individuals in this permanent and continuous field" (*Discipline* 177). In the film *A Clockwork Orange*, the uniform Alex wears in prison blends in with the prison officers' uniforms and the suits worn by the government officials, thus suggesting that the prison officers and the government officials are 'imprisoned' by their work as well. Also, the uniforms in the film *The Shawshank Redemption* visually suggest that the prison officers and the prisoners are parts of the same system. In this movie, the prisoners wear outworn blue jackets, blue trousers, and shabby gray or light blue prison shirts. These blue prison uniforms blend in with the guards' blue uniforms (and perhaps even Warden Norton's blue suits); the differences lie in detail.

Films also use matching shots or costumes to stress that prison officers are imprisoned as well. For example, when Sean Nokes and the other three sadistic prison officers of the Wilkinson Home for Boys are introduced by the voice-over narrator in the film *Sleepers*, the camera moves in circles around a table at which the four guards play cards. This circular camera movement is used again later on, when Shakes and his three teenage friends sit at a table and discuss the question of whether they should tell anyone about the sexual abuse they endured at the detention center. Like the guards, they decide to remain silent about the torture. These matching shots present two different groups in the same way. More specifically, a certain similarity between guards and inmates is stressed by the way the two groups are presented cinematically. First, the guards are like the inmates because they have to follow the prison rules and regulations as well. Second, both groups are tied closely together by the sexual abuse and experience particular types of friendship. The guard buddies are united because they indulge in raping the boys together, while the boys are united in their wreaking of revenge on their former perpetrators. The two cases share a similar construction of group identity. Common victims intensify the group-internal relationships. Furthermore, both groups are linked because they remain silent about the rapes and, in the words of the voice-over after the first gang rape, try to bury the sexual abuse "as deep as it can possibly go." Interestingly, when the guard Ferguson (Terry Kinney) re-experiences the rapes in the course of his confession on the stand, we learn that he and Shakes are haunted by the same nightmarish visions. The film conveys their memory of the sexual abuse by means of (partly blurred) black-and-white mindscreens. Hence, when the voice-over informs us that we are about to view a movie about "a friendship that runs deeper than blood," he might actually refer to both the ties between the guards and the bond between the former inmates.

The verbal descriptions, dialogues, camera positions, camera movements, and costumes referred to above suggest that the situation of guards and the situation of inmates hardly differ. Both groups are forced to wear uniforms, which correlates with a loss of individuality, and both groups have to spend a considerable time in prison. Most importantly, both are subject to the unforgiving and relentless routine of prison life. On the other hand, guards usually decide to work in prison, and they can leave the institution at the end of their shift. Nevertheless, it is true that "during their working shifts, day and night," the guards too "are within the security perimeter of the prison, subjected to a routine reflecting that of the prisoners" (Morris "Contemporary" 253). Their boredom and the power they wield can occasionally drive prison officers to indulge in the subjecting of prisoners to degrading physical abuse.

The representation of the guards as victims of the prison system ties in with one of the the central arguments of twentieth-century prison narratives. They critique the 'traditional' and boring routines in prisons and argue in favor of more 'progressive' rehabilitative prisons. Almost all of these narratives present us with well-meaning guards who offer a glimpse of a different moral universe and foreshadow the idea of reformative incarceration.[25] The simultaneous representation of 'traditional' and 'progressive' attitudes among prison officers (essentially 'discipline' vs. 'humanity') correlates with the liberal-conservative consensus toward the prison which prison narratives of the twentieth century tend to express. Also, the binary arrangement of 'positive' (e.g., the prison as womb) and 'negative' metaphors of imprisonment (e.g., the prison as tomb or cage) in such narratives serves to underline the distinction between rehabilitative penal styles and discipline-based institutions. Furthermore, prison narratives of the twentieth century make relatively unambiguous statements concerning the question of who is to be sent to the reformative prison institutions they prefer. Since the members of the white and heterosexual middle class we are supposed to identify with are clearly innocent, they do not belong there. Rehabilitative prisons are primarily institutions for the galleries of 'real' criminals that surround the central protagonist. And since they are colored and/or homosexual, we are told that we need reformative prisons for colored and homosexual criminals. Finally, it is worth noting that after our central protagonists have endured numerous rituals of symbolic 'feminization' (through prison violence, rapes, and time in the 'hole'), they either escape from prison or we learn that they successfully resisted the prison authorities. Both types of ending correlate with the defence of traditional masculinity and the restoration of white, phallic power, which is what twentieth-century prison narratives are really about.

ENDNOTES

1. In *Down by Law*, Roberto (Roberto Benigni) is imprisoned because he accidentally killed another man by throwing a snooker ball which hit the victim in the forehead. Also, in the film *Cool Hand Luke* (1967), Luke (Paul Newman) is caught vandalizing parking meters, which is not a proper crime. Rather, this action is associated with the romance of outlaw culture.
2. In the film *Murder in the First* (1995), Henri Young (Kevin Bacon) has to spend three years in one of Alcatraz' dark dungeons because he had stolen five dollars to feed his starving sister and then attempted to escape from Alcatraz.
3. Hadley beats the inmate "Fat Ass" (Frank Medrano) to death and brutalizes the rapist Bogs Diamond (Mark Rolston) so severely that he is a cripple afterwards. Norton exploits the prisoners as slave labor and uses the ex-city banker Andy to run his various corrupt scams. When the innocent Andy wishes to get a new trial because the new young inmate Tommy Williams (Gil Bellows) told him that Elmo Blatch (Bill Bolender) had committed the crime for which Andy was incarcerated, Norton sends Andy to the 'hole.' Since Tommy declares that he would testify that Andy is innocent, Norton tells Hadley to kill Tommy.
4. The Ludovico Technique makes Alex incapable of acting violently because he begins to feel nauseous at the thought of violence and sex. The treatment is a form of brainwashing in which the inmate is drugged and forced to watch a succession of pornographic and violent films with the result that any thought of sex and violence, and, incidentally, the sound of Beethoven, cause him to suffer nausea.
5. Sobchack points out that in the film, "art and violence spring from the same source; they are both expressions of the individual, egotistic, vital, and non-institutionalized man" (98).
6. The following conversation in the novel corroborates this point: "'We've had very little trouble in the Isolation cell block recently, Warden,' said the deputy. 'Men don't make trouble when they have something to do,' said Stroud" (103). Toward the end of *I Am a Fugitive from a Georgia Chain Gang!*, the narrator also sanctions rehabilitative prisons by pointing out that it is a warden's "duty [...] to help reform and train men for a useful place in society" (257).

7. The novel *A Clockwork Orange* and its film adaptation, by contrast, are critical of the idea of state-imposed rehabilitation. While the novel argues that rehabilitation can only be achieved if it correlates with personal choice, the film glorifies Alex whose individuality must never be disciplined by society's conformist forces. Also, the film *The Loneliness of the Long-Distance Runner* argues that the attempt to rehabilitate inmates like Colin is pointless because his crime was motivated by social necessity. In other words, society's class structure and poverty are blamed for the existence of criminality.
8. For the overrepresentation of African-American and Hispanic inmates in American prisons see Norval Morris (240), Amnesty International (99), and Tonry (10). In 2000, the number of inmates in American prisons hit the 2 million mark. Currently, every seventh African American is in a US prison. For the overrepresentation of colored inmates in British prisons see Marian Fitzgerald (9).
9. This film deals with the horrendous treatment of prisoners at the southern Wakefield Prison Farm, which is modelled on the notorious Cummins Prison Farm in Oklahoma. Like Thomas Mott Osborne, one of the wardens of Sing Sing Prison, who pretended to be a prisoner in the Auburn Penitentiary for a week, the new warden Brubaker enters the prison by playing an inmate.
10. Exceptions exist of course. For example, both Langston Hughes' "On the Road" (1935) and Chester Himes' *Cast the First Stone* (1972) concentrate on African-American inmates. Also, Wideman's *Brothers and Keepers* (1985) presents us with an African-American narrator who tells us the tale of his imprisoned brother. As far as films are concerned, one could mention *Malcolm X* (1991), *Penitentiary I–III* (1979; 1982; 1987) and *Stranger Inside* (2001).
11. According to Richard Ellmann, "Wilde's litigiousness gave proof of a distraught mind rather than an indignant one" (409).
12. In borstal, the earning of increasing privileges through promotion was possible. The progressive stages were indicated by means of color, with the blue dress signifying the highest stage.
13. Unreliability is an interactional phenomenon based on sensorially perceived information located in the text and extratextual conceptual information in the reader's mind (Nünning 23–28). Red's narrative is full of textual signals that suggest unreliability. For instance, we are presented with explicit contradictions and other inconsistencies (103–4; 33–34); Red admits that his narrative is highly subjective, untrustworthy, and full of memory gaps ("memory is a pretty subjective thing" [19]; "you

may have noticed how much of what I've told you is hearsay" [37]; "I'm not sure" [56]; "my educated guesses run out, folks; from this point they become progressively wilder" [104]); the narrator frequently addresses the reader (12; 37; 48; 97; 104; 106); and we are confronted with a high degree of expressive markers like "yeah" (8) or "so, yeah" (48).

14. In contrast to the movie, the novella establishes a number of affinities between Andy and Red. Both suffer from suicidal tendencies (20; 55). Also, Red refers to himself in terms of "the guy who can get it for you" (11), and with regard to the prison library, Andy seems to play precisely the same role: "[...] if you couldn't find it, chances were good that Andy could get it for you" (51).
15. The first part is accompanied by pre-existent songs which were not composed for the movie. These songs include "Walk Like a Man" (1962) by Frank Valli and the Four Seasons as well as "Good Vibrations" (1966) by the Beach Boys.
16. In the film *Wilde*, the outside world is also depicted in bright and warm colors, whereas the prison is represented in cool, dark, and bluish tones. Similarly, the prison scenes in the film *A Clockwork Orange* are "rendered in cool, flat tones, as long takes and subtle camera moves create a somber and then clinical atmosphere" (LoBrutto 54).
17. One might read this shot as the officer's desperate attempts to look into the inmate as far as possible. This will later on be achieved by the Ludovico Technique which transforms Alex into a law-abiding citizen. Also, there is, of course, a clear visual resemblance between the prison officer who put the torch into his mouth and the long phallic nose of the mask Alex wears when he rapes Mrs. Alexander (Adrienne Corri) or when he kills the Cat Lady (Miriam Karlin). The implication of the torch in this scene might be that Alex will now be 'feminized' and metaphorically 'fucked' by the institution.
18. Similarly, in the film *Esacpe from Alcatraz*, the newcomer Frank Morris is approached by the rapist Wolf (Bruce M. Fisher) who announces that he is looking for a "new punk."
19. An episode is speeded up when its discourse time is considerably shorter than its story time. Story time refers to the fictional time taken up by the narrative, whereas discourse time refers to the time it takes a reader (or a viewer) to read (or view) a narrative.
20. Since the bull pen is snow-covered in the second shot but not snow-covered in the first and the third shot of the bull pen, we can conclude that the whole sequence is supposed to cover a period of at least one year.

21. See for example the photograph in Kermode in which "Andy cowers from Norton's Luciferian light" (66).
22. The latter two are cases of cinematic metaphor. The juxtaposition allows us to see the prisoners (or the wardens) *as* rats.
23. We are presented with an additional fourth temporal level, namely the 'now' of the older Shakes (Jason Patric), the voice-over narrator, who relates his story in the past tense.
24. There is of course a large temporal gap between the time of B, which is part of Shakes' childhood, and the time of C, the beginning of the touch football game in the reform school.
25. The guard Wilson in the novel *Sleepers* is an example of such a well-meaning guard: "Wilson was the only black guard in our cell block and the only guard who shunned the physical attacks enjoyed by his co-workers" (222). Wilson was transformed into the well-meaning guard Marlboro (James Pickens Jr.) in the film *Sleepers*. Other examples are Ransom in the film *Birdman of Alcatraz* and the guard Wiley (Don McManus) in *The Shawshank Redemption*.

Chapter Five

Prison Metaphors in Novels and Films of the Twentieth Century

'Positive' and 'Negative' Metaphors of Imprisonment

The Prison as Womb, Tomb, and Homosocial Club

The film *The Shawshank Redemption* represents the prison as a womb, a tomb, and a homosocial club. The representation of the prison as womb-tomb begins with Andy's entering the Shawshank State Prison. The newcomer's entry ends in complete darkness and this image evokes the idea that the building 'swallows' Andy. On the auditory level, the voice-over narrator Red compares the new fish, who have to undress during the induction process, to new-born babies ("They march you in naked as the day you were born, skin burning and half blind"), while later on, he argues that the prison takes the inmates' lives away ("They send you here for life and that's exactly what they take"). It is the interplay between the auditory and the visual level which evokes these metaphorical readings. More specifically, the target domain (the prison) is present visually, while the source domains (the womb and the tomb) are present verbally. Since the prison experience implies infantilization and dependency (but also the possibility of being reborn), the inward movement into prison may be seen as an entry into the maternal body. Also, since prisoners are withdrawn from life in the outside world and experience forms of civil or social death, one might see the inward movement into prison as an entry into a dark tomb.

These connotations centrally correlate with Andy's statement that ultimately, everything comes down to a simple choice: "Get busy living or get busy dying." This phrase is related to the presence or absence of hope, and serves as a reminder that if you do not keep moving in prison, you risk becoming part of the walls yourself. The metaphor that describes the prison as a womb is linked to the behavior of Andy and the African-American Red, while the metaphor that codes the prison as a tomb is connected with the prison regime of Warden Norton and the behavior of the old prison librarian Brooks Hatlen (James Whitmore). The metaphors of imprisonment in the film help to separate traditional or discipline-based prison regimes (like Norton's) from rehabilitative penal styles: "Andy strives to create a progressive apparatus within [...] [Norton's, J.A.] semi-feudal system, one founded on the possibility of redemption and legitimized by reference to the arts" (Jarvis 198).

The film contrasts Warden Norton's brutal prison regime, which tramples on the prisoners' hopes, and Andy's humanitarian approach of trying to stimulate them. Already at the beginning of the film, Norton's regime is critiqued by means of a distortion metaphor that alludes to the loss of the inmates' identity (and individuality) as well as their sense of insignificance in prison. More specifically, before Andy enters the prison, we are presented with a bird's-eye view of the identically-looking prisoners in the exercise yard. This high-angle shot accentuates that Norton's system turns the inmates into insignificant ants. Also, before Andy walks into the prison, we are confronted with a sequence in which wild prison inmates shake the fence of the arrival area. The juxtaposition of raving prisoners and fences allows us to see the prison as a cage for wild animals. This sequence critiques Norton's traditional regime because it turns the prisoners into violent beasts of prey. Furthermore, Norton is repeatedly juxtaposed with dead or suffering prisoners and these juxtapositions code him as an evil torturer or gravedigger. Norton exploits the prisoners as slave labor, and accepts the use of illegitimate violence to support his corrupt regime: see e.g., the fatal beating of "Fat Ass," the illegitimate use of solitary confinement in the case of Andy, and the murder of Tommy Williams.

The hard-working Andy, on the other hand, persistently tries to educate the prisoners about the importance of hope. For example, he builds a new prison library and helps the young Tommy Williams to achieve educational qualifications. Also, Andy's escape from prison evokes the association with a birth or rebirth. More specifically, the inmate has to crawl through a dark tunnel which leads to a tight sewage pipe, and these tubes are clearly reminiscent of a birth canal. Hence, the parallels between Andy inching his way head-first through dark and tight tunnels and the birth of a child are made very obvious by this visual trope.[1] When Andy emerges from the pipe in the middle of a rain shower, he strips off his shirt and extends his arms up from his half-naked body to the sky. The camera then pulls back to an overhead shot of Andy as the showery rain washes down on him. Later on, the voice-over argues that Andy "crawled through a river of shit and came out clean on the other side." The context of Andy's escape and the interplay between the visual and the auditory channel clearly invite us to see the escape as a spiritual rebirth and, by extension, the prison as a womb. Since we have been party to the brutal treatment the innocent Andy had to endure in prison, it is almost impossible not to feel that the rain washing down on him is more than physical, that it indeed involves a process of redemption and perhaps a restoration of justice.

At one point, Andy broadcasts music by Mozart on the prison's P.A. system. Red comments on this act of rebellion as follows: "It was like some beautiful bird flapped into our drab little cage and made these walls dissolve away. And for the briefest of moments, every last man at Shawshank felt free." Later on, he says about Andy: "Some birds aren't meant to be caged—their feathers are too bright." Andy is here associated with a bird which might symbolize hope. Indeed, throughout the film, Andy argues in favor of hope, as in the following conversation:

> ANDY: [...] There's somethin' inside that they can't get to, that they can't touch. It's yours.
> RED: What are you talkin' about?
> ANDY: Hope.
> RED: Let me tell you something, my friend. Hope is a dangerous thing. Hope can drive a man insane. It's got no use on the inside. Better get used to the idea.
> ANDY: Like Brooks did?

Andy will not lose himself in the prison system, or allow himself to give up hope and become institutionalized, i.e., to exist in terms of some sort of 'death-in-life.'

The film also contrasts the old prison librarian Brooks Hatlen with Red. More specifically, Brooks has internalized Norton's regime and is completely hopeless, passive, and fearful when he leaves the prison. Red, on the other hand, gradually begins to internalize Andy's ideas about hope, humanity, and self-confidence. When Brooks is paroled after fifty years, he deliberately attacks the inmate Heywood in order to be classified as dangerous so that he will not be released into the hurly-burly of the frightening world outside. As he puts it: "It's the only way they'd let me stay." Later on, Red says about Brooks:

> The man's been in here fifty years [...]. Fifty years! This is all he knows. In here, he's an important man. He's an educated man. Outside he's nothing. Just a used-up con with arthritis in both hands. Probably couldn't even get a library card if he tried. [...] These walls are funny. First you hate 'em. Then you

> get used to 'em. Enough time passes, it gets so you depend on 'em [...].

During his fifty years of imprisonment, Brooks got so dependent on the comfortable stagnancy of his womb-tomb that it is impossible for him to survive on the outside. When he is released, he steps cautiously through the prison's main gate and almost falls over. The old con then travels to Portland by bus and desperately clutches the bar of the seat in front of him, thus trying to stick to some sort of security or stability. In Portland, Brooks cannot cope with the speed of the outside world and is almost run over by a car. In a letter to the inmates, he states: "Dear fellows, I can't believe how fast things move on the outside." Brooks got used to the slowness of the prison routine and, because of its repetitive nature, is not used to the idea of progress: "I saw an automobile once when I was a kid but now they're everywhere. The world went and got itself in a big damn hurry." The parole board got him a room and a job at the Foodway Market. However, Brooks fails to create an existence on the outside. Brooks remains tied to the prison. The loss of willpower and hope becomes a psychological prison for the former inmate which finally leads to his suicide. According to Magistrale, Brooks' endeavor to function in the outside world underscores "the psychological pervasiveness of the prison yard and the manner in which inmates are affected by prolonged incarceration" (128). As a child of Norton's rotten regime, Brooks complements his hopelessness, i.e., the kind of inner death the prison initiated in him, by his physical death. The last words of his letter read as follows: "I don't like it here. I'm tired of being afraid all the time. I've decided not to stay."[2]

It is also worth noting that throughout the film, Red considers hope to be "a dangerous thing." When he is paroled, he remains psychologically tied to the ignominy of the prison. At first, the film constructs a number of similarities between Red and Brooks. Like Brooks, Red travels to Portland by bus, where he gets Brooks' former room and job. At the Foodway Market, the ex-con, who is still used to not doing anything without asking permission for it, always asks his superior whether he is allowed to "take a piss." Red has got difficulties coping with the outside world, too. Like Brooks, he yearns for the security and protection of the prison's womb-tomb:

> All I do anymore is think of ways to break my parole so maybe they'd send me back. Terrible thing to live in fear. Brooks Hatlen knew it. Knew it all too well. All I want is to be back where things make sense, where I won't have to be afraid all the time.

The scene in which he picks up the letter that informs him of Andy's whereabouts accentuates Red's prison taint as well. Before he reads the letter, the former prisoner instinctively looks around as though he were still observed by prison officers. Earlier in the film, Red tells Andy: "I don't think I can make it on the outside, Andy. I mean… I've been in here most of my life. I'm an institutional man now, just like Brooks was." However, in contrast to Brooks, Red finally manages to overcome his fears, buys a (symbolical) compass (to direct him out of his despair), and travels to Zihuatenejo in Mexico to meet Andy on a beach. He walks bare-footed on the sand toward the escape artist, who sands the old paint from the ancient surface of an old boat, which perhaps signifies that he is trying to overcome the past by creating a new identity. The final lines of Red's voice-over run as follows:

> I hope I can make it across the border.
> I hope to see my friend and shake his hand.
> I hope the Pacific is as blue as it has been in my dreams.
> I hope.

In contrast to the novella, where Andy is merely a fictional creation, the actual ex- banker of the film manages to educate Red about hope and allows Red to overcome his mental confinement.

The lexeme 'redemption' denotes "the action of freeing, delivering, or restoring in some way" or "the action of redeeming oneself from punishment" (<www.oed.com>). The title of the film might thus refer to Andy's redemption, i.e., to his escape which redeems him from his punishment in prison or, since he inflicts poetic justice on crooks like Norton and Hadley, to the restoration of some sort of moral order. The title might also refer to his awareness that he is partly responsible for the death of his wife. At one point, he tells Red that he killed her even though he did not pull the trigger. That is to say, he killed her metaphorically speaking because he did not "show her love, thereby driving her into the hands of another man" (Kermode 64).

'Redemption' also denotes "the action of clearing off a recurring liability or charge by payment of a single sum" (<www.oed.com>). From this perspective, the title might refer to the fact that Andy clears off Norton's 'debts' by taking the money from his corrupt scams. For me, Andy's financial redemption, i.e., his emerging from prison as a rich man, is not entirely unproblematic because the ex-city banker steals the money from Norton's various scams. At one point, Andy tells Red: "The funny thing is, on the outside, I was an honest man, straight as an arrow. I had to come to prison to be a crook." While Rafter thinks that in this film, "good triumphs over evil and the moral order is restored" (120), I argue that the film actually glorifies the restoration of the clever white middle class. The film sanctions Andy's crime as a white collar crime, which is presented as being legitimate in the light of the horrors Andy had to endure and perhaps also in the light of what Andy did for the other inmates.

At first glance, Andy is a well-meaning, hard-working, perhaps even "Christ-like" (Magistrale 134–36) figure who tries to reintroduce the humanity which Norton's prison system has stolen from the prisoners. However, upon closer inspection, one realizes that Andy is a hypocritical Christian like Warden Norton.[3] A number of interesting similarities exist between Norton and Andy: both quote from the New Testament, and both use the Christian religion to cover up their scams. More specifically, the warden hides the safe which contains the evidence of his financial tricks behind a framed piece of needlepoint of the saying "His Judgment Cometh and that Right Soon," while Andy uses a bible to conceal his rock hammer. Also, by taking the money from the various scams, Andy (like Norton before him), feathers his nest at the expense of other people. On the other hand, Andy is obviously not as bad as Norton because he merely beats the warden at his own game. Nevertheless, it is worth noting that at the end of the film, society's traditional hierarchies are restored. The educated and clever middle-class banker Andy wins out and manages to fool all the others.

The film's title might also refer to Red's redemption. He is redeemed from both his actual and his mental confinement, which was constituted by fear and feelings of impotence. At the end of the film, Red actually regrets the murder he committed, and is paroled by the 'new' parole board ("There's not a day goes by I don't feel regret"). This is the first instance in which he confronts himself. And after he has learned 'the error of his ways,' Red gradually moves from Brooks' position ("get busy dying") to Andy's position ("get busy living"). In other words, Red begins to understand the redemptive power of hope. The film employs colors and space in such a way as to present us with a visual journey that matches Red's inner journey from the confines of the prison and his feelings of hopelessness to freedom and hope. Darabont said about the final sequence on the beach in Mexico:

> We wanted to start off in tight, cramped spaces and end finally in an endless horizon. We wanted to go from grays and monochrome to this blazing color. It's interesting to see how color creeps into this story more and more as you go on and how the spaces start widening out. (qtd. in Probst 68)

The theme of redemption is also conveyed by the film's processional tone, which is an effect of the reflective timbre of Red's voice-over and the slow (non-diegetic) synthesizer sounds that dominate the movie. John Bailey argues that you leave the film feeling "renewed, buoyant, sanguine" (83). However, it is worth noting that the story of the African-American Red is clearly subservient to the master narrative about the white Andy. The African-American is educated by the white escape artist, and one of his functions is to increase our admiration of this prisoner-hero.

The Shawshank Redemption tacitly approves of white collar crimes committed by the middle class and considers Andy's narrative to be superior to Red's story. The film also participates in further cultural demarcations by constructing the prison population as a homosocial club which includes African-American inmates like Red, stuttering inmates like Heywood, old inmates like Brooks, young inmates like Tommy, but excludes homosexual prisoners like Bogs and his 'sisters.' The term 'homosocial' is here applied to "such activities as 'male bonding,' which may [...] be characterized by intense homophobia, fear and hatred of homosexuality" (Sedgwick 1). By means of strategies that involve 'male bonding' (like beer-drinking), Andy gradually makes his way into the club, even though Red at first feels that he looks "like a stiff breeze would blow him over." Andy represents an updated and more 'sensitive' version of masculinity. He is an introspective middle-class intellectual who is interested in music, books, chess, etc. Andy's post-feminist masculinity presents us as viewers with a more culturally acceptable form of manliness which is nevertheless still masculine enough to avoid being confused with Bogs' 'deviant' homosexuality.

On the other hand, it is worth noting that the rather intense friendship between Andy and Red has a sexual connotation, and their homosocial friendship borders on homoeroticism—in particular at the end, when they warmly embrace each other on a sunny beach. This suggested homoeroticism could have been counterbalanced by the presence of a new girlfriend or wife, but a female person is significantly absent. Also, as in the rape scenes, the camera quickly pulls back as if two men embracing each other was as unrepresentable as homosexual sex. Following Sedgwick, we can draw the 'homosocial' "back into the orbit of 'desire,' of the potentially erotic," which means "to hypothesize the potential unbrokenness of a continuum between homosocial and homosexual—a continuum whose visibility, for men, [...] is radically disrupted" (1). In other words, the film illustrates that intense homosocial friendships can gradually merge with homoeroticism. Nevertheless, it clearly separates heterosexuals from 'deviant' homosexuals.

When Andy learns that the prison's rapists have taken quite a liking to him, Andy states that he is "not homosexual." Red replies: "Neither are they. They'd have to be human first. They don't qualify. Bull queers take by force. It's all they want or understand." While O'Sullivan believes that the film "tries to make clear" that its rapists "are not intended to be a representation of gay sexuality" ("Representations" 332; fn 8), Joe Wlodarz comments on this statement in a more insightful way. For him, such "nods of tolerance basically acknowledge" a "dangerous slippage [from rape to homosexuality, J.A.] […] and yet fail to curb that very slippage" (79). Indeed, like most twentieth-century prison narratives, *The Shawshank Redemption* codes rapes as homosexual acts because they constitute the one and only existing form of homosexuality in prison. Interestingly, in this respect, King's novella "Rita Hayworth and Shawshank Redemption," on which the film is based, differs radically from the film version. The novella's narrator distinguishes various forms of homosexuality which he contrasts with homosexual rape. Surprisingly, these two consensual types of homosexuality are left out in the cinematic version:

> Homosexuality, like straight sex, comes in a hundred different shapes and forms. There are men who can't stand to be without sex of some kind and turn to another man to keep from going crazy. Usually what follows is an arrangement between two fundamentally heterosexual men, although I've sometimes wondered if they are quite as heterosexual as they thought they were going to be when they get back to their wives or their girlfriends. There are also men who get 'turned' in prison. In the current parlance they 'go gay,' or 'come out of the closet.' Mostly (but not always) they play the female, and their favors are competed for fiercely. And then there are the sisters. They are to prison society what the rapist is to the society outside the walls. (29–30)

The critic Kermode, who compares the novella with the film, does not address the interpretive consequences of this omission, and merely argues that Red's "discussion is compacted and clarified somewhat by Darabont's adaptation" (25).[4] In contrast to Kermode, I argue that this omission is significant in so far as it codes rapists as homosexuals. This coding is enhanced by the filmic representation of Bogs. He constitutes a rather bizarre synthesis of attributes that are usually associated with woman-like gay men and qualities that are typical of rapists. When Bogs approaches Andy in the shower room, he displays the effeminateness that is stereotypically associated with homosexuals. His 'feminine' facial expressions and gestures make him a 'faggot.' It is also worth noting that the film feminizes the prison's rapists by calling them 'sisters.' This is significant because most rapists in prison practise a perverse cult of masculinity, and their nicknames ("jocker," "stud," "old man," etc.) never allude to feminine qualities (Büssing 61 and Mariner 70).

At one point, the voice-over announces that an important change in Andy's routine with the 'sisters' took place when Red and Andy are selected to resurface the roof of the license-plate factory. For me, this resurfacing is metaphorically related to the resurfacing of Andy's masculine identity. More specifically, the context of the homosexual rapes allows us to see a link between the cracks on the roof and Andy's tainted masculinity. On the roof, Andy regains his manliness by boldly confronting Captain Hadley, who complains about government taxes he has to pay after receiving an inheritance. Andy slowly approaches the guards and we witness the following conversation:

> ANDY: "Mr. Hadley, do you trust your wife?"
> HADLEY: "Well that's funny. You're gonna look funnier suckin' my dick with no teeth."

Andy even risks being thrown down the roof by Hadley, who thinks that Andy is calling his manliness into question. While dangling precariously from the roof, the former banker explains that if Hadley did trust his wife, he could give the money from the estate to her. Andy proposes to set up a tax-free gift for him. For his part in the bargain, he demands "three beers apiece for each of my co-workers." Then, he adds: "I think *a man* workin' outdoors *feels more like a man* if he can have a bottle of suds" (my emphasis, J.A.). The question of a man's 'proper' identity or masculinity seeps into the film again and again. In this particular sequence, the homosocial club accepts Andy as a member because he has confronted Hadley, thus enabling the prisoners to indulge in the homosocial activity of beer-drinking. Interestingly, Red speculates about Andy's motivation: "I think he just did it to feel normal again." And, the notion of 'normality' is here clearly linked to Andy's regaining of a sense of 'proper' masculinity.

The rapes by the 'sisters' are also coded as homosexual acts because they are permanently contrasted with the 'normal' homosocial behavior of the other men. Desiring the female body is presented as being quite acceptable (perhaps even 'natural'), whereas the only existing form of desiring the male body is clearly 'deviant.' In one significant sequence, the inmates' reaction to a sexy pose of Rita Hayworth in the film *Gilda* (1946) is juxtaposed with a homosexually suggestive scene. When Rita appears in the film-within-the-film, the convicts begin to whistle and scream out of excitement, and we see their vibrant faces. This 'normal' behavior is then contrasted with Bogs' actions in the projectionist's booth. Bogs, who is joined by three other 'sisters,' demands oral sex from Andy. Since Andy seems to prefer masculine aggression to homosexual desire, he uses his wits and manages to transform Bogs' sexual yearning into an outburst of violence. Red's voice-over informs us that they "beat him within an inch of his life. Andy spent a month in the infirmary. Bogs spent a month in 'the hole.'"

When Bogs is released from the 'hole,' Hadley and another guard brutally beat him up with a baton. The voice-over then announces that

> […] two things never happened again after that. The 'sisters' never laid a finger on Andy again. And Bogs never walked again. They transferred him to a minimum security hospital upstate. To my knowledge, he lived out the rest of his days drinking food through a straw.

The voice-over presents the fact that the 'sisters' never touched Andy again as a desirable consequence of the fact that Bogs is now a cripple. As if this were not enough, the inmate Heywood is shown smiling when he witnesses the bandaged Bogs who is transferred to another institution. Finally, Red does not care about the brutalization of this 'faggot' either and is more interested in providing "a nice welcome back" for Andy "when he gets out of the infirmary." Hence, the film (in contrast to the novella) not only codes rapists like Bogs as homosexuals by ignoring all other (less violent) forms of homosexuality. It additionally sanctions the brutal treatment and exclusion of such 'deviant' forms of masculinity.

Once the homosocial prison club has managed to rid itself of Bogs, another 'resurfacing' of Andy's masculine identity can begin. This time, the reconstitution is related to the Rita Hayworth poster which Red managed to get for Andy. The pin-up comes with a small note: "No charge. Welcome back." That is to say that Andy can 'have' the 1940's love goddess for free. This figurative 'shag,' which is free of charge, correlates with the 'resurfacing' of Andy's masculinity, which was so badly tainted by the homosexual Bogs. In other words, the poster allows Andy to feel like a man again because the poster perhaps makes it easier for him to indulge in fantasies of heterosexual desire.

Finally, it is worth noting that the sexual assaults, which are coded as homosexual acts, are exclusively enacted upon the white Andy. In contrast to the novella, the film nowhere indicates that the African-American Red was ever raped by the 'sisters.' In the novella, on the other hand, Red is white[5] and was likewise raped in prison: "[...] am I speaking from personal experience [concerning rapes, J.A.], you ask?—I only wish I weren't" (31). The fact that the film adaptation transforms Red into an African American must be significant. One might feel that this transformation moves the film closer to the experiential realities of American prison life, which is dominated by African-American prisoners. Nevertheless, the film and the horrors of prison life still centrally focus on the fate of the white inmate Andy. Red is significantly distanced from any sexual victimization. Hence, it is notably white masculinity which is threatened by the homosexual 'sisters' in the movie.

The metaphors of imprisonment in the film, i.e., the description of prison as a womb and a tomb, serve to contrast Norton's rotten regime and Andy's rehabilitative penal style but also to highlight different attitudes among the inmates. The film additionally represents the prison population as a homosocial club from which homosexuals are excluded. Furthermore, it is significant that the homosexuals in the film threaten only white masculinity. One may link the film's delimitations—the brutalization and exclusion of Bogs, the distancing of Red from the rapes, Andy's middle-class background, and the 'inferiority'of Red's narrative—to wider cultural demarcations. Like most twentieth-century prison narratives, the film constructs the prison as a space in which society's homophobia and the cultural hegemony of the white middle class are reproduced. Moreover, since the image of the escaped and spiritually reborn Andy in the cleansing rain shower ultimately correlates with the restoration of the phallic power of the white and heterosexual middle class, the film ultimately glorifies, reinforces, and stabilizes the cultural hegemony of straight white men from the middle class, whom we are invited to forgive for engaging in white collar crimes.

Forms of Rehabilitation and Positive Prison Images

The novel *Birdman of Alcatraz* and its 1962 film adaptation are about the life of Robert F. Stroud, who was sent to McNeil Island Penitentiary in 1909 because he killed a man who had beaten up his girlfriend, a prostitute. At first Stroud was a model prisoner but due to a fight with another prisoner he lost any chance of parole. In 1912, he was transferred to Leavenworth, Kansas, where he began to study mathematics and engineering. Four years later, Stroud's brother Marcus Stroud travelled all the way from Alaska to Leavenworth to see Stroud but was refused admission because he arrived on a no-visiting day. The prisoner became angry and was put on report for talking during a meal by a malevolent guard. Later on, Stroud killed this prison officer, and his sentence was commuted to life imprisonment in permanent isolation. In solitary confinement, Stroud became a leading ornithologist, also known as the 'Birdman of Alcatraz.'[6]

The novel presents us with a fairly accurate rendering of these events but seems to grossly distort or misrepresent the prisoner Stroud. In the novel, the higher echelons of the prison administration attempt to turn him into a conformist automaton, although the inmate shows signs of reform and rehabilitation. According to the criminologist Becker-Kavan (53), the prison files speak a different language. They describe Stroud as a violent and unruly inmate who had to be isolated because of his aggressive homosexual diposition. Like the novel, the film adaptation depicts Stroud as a prisoner with a heart of gold and misrepresents even more aspects of his life-story:

> The movie made some adjustments to truth for the sake of dramatic impact. For example, although it was Marcus Stroud who had been turned away from the prison in 1916 after travelling many miles to see Robert, the movie decided the scene would carry more impact if this happened to Bob's mother, Elizabeth Stroud (Thelma Ritter). (Crowther 54)

As Duncan (24) has shown, the student of fictional prison narratives cannot fail to be startled by the repeated characterization of prison as a peaceful and safe place. This is true of both the novel and the film. For example, at one point, the narrator of Gaddis' novel refers to Stroud's cell at Leavenworth penitentiary in terms of the "recesses of his stone womb" (170). In this case, the metaphor is supposed to stress that the inmate Stroud finds himself in a sheltered place of ascetic conditions that allow him to pursue his bird studies.

The positive image of prison as a secluded place of calm amidst the hurly-burly of life also appears in the film *Birdman of Alcatraz*. At one point, the sparrow Runt, Stroud's first bird, returns to the convict's cell. The prisoner then asks the bird: "Too tough out there, ha? Come back for a little prison security?" The interplay between the auditory and the visual level invites us to see the prison as a place of refuge, and this representation of the prison as a calm place in the midst of turmoil ties in with a comment on escaped birds by Victor Brombert:

> [...] the bird, in its free flight, brings to mind the cage from which it might have escaped, the cage that awaits it, the cage that it perhaps regrets. If indeed the quest for spiritual freedom and the redemptive thrust carry toward an elsewhere, a reverse impulse tends toward the still center, toward another form of release, a deliverance from the causal world of phenomena. (13)

Moreover, in some persons, incarceration fosters intellectuality with the consequence that they embark on systematic studies. Indeed, for Stroud, the place of punishment is at the same time the place of intellectual development. Parish argues that the so-called 'Birdman of Alcatraz' "survives years of deprivation [...] to emerge a learned man with advanced knowledge in many areas" (39). The narrator of the novel comments on Stroud's attempts to cure his sick birds with the following image: "Out of the fire which consumed the prisoner, phoenix-like, a scientist was born [...]" (124). This metaphorical passage portrays prison as the set for a drama of dying and being reborn. For Stroud, the prison becomes a rite of passage which transforms him into a scientist, a bird doctor. In the novel, the metaphorical 'growth' of Stroud's scientific personality, which correlates with intellectual freedom, finds its parallel in the literal growth of his cell into a 'prison suite': "a full-sized open doorway was cut between the two cells of Stroud's new home. The cells were wired with thirteen electric outlets" (153). In the film, the inmate tells the guard Ransom that since one of his canaries is male and the other female, there will be "procreation, new life, birth" in prison. This statement and the sequence in which we are shown the hatching of a canary chick clearly parallel Stroud's own spiritual rebirth.[7]

In both the novel *Birdman of Alcatraz* and its film version, Stroud's daily routine gradually becomes like the life-style of a "dedicated scientist" (190), while his cell becomes the study room of an ornithologist:

> Living in a small barred room with a tame sparrow and a score of warbling canaries, Stroud was forging obligations and

> responsibilities that kept him busy day and night. He fed his birds, talked to them, built cages for them and studied their habits. He made a schedule and within the bounds of his tiny empire, he rose, washed, ate, worked, exercised, rested, studied, read and slept like a citizen of the world outside. [...] Stroud's six-foot-wide cell was lined solid with cages and equipment. [...] He had perfected his cage-making technique and had invented a non-sag suspension device which he considered patentable. [...] After feeding and watering 300 birds, he would clean their cages, examine each canary with meticulous care for mites, fever, swellings, feather problems, egg trouble and diet deficiency. [...] While other prisoners sank into a sea of stupor, the lean Stroud could not find enough time for his activities. (111–29)

When Stroud is finally transferred to Alcatraz, the "handcuffed bird doctor" gestures "around his cell, his laboratory, his books, his microscope, his slides, his microtome" (200). Similarly, in the film, the juxtaposition of Stroud's equipment and his cell codes the prison as a laboratory. In both narratives, the prison becomes a study room or 'academy' for Stroud.

The film does not only represent the prison as an academy but also as a catalyst of intense friendship. More specifically, for Stroud, imprisonment offers an opportunity to renounce both arrogance and separateness. As the prisoner learns to care for his birds, he becomes more and more sensitive and even learns to develop an ability to form human relationships. As the following dialogue illustrates, the prisoner begins a cautious friendship with the guard Ransom:

> RANSOM: "I may be just a uniform to you but you've got no pattern on feelings. I'm a man—the same as you—and I wanna be treated like one." [*long pause*]
> STROUD: "Mr. Ransom [...] You know what I think, Bull? [...] I think you're absolutely right. I admire you for sounding off like that. [...] You always treated me square—you've been good to me. So there's something I wanna do. I wanna apologize to you. I haven't apologized to anybody for twenty years."

In the film, the metaphorical growth of Stroud's personality is conveyed by the off-screen sound of a jackhammer. The jackhammer, which we can hear during a visit by Stroud's mother, cuts a doorway between Stroud's cell and the neighboring cell so that Stroud will have more space to pursue his bird studies. In contrast to the novel, the film additionally establishes a clear parallel between the enlargement of Stroud's cell and Stroud's liberation from his overprotective and jealous mother. The enlargement of Stroud's cell correlates with a slight increase of physical freedom, while his liberation from his mother implies an increase of mental or psychological freedom. In the film, Elizabeth Stroud is so overprotective that she cannot forgive her son for having married Stella Johnson. Stroud's mother argues that his "association with her will bring [him] nothing but trouble," and asks him to "get rid of her." However, Stroud is not willing to "give her up" or to "forget her."

With regard to the relationship between Stroud and his mother, the prison serves as the source domain, while motherly love serves as the target domain. The off-screen sound of the jackhammer suggests that Stroud begins to break out of the psychological prison of motherly love.[8] The off-screen sound of the jackhammer is heard again at the end of their conversation when Elizabeth Stroud prepares to leave the visit room and her son for good. On the outside, she turns bitter and voices damning statements to the press which militate against her son's bid for parole. "My son is where he belongs. I shall do nothing to attain his release from the penitentiary. […] He is safe where he is." In his newly enlarged cell, Stroud then symbolically burns his mother's photograph. For me, the movie clearly suggests that Stroud breaks out of the emotional or metaphorical prison of his relationship to his overprotective mother.

Despite the many positive associations with prison, the novel *Birdman of Alcatraz* and its film adaptation do not idealize the prison. Rather, the positive images serve to oppose Stroud's rehabilitation to the strict rules and regulations which are imposed on him at Leavenworth and Alcatraz. It is in spite of the prison system (rather than because of it) that Stroud goes through a process of reform. Throughout the novel and the film, Stroud has to struggle with the discipline-oriented prison authorities in order to keep his birds and continue his research (143–51). In the novel, we learn that in 1944 the *Kansas Star* wrote about Stroud that he has the "attitude of experimentation and originality rather than respect for accepted opinion and tradition" (210). This statement provides a clear contrast between the free thinker Stroud and the strict prison authorities who merely want him to follow rules. The positive images of carcerality in the novel and the film serve to underline the contrast between Stroud, who achieves a form of reformative incarceration, and the conventional prison experience which is based on routines and discipline.

For instance, when Stroud in the film arrives at Leavenworth, Warden Shoemaker tells him: "You'll conform to our ideas of how you should behave." When the guard Kramer denies Stroud a visit from his devoted mother, Stroud questions Kramer's attitude of "I just follow the rules" by asking, "Is that all you've got inside of you—rules?" Later on in the film, Stroud's and Shoemaker's attitudes clash again:

> STROUD: "I won't lick your hand and that's what eats you, ain't it keeper? A man ain't whipped 'til he quits and I'll never give you that pleasure."
> SHOEMAKER: "I'll never forget you as long as I live. No matter what happens to me, no matter where I am, if I ever get a chance to punish you further, I'll do it."

Finally, at Alcatraz prison, Shoemaker blames Stroud for not showing "a sign of rehabilitation," to which Stroud replies: "I wonder if you know what the word means. Do you?" Shoemaker's answer is "Now don't be insulting." In the following monologue, Stroud is presented as being much more thoughtful and understanding with regard to the prison institution than the warden:

> The Unabridged Webster's International Dictionary says it comes from the Latin root *habilis*. The definition is 'to invest

> again with dignity.' You consider that part of your job, Harvey, to give a man back the dignity he once had? Your only interest is how he behaves. You told me once a long time ago, and I'll never forget it: 'You'll conform to our ideas of how you should behave' and you haven't retreated from that stand one inch in thirty-five years. You want your prisoners to dance out the gates like puppets on a string, with rubber stamped values impressed by you—with your sense of conformity, your sense of behavior, even your sense of morality. That's why you're a failure, Harvey, you and the whole science of penology, because you rob prisoners of the most important thing in their lives, their individuality. On the outside, they're lost, automatons just going through the motions of living, but underneath is a deep, deep hatred for what you did to them. The first chance they get to attack society, they do it. And the result: more than half come back to prison.

The metaphors of imprisonment in these two prison narratives critique the attempt to destroy the inmate Stroud, a potential genius and non-conformist scientist, by means of abstract prison rules and regulations. Furthermore, the positive images of carcerality, i.e., the representation of prison as a place of refuge, academy, laboratory, or catalyst of intense friendship, serve to oppose potentially rehabilitative penal styles and discipline-based institutions like Leavenworth and Alcatraz. In other words, like most prison narratives of the twentieth century, these two narratives argue in favor of reformative incarceration, which, by giving the inmates an occupation (like bird-breeding), allows them to rehabilitate. In this context, it is worth noting that the novel and the film use further negative metaphors of imprisonment to critique traditional and discipline-based prisons.

Disciplinary Prisons as Cages for Wild Animals

In both the novel *Birdman of Alcatraz* and its film adaptation, the rigid prison system at Leavenworth is depicted as a cage for animals. For example, in the novel, the prison is described as a zoo for allegedly dangerous beasts of prey. At one point, the narrator describes Stroud as "a man in a steel cage inside a stone prison, itself secured behind a mighty wall. Ironically enough, this triple-caged man had willingly constructed yet another cage" (94). Observing his birds, Stroud notes that "when caged with other males," fit canary males "will try to make love to them. Fights follow the repulsing of his advances" (105). Stroud argues that caged canaries react precisely like imprisoned men. Sexual deprivation turns some of them into violent animals:

> He noted a parallel between jailbirds, avian and human. Long before he had seen a canary, he had watched the merciless yaffling of young prisoners by older ones, by cajolery or at knifepoint. He had seen the wolves and the lambs, the pathetic and fantastic 'marriages' between prisoners. (105)

Stroud uses the metaphor of the 'jailbird,' thus defining the disciplinary prison at Leavenworth as a cage for animals. Additionally he refers to rapists in terms of wolves, while he describes the rape victims in terms of lambs. In other words, confinement turns human beings into jailbirds, and sexual deprivation then turns some of them into wolves.

In the film, prisoners are associated with animals as well. For example, when Stroud is sent to 'the hole' of the penitentiary at Leavenworth after a tussle with a fellow inmate, a close-up of a rat is juxtaposed with a shot of Stroud lying on the floor. This juxtaposition of disparate entities illustrates how the guards view the inmates, namely as rats or beasts.[9] When Stroud is sent to the 'hole' again in the film, we witness the following conversation with Warden Shoemaker:

> SHOEMAKER: "No remorse, ey? No pity. Just an animal."
> STROUD: "Ain't that what these cages are for? Animals?"

In this case, the interplay between the auditory and the visual channel codes the prison as a cage for wild animals. The film thus constructs the disciplinary prison at Leavenworth as a jungle where the inmates are treated like animals and have to struggle to survive. Additionally, the juxtaposition of Stroud's wooden bird cage and the bars of his cell (for example in the scene in which he has completed his first cage) involves an interesting intermingling of categories, which defines Stroud as a harmless bird locked up in a cage.

Other prison narratives of the twentieth century represent traditional prisons as cages for wild animals, too. For example in *I Am a Fugitive from a Georgia Chain Gang!*, the narrator points out that the exhausting labor and lack of food reduce the prisoners of the chain gang "to the same level, just animals, and treated worse than animals" (56). Similarly, when the inmates are being chained on the trucks in the film version *I Am a Fugitive from a Chain Gang*, the movie cuts to donkeys that are being chained. The rings on the inmates' ankles and those on the donkeys' noses are threaded with chains which illustrate how their keepers view them. Both the donkeys and the prisoners are used as animals of labor. In this case, the focusing on the same entity in two different scenes evokes a metaphorical reading. More specifically, the film places the donkeys and the prisoners markedly side by side, and establishes a connection through the use of chains. In the zoo of punishment in this film, the men are reduced to beasts of burden, chained together in the same way as the camp's donkeys. The inmates have to undergo backbreaking labor, are given unpalatable food (which even causes one inmate to throw up) and are whipped like animals if the guards are not satisfied with their performance at labor. Furthermore, the inmates' bodies are chained to their beds and to one another in a large bunkhouse, allowing for no mobility or privacy. A long chain that feeds through each man's leg irons is removed each morning only to be pulled back through when the men are pushed onto the truck which transports them to the quarries or the roadside. Every morning, the inmates are awakened at 4:20 A.M. Like animals, they are fed and herded to the worksite. At 8:20 P.M., they arrive back, have their chains inspected, are fed and shackled into bed. Human communication is reduced to terse orders—"All right, pick 'em up"; "Come on, pull 'em through"; etc. At one point, the film cuts from the chained prisoners to the guards' chained bloodhounds, thus establishing another parallel between the treatment of prisoners and animals.[10]

The representation of prison as a cage serves to critique the cruel treatment of inmates in 'traditional' or discipline-based institutions like Leavenworth and the chain gangs in the south of the US. This image of carcerality highlights processes of dehumanization and depersonalization in prison. In some prisons, the inmates are treated like animals of labor, and it should come as no surprise that this treatment turns some of them into violent animals or beasts. Most prison narratives of the twentieth century disapprove of such punitive forms of incarceration and argue that the 'real' criminals who undoubtedly exist should be sent to reformative institutions.

The Prison as Hell

Moreover, many twentieth-century prison narratives go one step further and critique traditional prison regimes that are dominated by sadistic guards by representing them as hell. The recurrent figuring of prison as hell introduces to the carceral world a religious slant. For example, Red, the imprisoned narrator of "Rita Hayworth and Shawshank Redemption," describes the situation of new inmates in prison as follows: "Old life blown away in the wink of an eye, indeterminate nightmare stretching out ahead, a long season in hell" (98). In this image of carcerality, the source domain (hell) and the target domain (prison) are rather similar, and the only crucial resistance to a one-to-one mapping is presumably the lack of heat in prison. As Fludernik ("The Prison as World" 152) has shown, both the prison and hell centrally correlate with confinement, suffering, and darkness. Also, "historically, Christian hell has traditionally been figured in scenarios that both anticipate later prisons and echo features of medieval carceral spaces" (ibid.). The primary function of the description of prison as hell is to highlight the prisoner's suffering, which may correlate with his being exposed to sadistic or devilish authorities.

The film *Sleepers* visually constructs the Wilkinson Home for Boys as hell, while the world outside is represented as heaven. Like heaven and hell in religious discourse, the closed world of the prison and the world outside function as counter-images of each other. In what follows, I use the metaphor of imprisonment which describes the prison as hell as the starting point of my interpretation of the film. Furthermore, this interpretation differs from Joe Wlodarz's reading of it. Wlodarz argues that the film symbolically codes male rapes in prison as homosexual acts. For him "it is clearly the overdetermined anal violation and its associations with emasculation and homosexuality that is set apart by the film [...] as the most avengeable trauma of all" (68). This interpretation is not convincing because the film is about mature *men* raping young *boys* and not about homosexual acts between adults. Second, the rapist Nokes and his gang of sadistic guards do not have any homosexual features. Rather, throughout the film, they consider themselves to be tough and masculine. Third, Nokes' abuses are frequently not sexually motivated. Like a devil, he appears to be primarily interested in degrading and tormenting the boys. These three points render Wlodarz's statement that "films like *Sleepers* [...] give license to the demoralization, prosecution, brutalization, and even murder of 'fags'" (73) highly questionable. When Tommy and Michael shoot the guard Nokes at the end of the film, they murder him because he tortured and raped them when they were children, and not because he is homosexual.

The film is not about homosexuality but about the difficulty of achieving justice. When the Catholic priest Father Bobby (Robert de Niro) thinks about whether he should commit perjury and provide the necessary alibi for Tommy (Billy Crudup) and John (Ron Eldard) on the night of the murder, he is centrally confronted with the question of whether the murder of a child abuser can be morally justified. The movie opposes the just and religious world of Hell's Kitchen, which is dominated by Father Bobby,[11] to the unjust and hellish Wilkinson Home for Boys, which is dominated by the devil-like guard Nokes. And in the visual representation of these distinct worlds, the film invokes the antonymic relationship between heaven and hell (light/darkness; joy/torment).

To begin with, the film constructs a rather idyllic image of the boys' childhood. The voice-over narrator speaks of the "children we were" and argues that Hell's Kitchen was a paradisiacal "place of innocence." As Wlodarz correctly notes, the 'lost paradise' is visually suggested by "the bare sunbathing torsos of the boys lying side by side in a near fusion of flesh" (69). Additionally, the innocence of the boys' childhood is repeatedly symbolized by an image of the boys frolicking in a gushing stream of water from an open fire hydrant. At Hell's Kitchen, Father Bobby, a loving father figure, cares for the four boys. For example, he plays basketball with them; and he is also the one who comforts Shakes before he is sent to the hellish reformatory; and he finally commits perjury to get Tommy and John acquitted in their criminal trial. Also, Father Bobby is very concerned about the unjust treatment of the boys. For instance, he warns John's big abusive stepfather that if he beats up John again, he will give him such a trashing that he "won't need a doctor" but "a priest."

Once the boys are sent to the reform school, where they will be abused and tortured, the nature of the images changes drastically. The "warm look" of Hell's Kitchen, which appears "kind of pretty and exciting," is diametrically opposed to the "cool, dark look" of the reform school where everything is "bluish and contrasty" (Turner 36–38). Additionally, in a segment which might be said to highlight the descent into the depths of hell, the camera slowly moves down the dark exterior of the gothic reform school and into its lowest point, the basement. The tight, dark tunnels in the reform school's basement, where the first gang rape takes place, suggest some kind of underground obscurity and metaphorically code the prison as hell. More specifically, the spare lighting, i.e., the cool, dark look of the detention center, in combination with the long, dark tunnels invite us to see the prison as an underworld setting.[12] The reverberating agonized wailings of the boys who are being raped by pedophile adults provide an additional link between the prison and the underworld (or hell) because they evoke the haunting voices of the sinners who are punished in Dante's *Inferno*.[13] Also, occasionally, the film even makes the demonized rapist Nokes look like Satan. For example, before the first gang rape, we are presented with a close-up of the guard's face as he blows cigarette smoke through his nostrils. It is also worth noting that in this shot, the lighting from below gives Nokes a particularly lugubrious appearance.[14] Furthermore, the film evokes the association of prison with hell by contrasting the religious Father Bobby with the sadistic guard Nokes. In other words, *Sleepers* represents religion as a just institution which contrasts sharply with the appalling brutalities committed by the guards at the reform school. The detention center is a closed space and as in hell, justice, and religion do not play any role at all. For example, the sadistic guard Nokes forces Shakes to take off his Virgin Mary charm. Shakes points out that Mary is "the mother of God," to which Nokes replies: "I don't give a fuck whose mother it is—take it off!"

The film plays with other metaphors of imprisonment as well. For instance, when Shakes is thrown into the 'hole' of the reform school, we are presented with an overhead shot of Shakes lying on the floor of his cell together with a rat. This shot evokes associations of the 'hole' (and by extension the prison) with a womb and a tomb, and it also codes the prisoner as vermin. First, the position of Shakes' body which is crouched in the fetal position gives the 'hole' a womb-like appearance and suggests the possibility of some kind of rebirth. Second, the darkness of the small 'hole' and the fact that the body at the end of its life is inclined to curl up on itself in the posture of Shakes' body gives the 'hole' a tomb-like appearance. The voice-over narrator adds to this coding of the 'hole' as a coffin by saying: "all I wanted to do was die." Third, as in the films *Birdman of Alcatraz* and *The Shawshank Redemption*, the juxtaposition of the inmate with a rat metaphorically codes the prisoner as beast or rat.

In the third part of the film, the associations of prison with a womb and/or tomb are extended to cover the post-imprisonment life of the four boys. More specifically, the suffering at the reform school rewarded the former inmates with a friendship that is purer and more enduring than the friendship experienced by 'normal,' law-abiding citizens. Already at the beginning of the film, the voice-over narrator informed us that the film is about "a friendship that runs deeper than blood," which means that the boys' friendship is even more profound than family relationships. Moreover, one might correlate John's and Tommy's shooting of Nokes in the third part of the film with some sort of redemption. The two former inmates, who have become vicious criminals,[15] first refresh Nokes' mind about his abuses.[16] Tommy then shoots him in the crotch and asks him: "Did that hurt, Nokes?" This question is followed by numerous bullets from the guns of the two criminals, while we as viewers are presented with extended slow-motion shots of Nokes' agony. At the end of the film, we learn that three of the four boys have actually succumbed to their experience at the reform school. John and Tommy are dead—John died of alcoholism—and Michael (Brad Pitt) gave up his job as an attorney and lives in quasi-solitary confinement alone in the English countryside, occasionally working as a carpenter.

The film represents the reform school as hell. More specifically, the long dark tunnels at the basement of the detention center and the boys' suffering (as it is highlighted in their reverberating agonized wailings) evoke the association of prison with an underworld setting. The hellish horror at the detention center functions as a catalyst of intense friendship, which in turn allows the former inmates to pursue their quest for justice. For me, the film is about the question of whether the killing of one's former perpetrator can be justified in a Catholic context. When Father Bobby decides to commit perjury by testifying that John and Tommy were with him at a basketball game on the night in question, he ultimately decides in favor of the line "An eye for an eye" (Matthew 5.38). If one extends this Christian approval of revenge, one can perhaps argue that the film offers, at least implicitly, an argument in favor of the 'lynch law' or maybe even the death penalty.

One of the central arguments of twentieth-century prison narratives is that the 'new' pentinetiaries we are presented with are possible sites of reformative incarceration (if they are run by well-meaning individuals). In other words, the inmates of these prisons may achieve rehabilitation (or some sort of redemption or spiritual rebirth) if they are not merely exposed to boring routines but are given an occupation that allows them to develop (as in *Birdman of Alcatraz* and its film adaptation) or if they manage to make an effort to confront themselves (like Andy and Red in *The Shawshank Redemption*). The 'negative' metaphors of imprisonment, on the other hand, primarily serve to critique the discipline-based institutions in which the narratives are set. More specifically, the description of prison as a tomb does not only imply that the prison newcomers experience a civic or social death. It additionally stresses that in purely discipline-oriented prisons, the inmates frequently experience some sort of spiritual death and lose all their hopes. The representation of prison as a cage primarily critiques the treatment of prisoners, who are placed behind bars or chained like animals of labor. Finally, the association of prison with hell critiques the prison by highlighting the unjust suffering of inmates—like the boys in *Sleepers* who are raped and tortured by devilish pedophiles.

Metaphors of imprisonment focus on the experience of imprisonment from the perspective of prison inmates. One may also deal with the prison from a slightly different angle, e.g., by showing how certain features of society (like conformism, the class system or racial discrimination) are reproduced in prison or by demonstrating how and why certain situations in the world outside can be perceived in terms of imprisonment.

THE PRISON AS WORLD—THE WORLD AS PRISON

Conformism and Individualism in Prison

Both Sillitoe's "The Loneliness of the Long-Distance Runner" and its 1962 film version address the relationship between society and the prison by assuming a homological structure between these two social systems. The novella is about the confrontation between Smith's defiant individualism and society's demands of conformism, and shows how society's conformism is reproduced in borstal. The film, on the other hand, argues that society's class conflicts are reinforced in borstal, and represents the situation of the English working class as a prison.

In the novella, the dialectical tension of 'them versus us,' of "In-law blokes" (or conventional law-abiding citizens) being "on the watch for Out-law blokes" (or non-conformist criminals) (10), is accentuated again and again. When Smith recalls his first meeting with the governor, the head administrator addresses the new inmate by using second-person singular pronouns, but when talking about himself employs first-person pronouns in the plural. This gives readers a first sense of the conflict between the individualism of the prison subject and the collective identity of the borstal staff:

> If you play ball with us, we'll play ball with you. [...] We want hard honest work and we want good athletics [...]. And if you give us both these things you can be sure we'll do right by you and send you back into the world an honest man. (9–10)

Since this is a private meeting, Smith (perhaps ironically) wonders who else might be in the room: "And when the governor kept saying how 'we' wanted you to do that, I kept looking around for the other blokes, wondering how many of them there were" (10). Smith also dislikes the fact that the policeman who questions him on the robbery of the bakery permanently uses the pronoun 'we': "They always say 'We' 'We,' never 'I' 'I'—as if they feel braver and righter knowing there's a lot of them against only one" (32).

The narrator posits a homological structure between the microcosm of the borstal and the world outside. For him, the disciplining of the borstal regime is like social conformism in general. For Smith, "the coppers and Borstal bosses" are two groups within the larger group of the "bastard-faced In-laws" (12) he despises. Furthermore, he relates the existence of prisons to the fact that In-law blokes (like the governor) have a different concept of honesty than Out-law blokes (like the narrator himself). More specifically, honesty in the sense of law-abiding citizens correlates with conformity, i.e., the idea of conforming to laws and of reporting the misbehavior of others, while honesty in the sense of Out-law blokes correlates with individuality, i.e., the idea of being honest to oneself and of being able to tell others what one really thinks of them.

For instance, conformist In-law blokes are honest in the sense that they only wait "to phone for the coppers as soon as we [i.e., Out-law blokes, J.A.] make a false move" (10). Smith considers the governor's concept of honesty to be related to leading a life of conformity. In what follows, Smith ponders about the head administrator's introductory speech: "Be honest. It's like saying: Be dead, like me, and then you'll have no more pain of leaving your nice slummy house for Borstal or prison" (14). For Smith, the governor's honesty is ultimately a kind of deceit. The head administrator not only cons Out-laws into becoming In-laws. He additionally deceives himself, which is the ultimate dishonesty in Smith's eyes. Recognizing that the governor wants the long-distance cup only for the glory it reflects on him, and that he is never aware of his real motivation, Smith concludes that he (i.e., Smith) is both more honest and more insightful than the governor: "I'll win in the end even if I die in gaol at eighty-two, because I'll have more fun and fire out of my life than he'll ever get out of his" (13). On the other hand, Smith considers his mother to be "honest" in his (individualist) sense because "she really told that copper what she thought of him and called him all the dirty names she'd ever heard of, which took her half an hour and woke the terrace up" (43). If Smith had won the cross-country race he would have given in to the governor's concept of honesty, which would have been tantamount to selling his soul. Consequently, he decided not to win it:

> [...] if I kept on being honest in the way he [the governor, J.A.] wanted and won my race for him he'd see I got the cushiest six months still left to run; but in my own way, well, it's not allowed, and if I find a way of doing it such as I've got now then I'll get what-for in every mean trick he can set his mind to. (45–46)

For Smith, the social institution of the borstal functions as a political force which reproduces the conformist concept of honesty according to society's In-law blokes:

> Because another thing people like the governor will never understand is that I *am* honest, that I've never been anything else but honest, and that I'll always be honest. Sounds funny. But it's true because I know what honest means according to me and he only knows what it means according to him. I think my honesty is the only sort in the world, and he thinks his is the only sort in the world as well. That's why this dirty great walled-up and fenced-up manor house in the middle of nowhere has been used to coop-up blokes like me. (15)

Smith also associates conventional law-abiding citizens with corpses, while he imagines his criminal freedom and individuality in terms of fire and heat. For example, Smith describes the conformist governor as a "dead bloke" (14). At the end of the novel, when we learn that Smith is still a successful criminal, he characterizes his criminal vitality and individuality in terms of fire and heat: "I'm out now and the heat's switched on again [...]" (54). Smith might mean that In-law blokes lack the vitality of Out-law blokes. Nothing happens when you're dead—similarly, nothing really happens when you're a conformist and "settle down in a cosy six pounds a week job" (14). Fire, on the other hand, like freedom and individualism, is interesting and challenging. However, you might face the danger of burning yourself like Smith when they caught him "after that bakery job" (7). These metaphors of death and fire are present throughout the novel:

> Everything's dead, but good, because it's dead before coming alive, not dead after being alive.[17] [...] I'm going to be warm, by the time I get to the main road and am turning on to the wheatfield footpath by the bus stop I'm going to feel as hot as a potbellied stove and as happy as a dog with a tin tail. (11)

Smith argues that as soon as people are in a position to exercise power over others, they automatically become conformist, i.e., 'dead': "At the moment it's dead blokes like him [i.e., the governor, J.A.] as have the whip-hand over blokes like me [...]. Maybe as soon as you get the whip-hand over somebody, you do go dead" (14). Smith's basic metaphor for the interrelationship between the In-law blokes and the Out-law blokes is that of warfare. The inmate has dedicated his cunning to a life of criminal rebellion and argues that "if the In-laws are hoping to stop me making false moves they're wasting their time. They might as well stand me up against a wall and let fly with a dozen rifles" (10). Furthermore, Smith feels that "by sending [him] to Borstal," society has "shown [him] the knife," and that "once you've seen the knife you learn a bit of unarmed combat" (16). The narrator concludes that now he knows "that it's war between me and them"

(16). The war and death metaphors coalesce when Smith argues that he is "in a different sort of war" because "the war they [i.e., In-law blokes, J.A.] think is war is suicide […]" (16). This image seems to suggest that law-abiding citizens fight their true selves by conforming to abstract rules and regulations, and in a sense kill themselves. By extension, the same is true of borstal inmates who decide to obey rules.

By means of the association of the life of conformist law-abiding citizens with death (or suicide), the homological relationship between society's conformism and the borstal's disciplining begins to turn into a critique of society in general and the microcosmic borstal world in particular. Since the governor wavers between the closed space of the borstal and the outer space, the description of the governor as a 'dead' bloke creates a whole mosaic of images. On the one hand, he represents society's conformism which metaphorically correlates with death or suicide. On the other hand, since the 'dead' bloke's attempts to make the inmates conform with his rules ultimately results in killing their true selves, his attempts evoke the association of borstal with a tomb.

The description of the governor as a dead bloke might also correlate with the governor's state of mind. The governor appears to be so obsessed with his stubborn attempts to discipline Smith that one might even classify him as a prisoner of his own mind. For example, the narrator informs us that after Smith has lost the cross-country race, the governor

> […] had me carting dustbins about every morning from the big full-working kitchen to the garden bottoms where I had to empty them; and in the afternoon I spread out slops over spuds and carrots growing in the allotments. In the evenings I scrubbed floors, miles and miles of them. (53)

Smith also points out that the governor "would have made it grimmer if he could" (53).

A fascinating alternative interpretation of the novella would be to argue that Smith's stubbornness with regard to his insistence on his individuality and his hatred of the governor also constitute a type of mental confinement. Ultimately, Smith is as stubborn in his unwillingness to obey rules as the governor is in his obsession to make the trainees conform. The narrator even argues that for him, "it's not allowed" (46) to give in to the governor. This statement evokes the strict rules and regulations that are typical of prison. One might get a sense that Smith is imprisoned by his stubborn insistence on individualism, which is reminiscent of solitary confinement: "As for me, the only time, I'll hit that clothes-line will be when I'm dead and a comfortable coffin's been got ready on the other side. Until then I'm a long-distance runner, crossing country all on my own no matter how bad it feels" (52). At the end of the day, it does not seem to matter whether you are an individualist or a conformist: stubbornness seems to constrain both Smith and the governor.[18]

Smith's running in the cross-country race is metonymically related to the borstal's and, by extension, society's conformism, while his solitary training sessions correlate with freedom and individuality.[19] Smith argues that the situation of borstal runners is similar to that of race horses, only slightly worse: "They give us a bit of blue ribbon and a cup for a prize after we've shagged ourselves out running or jumping, like race horses, only we don't get so well looked-after as race horses, that's the only thing" (9). By contrast, he feels free when he can do his training on his own because he exploits his running for the purpose of reflection. Sometimes the inmate thinks "that [he has] never been so free as during that couple of hours when [he's] trotting up the path out of the gates and turning by that bare-faced, big-bellied oak tree at the lane end" (9). This (second) type of running can be said to emphasize Smith's fight against dehumanization and his quest for individuality. For instance, at the beginning of the narrative, running is represented as a way of escaping society's forces of law and order: "running had always been made much of in our family, especially running away from the police" (7). Smith also fears that his life might be ended by a bullet, which one might also see as a symbol of conformism:

> I had a picture in my brain of me running and beating everybody in the world, leaving them all behind only I was trotting across a big wide moor alone, doing a marvellous speed as I ripped between boulders and reed-clumps, when suddenly: CRACK! CRACK!—bullets that can go faster than any man running, coming from a copper's rifle planted in a tree, winged me and split my gizzard in spite of my perfect running, and down I fell. (40)

It is perhaps also worth noting that at one point Smith announces that he "didn't suffer in Borstal at all. [...] They fed me, gave me a suit, and pocket-money, which was a bloody sight more that I ever got before, unless I worked myself to death for it [...]" (15). The inmate here describes himself in terms that evoke the image of a small child. Borstal allows him to be passive, sheltered, and idle because he is cared for by the institution. The borstal here evokes the association with a mother who provides and protects. The dependence on others for food, clothes, pocket-money, and shelter links Smith's borstal experience to an idealized image of infancy. Within the context of my interpretation of borstal as being homologous with society's conformism, this metaphor of imprisonment might link conformism with security and stability. Like children, borstal inmates and conformists do not have to make decisions on their own because they are ultimately cared for (by the borstal institution or their conformist ideology).

While the novella focuses on the tension between defiant individualism and conformism, the film defines its major protagonist much more clearly as an exceptional member of the working class, and shows how the class system is reproduced in borstal. In other words, Colin is constructed as an individual with a special understanding of the borstal system, which others clearly lack. The film presents us with various images in which Colin as an individual is juxtaposed with conformist groups in the outside world or groups of rule-obeying borstal boys. For example, when the governor talks to the inmates before the concert, we are confronted with shots in which we see groups of inmates who all look alike. These shots are contrasted with close-ups of Colin's face. The fact that Colin is alone in the camera frame clearly suggests that he is an individualist, while the fact that the other inmates are always represented as a larger group suggests that they lack individuality and only exist as a homogeneous collective entity. Later on, we are presented with shots of the lads enthusiastically singing the patriotic British hymn "Jerusalem," thus (ironically) celebrating the promise of a free country. However, we are not presented with a single image of Colin participating in the collective activity of singing. The most dramatic moment with regard to the confrontation between Colin's individualism and the others' conformism is the scene in which Colin deliberately stops before the finishing line of the cross-country race. Shots of Colin standing alone are contrasted with shots of the raving crowd and the borstal staff.[20]

In the course of the film's numerous flashbacks which deal with the world outside borstal, Colin is represented as a strict non-conformist as well. For example, we learn that he does not like staring at the television set like all the other members of his family. Additionally, when Colin's mother gives him a five pound note from his dead father's insurance money, he slowly burns it, and we see him alone in his room before a picture of his father. This action is of course more than a simple gesture: "It is a symbol of intellectual independence and of power over the social and material realities of the world, but it is also a defiant gesture of self-assertion" (Horne 117).[21] Colin's father was partly a conformist worker who slaved at the factory, and partly an individualist because he refused to go to hospital. Colin presumably admires his father for his non-conformist behavior. Interestingly, the doctor who comes to see his father is reminiscent of the governor of the borstal. While the doctor tries to heal the father's cancer without really knowing its causes, the governor attempts to rehabilitate Colin, i.e., cure him of his criminal impulses, without understanding where they come from.[22]

The film also presents us with images that link Colin's running in the cross-country race with conformism, while other images link Colin's solitary training with freedom and individuality. To begin with, in the course of Colin's first solitary training session, we are presented with various POV-shots of the winter sky and the barren tree branches whirling about, which convey a sense of subjectivity and individuality. Then, as the camera tracks parallel to him, he runs away from it, only to return and move away again, finally becoming smaller and smaller. This freedom of movement in relation to the camera reflects Colin's joy of being alone. At one point, the trainee slides playfully down a slope on his back and allows himself to settle in a bed of damp leaves. "We then move to a close-up of Colin's face; the sky swirls above his head and with a sigh of relief, he sinks into reflection" (Rollins 182). These shots in combination with the musical score convey a sense of freedom. On the auditory level, playful syncopated jazz music, which perhaps only Colin can hear, accentuates his feeling of release. Colin's facial expressions tell us clearly that he finds salvation during his solitary runs. Also, we are presented with a cross-cut from a shot of Colin running away from a policeman (i.e., society's conformism) to a shot of Colin during his training sessions. This visually codes running as a way of escaping the conformist forces of law and order, and, by extension, as a way of achieving freedom and individuality. By contrast, the cross-country race is represented as a circus-like event. For instance, we are confronted with shots of the cheering crowd waving streamers and manically chanting "run, run, run!" Also, on the auditory level, we can hear the school band "clamouring a victorious tune from the bleachers" (Rollins 185). This diegetic music obviously contrasts sharply with the playful jazz tunes heard during the training, and these two musical styles accentuate the difference between individualism and conformism on the auditory level. The interplay between the auditory and the visual level is significant because one might correlate the jazz tunes with a glimpse of a different universe, a different mode of existence where individuality is possible.

The Class System in Prison versus Class as a Prison

The British class system is clearly alluded to in the novella but plays a more prominent role in the film. In the written version, Smith is repeatedly encouraged to "win them the Borstal Blue Ribbon Prize

Cup for Long Distance Cross Country Running (All England)" (12) by the borstal's governor, an 'owner' who, like stereotypical capitalists, is a "pot-bellied pop-eyed bastard" with a gray moustache and "lily-white workless hands" (13; 9). One can argue that this description of the governor establishes a contrast between the 'capitalist' governor and the 'working-class' borstal inmate. It is perhaps also worth noting that the head administrator never suggests that the athlete should win for himself, i.e., that the laborer should receive the reward of his toil (Hutchings 37). From this perspective, there is certainly an element of class revenge in Smith's account: "I only want a bit of my own back on the In-laws and Potbellies by letting them sit up there on their big posh seats and watch me lose this race" (45). Also, in the novella, the 'worker' Smith is physically superior to members of the upper class, whom he refers to as "pot-bellies," i.e., as ugly and unfit for his kind of 'work':

> They're training me up fine for the big sports day when all the pig-faced snotty-nosed dukes and ladies—who can't add two and two together and would mess themselves like loonies if they didn't have slavies to beck-and-call—come and make speeches to us about sports being just the thing to get us leading an honest life. (8)

However, the expropriation of the athlete in the novella is not exclusively economic. Its basis is more broadly social, having its origins in the power of conformists to "have the whip-hand over" (14) individualists. Additionally, as illustrated by one of the narrator's pertinent remarks, not all members of the working-class are automatically Out-law blokes, with whom Smith identifies: "even in a street like ours there are people who love to do a good turn for the coppers, though I never know why they do" (29). Consequently, when Smith speaks of his father's death, which he clearly admires, he does not equate "his father's debilitating cancer and wretched end" with "the capitalists' misuse of the labor force," as John S. Slack (6) has it. Rather, he perceives his father as an individualist fighting the conformist forces of the hospital:

> [...] I'm still thinking of the Out-law death my dad died, telling the doctors to scat from the house when they wanted him to finish up in hospital (like a bleeding guinea-pig, he raved at them). He got up in bed to throw them out and even followed them down the stairs in his shirt though he was no more than skin and stick. They tried to tell him he'd want some drugs but he didn't fall for it, and only took the pain-killer that mam and I got from a herb-seller in the next street. (50)[23]

In contrast to the film, the narrator of the novella does not mention any similarities between the borstal and the factory at which his father worked. In the novella, Smith sees affinities between borstals and the army:

> [...] when they let me out of this [...] they'll try to get me in the army, and what's the difference between the army and this place I'm in now? They can't kid me, the bastards. I've seen the barracks near where I live, and if there weren't swaddies on guard outside with rifles you wouldn't know the difference between their high walls and the place I'm in now. (12)

The novella is thus hardly "about the class struggle per se nor is Smith a class symbol, as some critics apparently believe" (Vaverka 58). Rather, the short story asserts individuality and an attitude of persistence and defiance in a mechanized conformist world. Furthermore, Sillitoe's novella illustrates that both the borstal and society are based on conformist rules and regulations. Smith's "thoughts and secrets and bloody life" (11) inside him include the essential freedom not to conform, not to win for the benefit of others, and not to live according to others' expectations and desires. However, although the narrator does succeed to a certain extent in his efforts to maintain his sense of personal worth within the confines of a conformist society, these efforts do not ultimately lead to an improvement of his situation.

In the film, on the other hand, the borstal clearly serves as a microcosm which reproduces the class conflicts of English society. First of all, in contrast to the novella, it is Colin's working-class background that sends him to borstal. More specifically, Colin's motivation for robbing the bakery is his mother's 'order' not to return home without some money. While Smith's crime in the novella is simply a spontaneous act of criminality (or defiance against conformist society), the film stresses that the mother's melodramatic announcement drives Colin to rob the bakery.[24] Hence, the class system is argued to be responsible for the existence of criminality. Second, in contrast to the novella, the long-distance runner Colin, a member of the working class, has to compete with runners from an elite public, i.e., private, school. The movie's cross-country race pits Colin's borstal Ruxton Towers against Ranleigh school, an elite local public (i.e., private) school, whereas in the novella the battle involves only a competition among sister borstal institutions. That is to say, the contest in the film is staged as an antagonistic struggle between the working and the ruling class. The contrast between Britain's elite and the working class is visually accentuated by the physical differences between the good-looking, tall, and fair-haired actor James Fox, the public-school boy whom Colin overtakes in the race, and the 'anti-movie star' Tom Courtenay who is a wiry and not at all good-looking member of the working class. Third, in contrast to the novella, the governor of the film is clearly associated with Britain's elite because he "habitually wears a blazer emblazoned with the coat of arms of one of the public schools that train Britain's elite" (French 118).

Even though the film establishes a number of parallels between public (i.e., private) schools and borstals,[25] the introduction of elite schools (in combination with the 'explanation' of Colin's crime) gives Colin's refusal to win the cross-country race a new quality. It demonstrates Colin's awareness of something the governor will never understand: "in real life the boys from the public school will always be first across the line. In real life it is class which counts; skill and ability have nothing to do with success" (Crowther 34). In other words, Colin illustrates that in the outside world, which is dominated by class, the quality of his work does not matter at all. He will always be inferior because he was born into the wrong class: Colin will always be a member of the 'lower' working class. He may work as hard as he can. However, this will not alter his situation because he will remain imprisoned by the class system.

Indeed, in its various flashbacks, the film illustrates that in most areas of human activity outside prison, Colin was treated like a prisoner. The movie establishes various (mostly visual) parallels between the detention center and the working class area in Nottingham, thus visually imputing to class itself the qualities of a prison. For instance, once Colin's father has died in the film, we see the family entering their small house in Nottingham's working-class district. The tiny family house is surrounded by extremely high walls, which are reminiscent of the imposing walls and towers of HM Borstal Ruxton Towers. Second, when Colin and his friend Mike (James Bolam) 'borrow' a car, and convince Audrey (Topsy Jane) and Gladys (Julia Foster) to join them, they stop on a hillside overlooking the smoking factories of Nottingham. When Colin and Audrey kiss for the first time, we see barbed wire behind them—a detail of the *mise-en-scène* that visually comments on the confinements of industrial Nottingham, thus providing a link to the borstal, which is also framed by barbed wire. Third, when Colin and his mother visit the superior of Colin's father at the factory in order to collect the father's insurance money, a worker opens the gate of the factory for them. This may remind viewers of the opening of the borstal's gate at the beginning of the film.

The representation of these details of the *mise-en-scène*—the high and imposing walls, the barbed wire, and the gate—allows us to see Nottingham (and by extension the situation of the working class) as a prison. The mentioned details are metonyms of the borstal which are employed to assert some sort of identity between the situation of an inmate in borstal and the situation of a British worker. Both borstals and factories are disciplinary spaces which 'mould' individuals in certain ways to make them 'conform.' For instance, we learn that Colin's father was a useful conformist when his former superior says that he was a "jolly good worker and served the firm well." However, the father died of cancer of the throat,[26] which was an effect of his working in the factory, and Colin does not wish to follow his example. The final shot of the film is a close-up freeze frame of Colin producing a gas mask, which one might read as a final comment on the fact "that the boys are being methodically asphyxiated by their environment" (Rollins 186), i.e., the borstal which reproduces the class system and punishes working-class kids who are not willing to toe the line. Also, the ending is quite pessimistic because it demonstrates that Colin's 'rebellion' has not changed anything.

Another similarity between members of the working class and borstal inmates is that both groups are depicted as being treated in a rather rude manner. When Colin buys a first-class train ticket, the booking office clerk (Frank Finlay) is very unfriendly to him and says: "Come on lad. I haven't got all day." The clerk seems to dislike Colin because of his working-class accent. Also, this statement is of course reminiscent of the prison officer urging Colin to move on by saying, "Come on lad. We haven't got all day" at the beginning of the film.[27] Later on, the film openly condemns industrial oppression and the exploitation of the working class. When his girlfriend Audrey tells Colin to find a job, the latter says:

> I don't want to get a job. It's not that I don't like work. It's that I don't like the idea of slaving my guts out so the bosses can get all the profit. It seems all wrong to me. My old man used to say that the workers should be at the profit.

The situation of workers as Colin describes it in this short speech is similar to his situation in borstal where the governor attempts to exploit his talents for personal gain. It is also worth noting that during the speech quoted above, which could be a paraphrase of a Labour Party candidate electioneering socialism at the time, Colin and Audrey "stand in front of a brightly lighted furniture store window displaying the material goods of a life they are shut out from" (Quirk 167). In other words, the store window displays goods which members of the upper class can afford to buy while members of the poorer working class are excluded from this form of consumerism. And this exclusion from consumerism is clearly another example of metaphorical imprisonment through class.

The novella assumes a homological structure between society and the borstal and shows that society's conformism is reproduced in borstal. Furthermore, the novella comments on the difficult situation of defiant individuals (or criminals) like Smith in a conformist world, and since Smith is an alienated and socially hostile individual, evokes the question of whether individualist thrill or conformist security are to be preferred. On the one hand, one might argue that Smith's defiant individualism correlates with freedom, adventure, courage, fire, heat, and life, and is thus preferable to the governor's hypocritical demands for conformism. On the other hand, one might stress the fact that Smith is a wicked criminal and that society has to be protected from such hoodlums. After all, conformism also correlates with peace, safety, security, and stability. Depending on one's perspective, one may sympathize with Smith or one may argue in favor of conformism.

In contrast to the novella, the movie shows how the borstal reproduces conflicts that are inherent to the class system. Colin's decision to lose the cross-country race against an elite public school, illustrates an awareness of the fact that in the outside world, ability does not count, whereas class matters very much. The film also explicitly criticizes the prison-like situation of the working class in England. It uses metonyms of the borstal to illustrate that Colin had already been metaphorically imprisoned by the class system before he was sent to borstal. Additionally, while Smith's criminality is a positive act of defiance against conformist society, Colin's crime is a defensive stance imposed on him by his family background and the class system.

Racial Oppression in Prison versus Society as a Prison

In both Robert E. Burns' autobiography *I Am a Fugitive from a Georgia Chain Gang!* and its film version *I Am a Fugitive from a Chain Gang!* the eponymous hero, an unemployed ex-World War I soldier, steals a few dollars because he is hungry. He is caught by the police and sentenced to serve time on one of the hellish chain gangs in the south of the US. The major protagonist manages to escape and gradually develops into a rich and hard-working citizen.

He is reincarcerated, and escapes again only to live in constant fear of being recaptured. Since the ex-soldier steals because he is hungry, the autobiography and its film version might be argued to focus on the social causes of crime. Furthermore, our hero's second imprisonment destroys an honest and successful businessman, i.e., one of the pillars of society.

However, there is more to the representation of prison in these two narratives than social criticism and the destruction of a successful businessman. In Burns' autobiography, the prison serves as a locus of racial discrimination, while the film visually presents society as a prison.

It is worth noting that historically speaking, the southern chain gangs took their inspiration from slavery:

> The [...] rise of the chain gang represented the continuation of slavery in another form, for it enabled white Southerners to exploit African-American labour while inflicting punishment and establishing social control. [...] In addition to solving the South's labour shortage, the chain gang served as a legal means of subordinating African Americans. [...] These men were subjected to treatment even more brutal than whites, as a comparison of their mortality rates makes clear. (Lewis 227–29)[28]

In Burns' autobiography, the white guards openly and explicitly reproduce racial oppression, which was a typical feature of American states like Georgia at the beginning of the twentieth century. The white inmate Burns, the first-person narrator, (perhaps unconsciously) constructs the prison as a space to distance himself from his Other, the African American. Burns permanently depicts himself as being superior to others, and in particular to African-American inmates. Burns' narrative participates in a discourse of strict racial differentiation, and renders the prison experience in such a way as to maintain the cultural hegemony of the white race. In the autobiography, the microcosmic world of the prison is like society because both are based on racial oppression. In other words, the prison, and the imprisoned narrator, reproduce society's racial oppression so that

African Americans are discriminated against everywhere. It is also worth noting that even though Burns does not realize this, society's racism is intensified in prison because the most cruel punishments are inflicted upon African Americans.

In his autobiography, the inmate Burns constructs himself as the man with whom his readers are supposed to identify. And, "though generally unacknowledged, his race is clearly white, and his awareness of racial dynamics is virtually elided" (Perreault 154). Burns by no means feels at one with his African-American fellow prisoners whom he refers to as 'Negroes,' thus strictly separating one race from the other. For instance, he points out that at the Campbell County chain gang, "we [i.e., white men, J.A.] worked with the Negroes" (59). Later on, Burns refers to "a certain Negro [...] who had been in the gang so long and had used a sledge so much he had become an expert" (62). While the term 'Negro' was common parlance at the time, Burns' frequent use of the word 'nigger' certainly attests to his racist views. At one point, he announces that he "spoke to this nigger" (63), and at another point he calls his fellow inmate Cowboy a "Nigger boy" (156–57) as do the white guards.

In a rare moment of recognition of the nasty treatment to which white guards expose African-American inmates, Burns describes the terror two "illiterate Negroes" feel of bloodhounds: "What a laugh the guards and the posse get out of this fear of Negroes of bloodhounds. It's hard to say who enjoys it the most, the dogs or the white men" (161).[29] As Perreault (158) correctly points out, beyond this expression of contempt, Burns offers no comment on the bestial conduct of the guards. What is more, their designation as "white men" clearly sets them apart from the unexamined and essentialist "fear of Negroes for bloodhounds" (161), and this is again typical of racist discourse. Earlier on, Burns expresses his essentialist beliefs about African Americans as follows. He argues that "friendship in misery is a special characteristic of Negroes" (158). Perhaps he is envious because he seems to be incapable of making friends among the prisoners. Generally speaking, it is quite striking that unlike his distinctness from other whites, which he also refers to (145–47), Burns' often marked difference from 'Negroes' is not based on moral character but on some unnamed Otherness.

Moreover, Burns frequently refers to 'Negroes' to underscore the injustice of his own position: "Garbed in the stripes of a desperate felon, I was engaged in the back-breaking toil of loading trucks with soil, keeping time with a gang of Negroes at the rate of sixteen shovelfuls a minute, thirteen hours a day" (167). Later on, when Burns protests against Georgia's violations of its own penal regulations, one of his complaints is that contrary to the law, blacks and whites are not properly separated during work: "[...] whites and Negroes worked side by side, which was another violation of state regulation" (176). At one point, Burns tells us that "all morning I had wearily kept pace with the sweating Negro beside me" (179). One might argue that Burns' suffering is intensified by the sexualized figure of "the sweating Negro." Since Burns stresses that he has to keep pace with him, he clearly perceives the inmate as being stronger or more physically potent. The "sweating" African American is not only an object of fascination but, since Burns feels inferior to his strength, also a potential threat to the white man's sexual identity, i.e., white masculinity.

It is also worth noting that throughout the text Burns never recognizes that "the privileges of his race, including economic advantages [...] were instrumental to the success of his daring escapes" (Perreault 159). For example, he owes his first escape to his lack of fear of the bloodhounds (which the 'Negroes' apparently suffer from).[30] Second, and more importantly, if Burns had been African-American, the white salesman in the Ford coupé would presumably not have given him the lift which allowed him to quickly get away from the chain gang (69–70). Third, his economic privileges, i.e., the cash he had, allowed him to buy "a suit of overalls, pants, and a jumper that fit, and a fifty-cent cotton shirt" (70). Also, the money allowed him to enter a barber shop to get a shave without questions (71). Furthermore, Burns never acknowledges that he could have never escaped without the help of the African-American inmate Sam. Sam hit Burns' shackles with a sledgehammer, thus bending them into elliptical shape. Moreover, the narrator owes his second escape to the money his family was able to send him which enabled him to bribe a white local into giving him a lift in his car (204–16). Again, this would presumably not have worked out if he had been African American. Generally speaking, Burns' arrogance and sense of himself as the civilized exception in the chain gang is one of the primary markers of the text.

In Burns' autobiography, the microcosmic world of the prison reproduces society's racism. While the white guards inflict the most cruel and arbitrary punishments upon African Americans, the white inmate Burns employs a number of narrative strategies that maintain the cultural hegemony of the whites. Burns' autobiography relies heavily upon the strict separation of whites and African Americans. The narrator participates in a cultural discourse of racial differentiation, thus linking the prison's delimitations to wider cultural demarcations. Burns constructs the prison as the space of the Other, the African American, and he believes that he does not belong there. Very rarely, Burns appears to be aware of the special oppression of African-American prisoners and to understand that their servitude is part of the history of a people. However, even in such moments, the narrator considers the African Americans' fight for freedom to be "exciting":

> Two illiterate Negroes, battling for freedom in the wilds of Georgia's swamps, hunted by white men like beasts of prey. For more than two hundred years the woods and swamps of Georgia have witnessed similar *exciting* scenes. And even before that in the wilds of Africa the tragedy was enacted, the purpose the same, the result foretold. (160–61; my emphasis, J.A.)

Burns is usually incapable of seeing beyond his own position. His prison narrative can be said to recreate the master-slave relationship and to reconstitute the segregated identities of African Americans and whites. Burns uses the prison to distance himself from the 'niggers.' He constructs the prison as a cultural space where society's racial oppression is reproduced and intensified. In the words of Lichtenstein, Burns' does not "ask Americans to confront the racial caste system that made the chain gang possible" (654).

At this point, I wish to turn to an analysis of the film *I Am a Fugitive from a Chain Gang!*. To begin with, by pushing "African Americans into the background of a segregated prison yard" (Lewis 236), the film also constructs the prison as a space for maintaining the cultural hegemony of the white race. The movie clearly foregrounds white prisoners. For instance, even though the African-American character Sebastian plays an important role in the film—he selflessly helps Allen to escape—the actor is not even mentioned in the opening credits. Furthermore, when Allen is sent to a second chain gang in the film, we are presented with a close-up of a blackboard which informs us that the prison population of the "Tuttle County Prison Camp" consists of 34 white convicts and 69 "negroes." These figures are not reflected in the (almost exclusively) white prison population on the screen. Furthermore, historically speaking, these figures are imprecise. African Americans actually "made up more than 75 per cent" of the inmates of the chain gangs in the southern states of the US (Rotman 176).

In what follows, I offer an interpretation of the film that differs from Roffman's and Purdy's reading of it. For them, the film plays with the metaphor DEPRESSION ERA IS PRISON. Roffman and Purdy argue that in American prison films of the 1930s, the prison was "the ultimate metaphor of social entrapment, where the individual disappears among the masses in an impersonal institution" (26). For them, the victimization of James Allen is "not merely a matter of being caught with his hand in the till, but more a matter of being caught in American society during the Depression" (30). Additionally, they argue that the end of the film summarizes the "paranoia, anger and despair" (80) of the Depression era in the thirties. At the end of the movie, Allen says a last dramatic goodbye to Helen (Helen Vinson), the woman he loves. In the course of the conversation, she asks him how he survives. He puts it as follows:

> ALLEN: "[…] I hide in rooms all day and travel by night. No friends, no rest, no peace. […] Keep moving. That's all that's left for me. Forgive me, Helen. I, I had to take a chance to see you tonight. Just to say goodbye. […]"

> HELEN: "I can't let you go like this. [...] Can't you tell me where you're going? [*He shakes his head.*] Will you write? [*He shakes his head.*] Do you need any money? [*He shakes his head again, still backing away from her.*] But you must, Jim! How do you live?"

As we hear the sound of an approaching car, Allen backs out of the light into the surrounding darkness, and his disembodied voice hisses the film's dramatic last line: "I steal," and his footsteps are heard running away.

If the film did actually represent the Depression era as a prison or a form of imprisonment, as Roffman and Purdy claim, the movie would need to consist of various shots in which the US in the thirties is visually represented as a prison (for example by means of metonyms of the chain gang). However, the film only visualizes the Depression era after Allen's second escape, i.e., at the end of the film. Admittedly, the final dramatic scene in which Allen slinks away like an animal into the dark and answers the question "How do you live?" by hissing "I steal," is full of paranoia, anger, and despair. However, darkness on its own is hardly sufficient to produce a cinematic metaphor. Additionally, darkness is not an important feature of the chain gang as it is depicted in the film. In contrast to Roffman and Purdy, I argue that the film first draws a homological structure between prison and society which then turns into a critique of society and defines society as a prison. In other words, the metaphor that is generated by the film is much more general and concerns society as a whole.[31] From our retrospective position, this may then condense into society during Depression.

At the beginning of the film, Allen complains about the "drab routine" he is confronted with in his life. Demobilized from the mechanical routine of the army, he is frustrated by his tedious job at a factory. Allen announces that he wishes to "get out, away from routine" and is unwilling to be bound by "a factory whistle instead of a bugle call." He quits his job to become an itinerant construction worker. Soon he is out of work. When Allen ends up at the prison camp for participating in a robbery of $6, he is exposed to an even harsher type of routine than in the army or the factory. The film also links the conformism inherent in life on the chain gang to that in the outside world. Allen complains to his family that everyone tries "to harness me and lead me around to do what you think is best for me." On the chain gang, he is exposed to an even stricter form of conformism. As the inmate Bomber (Edward Ellis) bitterly remarks, one even has to ask for permission to wipe off one's sweat, "but first you have to have their [the guards,' J.A.] permission to sweat." Thus, the chain gang represents in the extreme the oppressive rules and regulations Allen has attempted to get away from since he returned from World War I.

Once Allen has escaped, the film continues to parallel the prison to the outside world, and these parallels gradually turn into a critique of a malfunctioning society. For example, the counter where Allen buys a train ticket is framed by a wire-netting fence—just as the chain gang camp is framed by barbed wire. Additionally, during his first job outside, Allen has to work hard by using a pickaxe, which is precisely what he did on the chain gang. The wire-netting fence and the pickaxe are metonyms of the prison which reappear in the outside world, thus alluding to the carceral coordinates of society. Additionally, in the course of the film, we are repeatedly presented with high-angle long shots which make people appear insignificant. More specifically, the first shot of the World War I veterans, the first shots of the prisoners working in the quarries, as well as the first shot of citizens strolling through the streets of Chicago are all high-angle long shots that make the depicted people look alike. The repeated use of this angle of vision involves another connection. For me, these matching shots suggest that both the prison and the outside world (including institutions like the army) reduce people to insignificant cogs of a larger homogenous whole that destroys people's individuality. Moreover, Allen feels entrapped by his marriage to Marie (Glenda Farrell), who, upon discovering that he has escaped from the chain gang, forces him into marrying her. He explains to Helen that his life is like a prison from which there is "no escape [...], no freedom." And it is worth noting that pace Roffman and Purdy, all of this does not correlate with the Depression era: the soldiers returned in 1918, and by the time Allen escapes from the chain gang, the country is at the height of the twenties' prosperity.

Allen is tricked into returning to the chain gang with the promise of a pardon in ninety days. When Allen is imprisoned for the second time, vengeful state officials (including the governor) renege on their promise to pardon him because he attempted to expose the brutality of the chain gang. Shots of these suit-wearing crooks, who sit comfortably at their desks and discuss Allen's case, are contrasted with shots of the hard-working Allen on the chain gang. By presenting society's leaders as hypocritical crooks, the film foregrounds society's vices and failings. Allen argues that the world is upside down when he says that "the state's promise didn't mean anything. It was all lies! [...] Their crimes are worse than mine! They're the ones that should be in chains, not we!" As in *Little Dorrit*, the description of the prison as being homologous to the world turns into a description of the world as a prison (or a society of criminals). The film also associates Marie with the above mentioned bunch of crooks. Marie imprisons the rich and hard-working Allen by blackmailing him into marrying her and then begins to entertain sexual relations with other men. This lack of moral standards on her part clearly links her with the hypocritical state officials.

Social criticism plays an important role in the film. However, in contrast to Roffman and Purdy, who think that *I Am a Fugitive from a Chain Gang* plays upon the metaphor DEPRESSION ERA IS PRISON, I argue that the film makes a much more general statement about the relationship between the chain gang and society. On the one hand, the prison is depicted as being similar to society because both are based on drab routines and conformism, while the chain gang constitutes an intensification of routines and conformist rules and regulations. On the other hand, the film imputes to society itself the qualities of a prison. Society is a massive social system that is implacable, impersonal, and out of control. Its authorities are cast as brutal oppressors. Most importantly, the world is upside down because nearly innocent citizens like Allen are sent to the chain gang, while the actual criminals, i.e., hypocrites like the vengeful state officials (and perhaps Marie), rule this oppressive system.

Is the Whole World a Boring Prison?

The movie *Down by Law* deals with the disc jockey Zack and the pimp Jack who are set up in New Orleans and then meet in a cell at the Orleans Parish Prison. The cell soon receives another inmate, namely the warm-hearted Italian Roberto, also called Bob. Bob urges the other two to break out of prison through an underground tunnel which leads them to the bayou. The three fugitives wander aimlessly through the swamps until they reach a tiny hut called 'Luigi's Tintop.' Roberto goes inside, falls in love with Nicoletta (Nicoletta Braschi), and decides to stay with her. The next day, Zack and Jack depart down the road, each man going his own way.

The film presents us with a variety of scenes which suggest a homological structure between the outside world and the alien world of prison. The movie establishes numerous parallels between the experience of imprisonment and particular aspects of life in New Orleans. Additionally, after Zack, Jack, and Bob have escaped from prison and wander through the bayou, the film's description of the prison as being homologous to the world turns into a description of the world as a boring prison. In other words, imprisonment is seen as being emblematic of our being in the world. The prototypical features that are mapped onto the world are restraint, confinement, boredom, and monotony.

The first scenes of the film, which are set outside prison, evoke a world of frustration, lethargy, and passivity. The movie links life in New Orleans to a tomb or to death. "We open on a long, low hearse parked outside a cemetery, from which the camera takes off in a fast lateral glide past rows of box-like houses with elaborate porticos, like family mausolea" (Kemp 142). The juxtaposition of graves with dilapidated fronts of houses, idle huts, and empty balconies evokes the association of society with a graveyard or tomb.[32] We are then introduced to the land of the dead: "You're digging your own grave," Zack's girlfriend Laurette (Ellen Barkin) tells him, pausing in her task of throwing his personal property into the street below. A graffiti on the wall next to the door adds to Laurette's statement: "It's not the fall that kills you, it's the sudden stop." Zack argues, "Yeah well, that's right Laurette, we can't live in this prison forever," and Laurette throws him out of the flat. The interplay between the auditory and the visual channel codes his life as a prison.

Later on, the passive Zack is approached by a minor criminal who tells him that he can make some easy money by driving a stolen car around town. Zack realizes that he has been set up when the police stop him and discover a corpse in the trunk. Meanwhile, the pimp Jack slumps lifelessly in a chair, submitting to the sardonic jibes of an African-American prostitute, only rousing himself to walk blindly into a trap that sends him to prison. More specifically, Jack makes amends with a former enemy named Preston and Preston sets him up with a ten-year old girl. Since the police believe that Jack intends to prostitute the underage girl, they arrest him.

On a psychological level, Zack and Jack appear to be imprisoned by their self-centeredness, which makes them particularly oblivious to the feelings and needs of women. For example, the African-American prostitute tells Jack: "I can just lay here and talk forever and you won't hear a single word like you don't even speak English." Additionally, both are so lethargic and lifeless that the task of setting them up can be easily accomplished. Before the two become cellmates, we are presented with a dolly shot in the course of which the camera slowly and smoothly moves along the individual cells of prison. This shot is reminiscent of the dolly shot at the beginning of the film, in the course of which the camera moves smoothly and quickly along coffin-like house fronts in New Orleans. These two similar dolly shots are matching shots, i.e., shots that present two different entities in the same way, and invite us to look for aspects they might have in common. In this case, having to live in dilapidated houses is presented as being similar to imprisonment in a cell. This cinematic metaphor is created by combining two different settings with the same camera movement and angle of vision. The prison is represented as being like society because both correlate with lethargy and boredom. As we quickly learn, the prison experience carries the feelings of ennui and frustration to an extreme. In prison nothing happens at all.

We see Zack and Jack filmed through the bars of their cell—a juxtaposition which, apart from their literal confinement, also suggests their mental confinement. At one point, Jack tells Zack, "As far as I'm concerned, you don't exist," to which Zack replies: "You don't exist either. The walls don't exist. The floor doesn't exist. This prison's not here. These bunks aren't here. The bars aren't here. None of this is really here. None of this is really here at all." Into their cold antagonism irrupts the Italian Roberto who has some difficulty with the English language. Upon arrival, he says: "If looks can kill I am dead now." Later on, he insists that in the cell, there is "not enough room to swing a cat." On the one hand, he urges his two fellow inmates to literally break out of prison. On the other hand, he urges them to figuratively break out of their lethargic self-centeredness. For instance, he wants Jack and Zack to communicate with him (both for company and to provide information for his notebook), and despite their initial disinterestedness in others they do so. Later on, he wants them to play cards with him and even leads them in a chant of the 'circular' saying "I scream, you scream, we all scream for ice-cream," in the course of which the three inmates walk around in circles. At one point, Jack tells Roberto that he must look *at* the window he has drawn on the cell wall, rather than *out* of it. Roberto's linguistic difficulties gain larger significance when he leads them to freedom with near-magical ease. Since we never actually see how the three inmates manage to get out of prison, the breakout indeed appears to be accomplished by magic.

During their escape from prison, the three fugitives reach a tiny hut in the swamps. The bare interior of this hut looks exactly like their prison cell. In this case, the simile (THE WORLD IS LIKE A PRISON) is created by the *mise-en-scène* because the similarity between the hut and the cell is clearly a pre-existing visual one. This simile is then extended and becomes a metaphor which defines the world as a boring prison. Zack, Jack, and Bob are soon lost in the swamps where everything looks the same. The bareness of the trees in the swampy wilderness of the bayou not only correlates with the prison's lack of sensory stimulation and orientation, but additionally evokes and recreates the starkness of the near-identical prison cells. At one point, Zack announces, "we've been goin' around in circles, Jack," which is reminiscent of both the inmates' walking around in circles in prison and the dull routine of prison life. Furthermore, the scene in which the three fugitives watch the sinking of their small boat may be seen as a symbol of the lack of mobility which seems to be an essential feature of New Orleans, the Orleans Parish Prison, and the swamps of Louisiana. In short, the film defines the world as a bare prison where nothing really happens and people walk around in circles.[33] In the movie, nothingness characterizes both the boring world of the prison and the boring world outside, i.e., life in New Orleans and the swamps of Louisiana.

It is also worth noting that the film presents us with a way of temporarily countering the world's (and also the prison's) nothingness, and this temporary 'solution' correlates with the Italian character Roberto. With regard to Roberto's affection for the American poets Walt Whitman and Robert Frost, whom he quotes in Italian, and his references to what he has seen in (action-filled) American prison movies, the film clearly stresses the cross-cultural aspect of the encounter.[34] Also, at one point in prison, Jack tells Roberto, "Cigarettes won't help with hiccups, not in this country." The confrontation with the cultural Other, whose first line in the film is "it's a sad and beautiful world," reduces both the boredom of prison and the prison-like character of the world. In prison and in the course of the escape, Roberto urges the two American characters to break out of their self-centeredness which Zack's "every man for himself" aptly describes. While Roberto considers the world to be sad but beautiful, Zack and Jack consider it to be a boring prison. At first, Zack and Jack seem to dislike Roberto and refuse to talk to him. When they learn that he killed a man by throwing a snooker ball which hit the victim in the forehead, they become more and more interested in this bizarre character, who then leads them out of prison and out of their mental confinement. Jenkins argues that the "humour of Benigni's performance is played off against the more deadpan, cool presence of Lurie and Waits, with the result that the Italian character becomes almost an autonomous turn" (3). To my mind, Roberto is the most likeable character in the film. He allows the near-zombified Americans a temporary escape from their self-centeredness. In contrast to Zack and Jack, Roberto appears to be free from all types of constraint and does whatever he feels like doing. Kemp points out that the film's title *Down by Law* sounds as though it should mean 'sent to prison,' but is in fact street slang for 'in control' (142). And this is precisely what Roberto is, for all that he comes across as a naive buffoon. Whatever he wants, he gets—in the nicest possible way.

In contrast to the other two fugitives who ultimately remain oblivious to the feelings of others, Roberto manages to 'get' a woman at 'Luigi's Tintop.' He falls in love with Nicoletta, who has been left the place by her late uncle Luigi (who died on the day her boyfriend left her). In a moment of admiration, Jack comments on Bob: "He's from outer space." While Bob stays with Nicoletta, Jack and Zack return to their initial self-centeredness and pursue their solitary and divergent paths. One might argue that Bob follows the attitude of "get busy living" which Andy proclaims in the film *The Shawshank Redemption*, whereas Zack and Jack follows the attitude of "get busy dying," as it is proclaimed by Brooks Hatlen, the prison librarian who ultimately commits suicide. Indeed, at the end of the film, we do get a sense that the encounter with Roberto provided only a temporary release from the boring prison of the world and that Zack and Jack will go on to lead their lives by moving around in circles. Furthermore, since Roberto can only provide temporary release from the prison of the world, it is difficult to believe that the love of Bob and Nicoletta will endure.

The film *Down by Law* juxtaposes the dilapidated house fronts in New Orleans with graves, thus evoking the association of society with a tomb or graveyard, where nothing really happens. The film also uses matching shots, i.e., two similar dolly shots, to show that the prison is like society. More specifically, the general feeling of boredom or lethargy is intensified by the microcosmic world of the prison. The speed of the film slows down with the first dolly shot in prison. Once the three inmates have escaped from prison and wander aimlessly through the bayou, the world is represented as a bare and boring prison. Restraint, confinement, and monotony define the scenes in prison as well as the pre-prison scenes in New Orleans and the post-imprisonment scenes in the swamps so that culture and nature merge with the prison. The primary function of the character of Roberto is to temporarily counter the overall nothingness of both the prison and the world. He urges Zack and Jack to break out of the Orleans Parish Prison as well as the prison of their self-centeredness, to which they eventually return. Roberto makes the prison-like world of the film more beautiful. Notably, his first line in the film is: "It's a sad and beautiful world."

Like Dickens' later fiction, prison narratives of the twentieth century draw a homological structure between prison and society in order to critique society. For example, "The Loneliness of the Long-Distance Runner" illustrates that the demands of conformism in the macrocosm of society (and in the microcosmic world of the borstal) destroy all types of individualism and spontaneity. Similarly, the film *I Am a Fugitive from a Chain Gang!* critiques conformist society by demonstrating that, like the chain gang, it attempts to transform its citizens into socially acceptable and well-functioning automata. Other attitudes or eccentricities of society are shown to be reproduced in prison as well. The film *The Loneliness of the Long-Distance Runner* demonstrates that the borstal is ultimately a disciplinary space for working-class kids who are not willing to toe the line. The movie blames the English class system for the existence of criminality, and accentuates that all attempts to rebel against this system are doomed to failure. The borstal reproduces and intensifies the inferior position of working-class boys in relation to members of the upper class. Finally, in the autobiography *I Am a Fugitive from a Georgia Chain Gang!*, the prison system and the imprisoned white narrator reproduce society's racism. More specifically, by merely protesting that the harsh treatment of African Americans should not be extended to respectable subjects like himself, Burns constructs the prison experience in such a way as to maintain the cultural hegemony of the white race. Finally, in prison metaphors, the image of the prison is projected onto domains outside a legal context. The class system, society, or perhaps even the world may be represented as prisons because they correlate with restraint, confinement, boredom, loneliness, the feeling of being unable to freely decide on one's actions, etc. For example, by using metonyms of the prison (like barbed wire, high and imposing towers, gates, pick axes, etc.), the films *The Loneliness of the Long Distance Runner* and *I Am a Fugitive from a Chain Gang!* represent the situation of the working class in Nottingham and American society respectively as prisons. In the former case, the lack of opportunities for the working class is stressed, whereas in the latter case, society is represented as being dominated by immoral criminals. Finally, in the film *Down by Law*, the whole world is constructed as a prison because both nature and (American) culture are described in terms of monotony, lethargy, boredom, bareness, and lack of sensory stimulation. On the other hand, the film also argues that imprisonment in the world can temporarily be overcome by interesting cross-cultural encounters.

ENDNOTES

1. During the surprise inspection of Andy's cell, we see the word "MOTHER" scratched into the wall above the Rita Hayworth poster which Andy uses to cover the tunnel shaft in his cell. This juxtaposition suggests that Rita Hayworth is a mother figure and by extension, that Andy's escape (through the poster) is a birth or rebirth.
2. One might also mention the killing of "Fat Ass" and Tommy Williams to illustrate the connection between Norton's corrupt regime and death. Furthermore, even the warden himself commits suicide when he learns that Andy made public his corrupt scams and the brutal treatment prisoners receive at the Shawshank Prison.
3. I am not convinced by Kermode's various descriptions of Andy's bodily positions—on the roof of the license-plate factory, in the projection booth, or in his cell before his escape—as being Christ-like (31–32; 41; 58). These references are good examples of how a critic desperately tries to impose his interpretation upon the text, which might actually have nothing to do with it.
4. The general tendency of Kermode's analysis is to merge the novella and the film by frequently pointing out "that Darabont gets what King means" (34) or noting "an admirable devotion to King's source novella" (74). Kermode does not usually differentiate between the written version and the film adaptation.
5. We learn that as a kid, he had "a big mop of carroty hair" (55).
6. Since Stroud's birds had been taken away from him at the prison at Leavenworth before he was transferred to Alcatraz in 1942, he should actually be called 'Birdman of Leavenworth' rather than 'Birdman of Alcatraz.'
7. This film metaphor also involves an interplay between the auditory and the visual level. The metaphor's source domain ("new life, birth") is present on the auditory level, while we see the target domain, the prison, on the screen.
8. According to Crowther, "the movie's implication, that Stroud was an emotional prisoner of his mother, barely stands up to scrutiny; he spent too little time in her company for that" (56).
9. This juxtaposition metaphor is anticipated by Dickens' *Little Dorrit*, where the narrator points out that the prisoners Rigaud and John Baptist have to share their cell with "rats and other unseen vermin"

and then refers to the two inmates in terms of "the seen vermin" (16). It is perhaps also worth noting that in contrast to Dickens' novel, where Rigaud is a very ambivalent figure, Stroud is clearly a sympathetic prisoner. In other words, the metaphor in the film carries much more critical weight concerning the animal-like treatment of inmates.

10. One could also argue that since the shot includes bloodhounds and guards in the frame of the camera, it is the juxtaposition within the frame (rather than the cut) that involves an intermingling of categories, and thus metaphor. From this angle, the guards are defined as bloodhounds.
11. With regard to Father Bobby, Wlodarz argues that the "erasure of pedophilia from its most likely candidate [the Catholic priest, J.A.] allows the charge to shift to its other most frequent (and far less substantiated) target, the homosexual man" (72). This statement does not make much sense because the guards are pedophile rather than homosexual. Pedophilia is not entirely erased in the film; it is only that the guards (rather than the priest) are child abusers.
12. This is a distortion metaphor that invites us to see the detention center as hell.
13. "Now begin moans that, as they louder grow, force themselves on my ear: now I am come thither where many wailings strike me thro.' [...] When they [the sinners, J.A.] arrive at the brink o' the landslip, strong is the outcry there, wailing and lamentation" (*Inferno* 3, 25–35).
14. This is another example of a distortion metaphor which is achieved through this particular combination of the *mise-en-scène* and the lighting from below.
15. The voice-over narrator inform us that John "[...] had been in and out of jail since he was a teenager. He robbed and killed at will or at command and was currently a suspect in four unsolved homicides. He was an alcoholic and a cocaine abuser with a fast temper and a faster trigger. He once shot a mechanic dead for moving ahead of him in a movie line." Additionally, we learn that Tommy "was equally deadly. He had committed his first murder at the age of seventeen. In return, he was paid fifty dollars. He drank and did drugs. He had a wife he never saw somewhere in Queens."
16. Interestingly, before Nokes is shot, he still practices his perverse cult of masculinity by stating that his motivation for raping them was to make the boys "hard and tough," which, in contrast to Wlodarz's argument (73), clearly distances him from 'fags.'
17. This paradox seems to imply that a conformist can gradually develop into a criminal individualist.

18. Depending on one's perspective one may agree with Smith's defiant individualism, or one might instead stress the fact that Smith is a stubborn and wicked criminal who has to be locked away. From the latter perspective, the novella might argue in favor of borstals that are run by well-meaning individuals rather than hypocrites like the governor.
19. With regard to the cross-country race, which is a public activity, the runners have to follow clear rules and run along a given path, which links the race with conformism. On the other hand, during his solitary training sessions, Smith can make decisions concerning both the way and his speed, which in a sense links this type of running with individualism and freedom.
20. As in the novella, an alternative reading is possible which would see Colin as the prisoner of his individuality. Ultimately, Colin's stubborn insistence on his individualism correlates with complete loneliness and lack of contact with others; perhaps the loneliness of the individualist long-distance runner constitutes the ultimate metaphorical prison in the film.
21. The Smith of the novel, on the other hand, callously enjoys both television and his father's insurance money: "Night after night we [Smith and his mate Mike, J.A.] sat in front of the telly [...], while mam was with some fancy-man upstairs on the new bed she'd ordered, and I'd never known a family as happy as ours was in that couple of months when we'd got all the money we needed" (21).
22. More specifically, both the doctor and the governor are ignorant of the actual causes of the types of 'deviance' they are confronted with. The father's cancer was presumably caused by his work in the factory and, as I will show in the following section, Colin's crime was to some extent at least caused by the class system. In a sense both the doctor and the governor fail to tackle the root of the problem.
23. The contrast between the third-person pronouns in the singular, which refer to Colin's individualist father, and the plural pronouns, which refer to the conformist doctors, is of course reminiscent of the confrontation between Colin and the governor in the course of the induction process (10–11).
24. This is of course something neither the governor, who believes that the salvation of wayward youth is their participation in sports, nor the new housemaster, who is more interested in the trainees' "emotional readjustment," are capable of understanding. The new housemaster asks Colin to tell him all about himself. He also wants to know how he ended up in borstal, and records everything Colin says on a tape-recorder.

When Colin says, "I wasn't thinking anything. I was too busy breaking in," the new housemaster is irritated and does not grasp the real reason, namely the fact that Colin's working-class mother needed money. This sequence encompasses "the well-meaning ineptitude of the newly trained, socially aware officer, who is every bit as uncomprehending as the older traditionalists" (Horne 110).

25. For instance, in the dressing room, one of the inmates asks one of the public school boys what happens if they get caught smoking a cigarette. One of the boys says: "We get beaten on the backside." Surprised, the inmate asks, "Do you pay to go to this school?" to which the boy replies, "Our parents do."
26. In the borstal's workshed, the inmates have to dismantle gas masks, which provides an interesting link to the death of Colin's father.
27. The film here uses the same lines of dialogue to invite us to link these two different situations.
28. Franklin, Rotman (176), and Oshinsky also point out that the Southern chain gangs and prison farms were a continuation of slavery by other means. Davis and James (96) and Davis argue that the US prison system as a whole incorporated and sustained pre-existing structures and ideologies of racism borrowed from slavery.
29. As in the film, the guards clearly share features with bloodhounds.
30. In contrast to the 'primitive' 'Negroes,' who are full of "mortal terror" when they hear "the bay of the hounds" (161), the 'civilized' white man pretended to play with them as he ran (67).
31. On the other hand, I think that at the time, viewers certainly identified with Paul Muni in the film and related the chain gang to their own feelings of imprisonment by economic and social realities. Indeed, "readers and critics frequently interpret fictional prison scenarios as implying that the prison is a metaphor for our lives, for our society, for our times" (Fludernik and Olson xxvi).
32. Similarly, the narrator of *Little Dorrit* compares the architecture in London to a funeral: "It was one of the parasite streets; long, regular, narrow, dull, and gloomy; like a brick and mortar funeral" (317).
33. Bareness, lack of sensory stimulation, and circularity are metonymic features of prison life which are projected on to the world.
34. *Down by Law* may also be read as a humorous parody of American prison films.

Chapter Six

Conclusion

Since law-abiding citizens do not usually visit prisons or study historical material, prison files written by prison staff, government reports, or campaigning documents by penal reform organizations, one has to address the possibility that fictional prison narratives are an important source of the public's ideas and understandings. For this reason, I have decided to investigate the ways in which well-known fictional narratives like Charles Dickens' mature novels, twentieth-century fiction, and prison films narrate the prison.

The leading questions of this investigation were the following:

(1) Do the prison narratives of my corpus generate cultural understandings of the legitimacy or of the illegitimacy of the prison?
(2) How do they represent the experience of imprisonment and in what respect do they depart from the realities of penal practice?
(3) Which prison metaphors can be found in prison novels and films?

(4) What are the similarities, differences, and continuities between Dickens' novels, twentieth-century novels, and films?

(1) In contrast to the claims by Hale, Seltzer, Bender, Miller, and Grass, no direct link exists between purely narrative features and Jeremy Bentham's plans for a *Panopticon* (1791) or other structural attributes of the penitentiary idea. First-person narratives, authorial novels, and prison films (which are third-person neutral narratives) can all be used for a variety of different purposes. They may all critique or support the prison, and do not in themselves correlate with pro-prison ideologies. In order to determine the ideological underpinnings of prison narratives, one should therefore not investigate purely formal features but the ways in which they narrate the interrelationship between the prison and its inmates on the one hand, and the prison metaphors they use on the other.

During the course of my investigation, the 'conservative' Dickens surprisingly turned out to be much more critical of the prison than most prison narratives of the twentieth century. Dickens' mature fiction critiques the prison by presenting us with innocent and likeable inmates who suffer unjustly in prison. It is only occasionally that Dickens confronts us with vicious criminals (like Compeyson) who might justify the existence of prisons. It is also worth noting that even though Dickens' mature fiction focuses on individual inmates, they are not set apart from the 'other' prisoners. Characters like William Dorrit or Manette are not singled out because they are exceptional. Rather, they are used as representative examples to illustrate the general suffering of *all* prison inmates. In contrast to his non-fictional writings, which became slightly more reactionary as he grew older, Dickens' later fiction openly condemns the prison. The prison is depicted as a sickness that tries to 'infect' various human domains. It is a universal negative force that enters the minds of prisoners, the world outside prison, and even the psychological states of characters who have never been to prison.

Some prison novels of the twentieth century also shed a critical light on the prison by highlighting that prisoners may remain tied to the ignominy of the prison or by pointing out that the idea of rehabilitation always correlates with the destruction of the prisoner's individuality. However, most prison narratives of the twentieth century draw a qualitative difference between the suffering of *one* wrongfully convicted prisoner-hero and the 'other' prison inmates. Such narratives only question the legitimacy of the imprisonment of our identificatory figure but tacitly accept the incarceration of the 'deviant' others, and hence clearly sanction the existence of prisons. Since they do not manage to deconstruct the dichotomy citizen/criminal and solidify the role of the prison, one might in fact link them with late Victorian prison memoirs like the anonymously published *Five Years' Penal Servitude* (1877), which was written by Edward Callow, or Jabez Spencer Balfour's *My Prison Life* (1907). As Lauterbach ("From the Slums") has shown, such texts concentrate on gentleman prisoners who corroborate the demonization and animalization of 'common' criminals but exempt themselves from this class.

Many critics attribute a liberal-conservative consensus to Dickens. However, the idea of "wanting prisons as simply neither too hard nor too easy" (Tambling "Prison-Bound" 128) should rather be attributed to most prison narratives of the twentieth century. As a general tendency, one can say that since Dickens' later novels do not present us with a single inmate who goes through a process of reform in one of his gloomy dungeons, Dickens' mature fiction rejects the idea of rehabilitation in prison as such. Most prison narratives of the twentieth century, on the other hand, draw a distinction between a traditional prison system based on discipline and violence, which they critique, and a more progressive one, which they agree with. More specifically, they argue that if prisons are run by well-meaning individuals, the rehabilitation or reform of the prisoner is both possible and desirable. Sometimes such a reformative prison system is shown to develop in the course of the narrative, and sometimes it is alluded to through 'positive' metaphors of imprisonment or well-meaning prison officers.

(2) All fictional prison narratives occasionally depart from the actual prison experience and hence 'misrepresent' the prison. For example, Richard Maxwell says about Dickens' *Tale* that

> [...] Dickens understood full well that there were only seven prisoners in the Bastille when it was finally liberated [...] but chose to organize the novel around the fate of a Bastille prisoner whom he had invented himself and who represents an idealistic martyr to liberty, unlike any of the actual prisoners. (xviii)

Indeed, in Dickens' mature fiction, most imprisoned characters are idealistic martyrs who do not manage to escape the prison they have internalized. The primary function of such sentimentalized inmates is to condemn the prison by showing that they suffer unjustly in prison. It is also worth noting that even though the 'new' penitentiary had already replaced the 'old' prison system in the mid-nineteenth century, Dickens' novels continue to confront us with dark and filthy dungeons or anarchic places like the Marshalsea debtors' prison. Since Dickens was well aware of the 'new' prison system and its consequences (Dickens "Philadelphia" 99–109), one can hardly attribute this anachronistic aspect of his fiction to the time it takes until certain ideas make their way into fiction. Rather, the representation of 'old' prisons correlates with a temporal distancing that allows him to condemn the prison by dramatizing the suffering of his idealistic inmates in great detail because the prisons are 'safely' located in the past.

Prison narratives of the twentieth century draw extensively on real prisons and actual events, and usually present us with 'new' prison settings, i.e., bright and clean penitentiaries. However, they also ignore many components of the actual prison experience like the predominance of colored inmates in British and American prisons, and focus almost exclusively on white inmates. Second, even though the reality of being imprisoned today involves almost interminable boredom, prison novels and films of the twentieth century do not focus on the monotony in prison, and prefer to present us with prison violence, rape, or time in the 'hole.' Third, twentieth-century prison narratives concentrate almost exclusively on outbreaks of violence between prisoners and guards and tend to ignore inmate-on-inmate violence. Also, conflicts between inmates and distasteful companions in the cell appear to be too boring or insignificant to be represented (even though they occur almost daily in real prisons). Fourth, twentieth-century prison narratives tend to misrepresent homosexuality in prison. More specifically, they do not usually mention the wide range of consensual homoerotic practices that develop in prison. Furthermore, even though most prison rapists are (and view themselves as) heterosexuals, prison narratives have a tendency to blur the distinction between rapists and homosexuals so that rapists are frequently coded as homosexuals.

Since prison narratives of the twentieth century distort the experience of imprisonment in various ways, their primary goal is hardly to offer us "a window onto the inaccessible but riveting world of the prison" as Rafter has it (127). Rather, the way in which twentieth-century prison novels and films narrate the prison is clearly linked to wider cultural demarcations. Most prison narratives of the twentieth century focus on the unjust victimization of white and heterosexual members of the middle class whose 'proper' status is restored at the end when they are shown to regain their manliness. In the course of their stays at prison, our white prisoner-heroes have to endure numerous rituals that produce some sort of symbolic 'feminization' and constitute a threat to their masculinity. Most twentieth-century prison novels and films do not focus on monotony or the boring routine of prison life because the deadening sameness of prison life does not constitute a proper threat to the masculinity of our identificatory figures. The 'feminization' in the course of the induction process (e.g., the obligatory shower scenes or the inspection of orifices of the body) as well as the violence inflicted by sadistic guards with long batons or 'homosexual' rapists are of course much more apt to create a victim figure out of our prisoner-hero. The ravages of the 'hole' (in combination with all its associations of anality and excrement) continue the degradation of our prisoner-hero by turning him into an 'abject.' It is worth noting that our identificatory figures usually withstand and resist these threats and remain unbroken. Most of these prison narratives end with the reconstitution of the central protagonist's masculinity, and hence, clearly and openly reproduce tough-guy ideals.[1] Thus, prison narratives of the twentieth century do not actually address the real situation of inmates in British and American prisons. Instead, they present us with stories about the unjust victimization of wrongfully convicted members of the white and heterosexual middle class. Moreover, they contrast these 'innocent' prison newcomers with colored and homosexual inmates who are 'real' criminals, and argue that the latter belong into prison whereas the former do not.

(3) Metaphors of imprisonment highlight the prisoners' attitude toward prison. Such metaphors comment on the prison experience by providing an internal perspective on incarceration. The metaphors of imprisonment in Dickens' mature fiction stress the agony, misery, and infantilization of prisoners. Occasionally, being inside appears to be preferable to life outside, but even the descriptions of prison as womb or peaceful resting place evoke the prisoner's dependence on the prison and emphasize that inmates frequently get so used to the static world of the prison that they cannot live on the outside. The 'old' prison system and its images of dark dungeons persist in most metaphors of imprisonment in Dickens' later fiction. More specifically, most images focus on the inmates' suffering and entombment. The only metaphor that evokes associations of the 'new' prison or penitentiary is the description of prison as a greenhouse. This metaphor evokes the icy treatment, scientific detachment, and anonymity in typical Victorian prisons. Generally speaking, the images of carcerality in Dickens' mature fiction evoke rather negative associations and stress the inmates' suffering.

Prison narratives of the twentieth century, by contrast, confront us with both 'negative' and 'positive' metaphors of imprisonment. On the one hand, the prison is described as a counterworld or in terms of Otherness. Inmates are represented as an 'abject,' and the prison frequently evokes associations of death, hell, animality, or monstrosity. Such metaphors critique the prison system and the treatment of the inmates. The prison staff view the prisoners as rats or beasts and use them as animals of labor or expose them to cruel types of punishment. On the other hand, we are also confronted with prisoners who use the prison as a place of refuge from the hurly-burly of life, a matrix of spiritual rebirth, a catalyst of intense friendship, or an 'academy' or laboratory. These two different sets of metaphors suggest that the prison is not necessarily a place of suffering. Rather, individual prisoners are shown to achieve forms of rehabilitative incarceration that differ from the conventional prison experience. In other words, these narratives argue that certain forms of imprisonment can have positive effects on the inmate. This binary arrangement of 'positive' and 'negative' metaphors of imprisonment serves to underline the distinction between rehabilitative penal styles, which most prison narratives of the twentieth century agree with, and punitive or discipline-based institutions, which they critique. Furthermore, they argue that we need rehabilitative prisons for colored and homosexual inmates, while members of the white and heterosexual middle class do not belong there and escape.

The major function of the 'prison-as-world' simile in both Dickens and twentieth-century narratives is to demonstrate that certain attitudes are reproduced and intensified in prison, and this is usually done to critique society. For example, society's conformism may be shown to destroy people's individuality both inside and outside. In such cases, the representation of certain societal features in the prison correlates not only with a critical perspective on the treatment prisoners receive in prison. Rather, the simile allows us to re-evaluate life in the outside world. Society may force its citizens to live in accordance with drab rules and regulations and disallow individuality, spontaneity or autonomy. Furthermore, the replication of society's class conflicts in prison may offer us a critical perspective on class divisions in society. Poverty may be represented as the major 'crime' that sends protagonists to prison. Also, in twentieth-century narratives, society's racism may be reproduced in prison so that the prison continues and intensifies the general oppression of African Americans. Indeed, African Americans today see American prisons as epitomes of the continuing enslavement of their race, and given the gross racial imbalance in the American prison population, this view is not at all absurd.

At first glance, one expects prison metaphors (X IS PRISON) in narratives that have no legal or penal preoccupations. However, prison metaphors are also used in prison narratives in which they serve to corroborate or complement the narrative's major argument. For instance, the limitations and restrictions of prison settings may be extended to the world outside where people suffer from various types of metaphorical imprisonment or mental confinement. Generally speaking, prison metaphors highlight the feeling of constraint in the world outside prison and hence provide us with an internal perspective (as do metaphors of imprisonment). In particular the several prison-like settings or correlates of constraint in Dickens demonstrate that the prison may transcend its borders and 'infect' the world outside. Also, metonyms of the prison (such as bars, chains, fetters, etc.) are frequently used to project the image of the prison onto domains outside a legal or penal context. Prison metaphors critique certain elements of the world outside that constrain people (like the class system) or they accentuate the mental confinement of a character; and this may be done to critique the character's inability to act like a free person or to accentuate the character's difficult or problematic position in society.

It is also worth noting that novels and films do not actually differ with regard to their metaphorical potential. The following taxonomy of cinematic metaphor summarizes the major cinematic strategies of evoking metaphor. The stronger denotation, i.e., the one more fully present in the narrative, serves as the target domain, while the weaker or suggested one serves as the source domain. As in verbal metaphors, prototypical features of the source are then mapped on to the target.

Cinematic similes of the form 'A is like B' can be found in the following constellations. First, films may invite us to link two entities with some pre-existing visual similarity or well-known affinity. For instance, in *Down by Law*, the three prison escapees Zack, Jack, and Bob reach a tiny hut in the bayou, the interior of which looks exactly like the prison cell from which they escaped. The film uses this architectural similarity to link the world outside prison to the prison. Similarly, in the films *The Shawshank Redemption* and *A Clockwork*

Orange, the uniforms the inmates wear in prison blend in with the uniforms of the prison officers and wardens, thus suggesting that the prison staff are 'imprisoned' by their jobs as well. In these examples, the similarities are visual ones, and the *mise-en-scène* is more important than the camera movement or the angle of presentation.

Whereas cinematic similes direct attention initially to a pre-existing resemblance, proper film metaphors imply that the essence of something is not what we normally take it to be, but something quite different (A is B). The figurative interpretation follows from an awareness of the incongruity between two entities. Metaphorical readings can be evoked in seven different ways:

(a) First, film metaphors may emerge from the *juxtaposition of disparate elements*. However, not all juxtapositions automatically involve metaphor. Rather, the juxtaposition has to involve a surprising intermingling of categories to establish a special relationship between A and B. For example, the film *Down by Law* juxtaposes graves with dilapidated fronts of houses. This juxtaposition evokes the association of society with a graveyard or tomb. Similarly, Conway's film *A Tale of Two Cities* juxtaposes images of the Marquis' expressionless face and the gargoyles of his chateau, thus inviting us to see him *as* a stone-like character. Many prison films juxtapose prison inmates with rats, thus highlighting that the prison staff (and maybe also law-abiding citizens) view them as vermin.

(b) Second, cinematic metaphors can be generated by an *interplay between the auditory and the visual level*. In other words, the source domain can be introduced by spoken or written words, music, or sound, while the target domain is represented on the screen. For example, in Edzard's *Little Dorrit*, shots of the city of London are repeatedly combined with the sound of clinking coins, which is reminiscent of clinking chains in prison, and the sound of buzzing flies. The first juxtaposition defines London as a materialist city dominated by money and, by extension, a prison, while the second interplay between the auditory and the visual level codes the city as a dying carcass or tomb that attract flies. Also, in *The Shawshank Redemption*, the interplay between images of the prison and Red's voice-over ("They march you in naked as the day you were born, skin burning and half blind"; "They send you here for life and that's exactly what they take") codes the prison as a womb and a tomb.

(c) Third, metaphorical readings may emerge from *matching shots*, i.e., shots that construct a similarity between two different entities (e.g., by using the same camera angles or movements or the same lines of dialogue). For instance, the film *Down by Law* presents us with two similar dolly shots. In the first one, the camera moves along box-like houses in New Orleans. Later on, the camera moves along the individual cells of the Orleans Parish Prison in a similar fashion, thus suggesting a link between life in prison and life in New Orleans. In this case, the common feature is monotony or boredom. The film *I Am a Fugitive from a Chain Gang!* uses matching shots, too. More specifically, we are presented with numerous similar high-angle long shots which suggest that the prison and the outside world reduce people to insignificant entities and destroy people's individuality.

(d) Fourth, metaphors may emerge from *distortions*, i.e., deviations from what is normally expected in film. Distortions can be achieved in a variety of different ways: the *mise-en-scène* may play a role but also the use of particular lenses, camera speed, inserted cartoon sequences, etc. In distortion metaphors, the image on the screen must present an entity in such a way that the viewer is unsure which category the entity belongs to. For example, at the beginning of *The Shawshank Redemption*, we are presented with a bird's-eye view of the inmates in the prison yard and this shot allows us to see the prisoners *as* insignificant ants. Also, the long, dark tunnels in combination with the low-key illumination in the film *Sleepers* invite us to see the reform school as an underworld setting or as hell.

(e) Fifth, *the focusing on the same entity in two different scenes* may also evoke cinematic metaphor. In other words, the unexpected depiction of entities that usually belong to a different domain might involve an intermingling of categories. For example, the depiction of details of the prison (like barbed wire, high and imposing towers or walls, and so forth) in the working-class area of Nottingham, *The Loneliness of the Long-Distance Runner* invites us to see this district, and by extension, the class society *as* a prison. It is perhaps worth noting that the mentioned details are metonyms of the prison. However, these images do not fully shade off into metonymy proper because in these tropes, the imported item comes from a domain (the prison) which is, at least at first glance, utterly alien to that of the target domain (society or the world).

(f) Sixth, the *context* of a film may invite us to see one entity as another. For example, in *The Shawshank Redemption*, we are presented with an image of the escaped Andy in the rain shower. Since we have witnessed the brutal treatment he had to endure in prison, it is obvious that the rain shower is not just physical, that it additionally involves a process of redemption.

(g) Finally, cinematic metaphors can also emerge from the *superimposition* of two distinct images. For instance, the film *Wilde* presents us with a sequence in which prisoners working on the treadwheel are superimposed over the machine's cogwheels. This superimposition invites us to see the hard-working prisoners *as* turning cogwheels.

Thus, various ways exist in which films may evoke metaphorical readings. From a purely theoretical perspective, films can of course employ all types of metaphor. However, it is worth noting that certain metaphors do not occur in film. For example, no film codes the prison as a greenhouse. Maybe only extremely experimental cinematic ventures use such metaphors. In any case, the absence of certain metaphors in film does certainly not correlate with limitations of the medium but perhaps with viewer expectations: most viewers seem to expect realism and verisimilitude.

(4) While Paul Mason thinks that prison films emphasize the "effect" of the "prison experience [...] on inmates" ("The Screen" 291), I argue that this can be done much more effectively by first-person novels that allow us direct access to the thoughts, feelings, and motivations of prisoners. One advantage of prison novels is that they allow us to witness internal processes like the identity constructions which the prison initiates in the inmate. A very important facet of these constructions concerns the oscillating between hope and resignation. The prison experience usually creates split personalities. These consist of a hopeful prison self (that tries to resist the prison) on the one hand, and an 'institutionalized' and hopeless prison self (that has internalized the prison) on the other. Newcomers usually try to resist the internalization of the prison, which subsumes their former self, by distancing themselves from the 'other' prisoners who are perceived as 'real' criminals. More specifically, the newcomers construct themselves as heterosexual, educated, and civilized 'exceptions,' while the other prisoners are represented as homosexual perverts, primitive, and uncivilized country bumpkins, or truly vicious criminals who will never be rehabilitated.

Furthermore, the first-person accounts I have discussed illustrate that prisoners may internalize the prison and become mentally confined. By contrast, in saints' legends and Romantic poetry, we frequently come across the so-called 'freedom of the mind' trope. From this perspective, the walls of the prison may be physically impenetrable but they can be overcome by the free mind, i.e., active efforts at transcendence. Prison narratives of the nineteenth and twentieth centuries, by contrast, illustrate that the prison institution may gain power over the prisoner's mind and his identity constructions. In other words, the prisoner's former identity is frequently subsumed by his prison identity. Philip Collins refers to the case of a German prisoner on whom Dickens expended much sympathy. This prisoner was released after an inhumane period of time but at one point after his release desperately "rang the bell on the prison gate and begged to be allowed to come inside to die" (*Dickens* 51). In the light of first-person narratives that illustrate how the prison affects its inmates and their identities, this should come as no surprise.

One advantage of prison films is their visual concreteness. Prison films can confront us with extremely detailed images of the prison architecture, i.e., the cells of the inmates, the prison yard, the mess hall, the observation towers, the isolation unit, the warden's office, and so forth. Furthermore, they frequently use real prison locations and occasionally we see real prisoners, prison officers, and wardens on the screen. Also, according to Rafter, "about half of all traditional prison movies assert that they are 'based on a true story' or are 'fictionalized accounts of an actual event.'" She concludes that "no other genre so loudly proclaims its verisimilitude" (127). Even though films could use actual inmates, most prison films confront us with at least one superstar with whom we are supposed to identify. And by presenting us with representatives of cool masculinity (such as Paul Muni, Burt Lancaster, Paul Newman, Malcolm McDowell, Steve McQueen, Clint Eastwood, or Tim Robbins) they clearly distort the realities of penal practise. Another disadvantage of films is of course that they cannot present us with a character's thoughts, feelings, and motivations in the way fictional literature can. Hence, prison movies usually use external features to simulate the prisoners' internal states. Examples are facial expressions or submissive bodily positions but also cool colors, lugubrious sounds, and shabby prison uniforms, all of which allude to the dereliction of the new inmate's self-image. Furthermore, prison films often use static and claustrophobic shots of the prison's interior to convey a feeling of enclosed space. Also, they use low-angle shots of imposing towers or prison officers to accentuate the prisoner's feeling of being dominated by the prison system.

An interesting cinematic way of simulating interiority is offered in Edzard's film adaptation of *Little Dorrit.* The camera cuts across the distinction between internal and external focalization. We see the world from a third-person perspective but we perceive it in the way in which a character sees the world. This technique can perhaps be classified as a filmic version of free indirect discourse. More recent films like *Fight Club* (1999) and *A Beautiful Mind* (2001) carry this technique further and present us with unreliable forms of free indirect discourse. More specifically, they treat us to images of the world as it is experienced by schizophrenic characters. We appear to be presented with an external perspective while we simultaneously share the major character's deranged vision, i.e., his 'wrong' image of the world. Only gradually do we realize that certain characters do not really exist, and that certain events did not actually take place.

This takes me to literary history, i.e., the ways in which Dickens anticipates prison narratives of the twentieth century. The authorial novels *Little Dorrit* and *A Tale of Two Cities* anticipate the representation of the prison experience in prison films, whereas the embedded first-person accounts in these novels and the pseudo-autobiography *Great Expectations* foreshadow prison novels of the twentieth century, many of which are written from the perspective of a first-person narrator. Prison novels of the twentieth century abandon the authorial mode and, by concentrating on the interiority of the prisoner, focus on the ways in which he internalizes the prison. The first-person novel *Great Expectations*, in which the prison has been interiorized by almost all the characters (including the guilt-ridden first-person narrator Pip), serves as an important link between nineteenth-century fiction and prison novels of the twentieth century. Many more recent prison novels conform with the narrative situation of *Great Expectations*. They are also written from the perspective of a first-person narrator and present us with a mind's self-observation, thus allowing us access to the narrator's thoughts and feelings.[2] In this context, it is also worth noting that some newer prison novels are reflector-mode narratives which familiarize us with the internal processes of imprisoned characters.[3] These first-person and reflector-mode novels replace Dickens' panoramic vistas with narrower visions or interior movements.

Even though Dickens' novels are not inherently cinematic, a fundamental continuity connects the themes and techniques of his novels and twentieth-century prison movies. Dickens' prison novels and prison films of the twentieth century usually share the following thematic elements: (a) they deal extensively with the disciplinary space of the prison and its consequences, and frequently represent the prison experience by using metaphors of imprisonment; (b) the prison is usually depicted as being like society so that certain societal eccentricities are reproduced in prison; (c) people in the 'free' world are sometimes represented as criminals so that society becomes a prison (or a society of criminals).

Striking affinities also exist between the modes of narration of Dickens' novels and the cinematic techniques of prison movies. Prison films continue the panoramic vistas of Dickens' authorial novels. Both Dickens' mature fiction and prison films of the twentieth century present us with rather detailed descriptions of prisons and represent the prison and its inmates from a third-person perspective. Furthermore, both Dickens' novels and twentieth-century prison films tend to focus on the human face with its grimaces, frowns and innumerable tics to simulate interiority. Also, the vivid awareness of detail and the attempt to visualize internal states or ethical countenance by way of external features (like facial expressions, bodily positions, clothing, the behavior of characters) or the bleak atmosphere of environments is a trademark of Dickens and prison movies.

Despite these similarities, important differences exist, and the most important one concerns the ideological underpinnings of these narratives. Dickens' mature fiction idealizes and sentimentalizes his prisoners by arguing that they are innocent victims of an unjust society, and ignores the fact that vicious criminals may exist. Prison narratives of the twentieth century, on the other hand, are primarily sadomasochistic fantasies for members of the white and heterosexual middle class that allow them to vicariously experience (and perhaps also enjoy) processes of degradation, dehumanization, and victimization in an exotic setting from the safety of their homes. Luckily enough, at the end of such fantasies, everything is back to normal. The recipients and their identificatory figures are free, while their Others, i.e., the 'truly guilty' colored and homosexual inmates are still incarcerated. And average viewers will not care about these 'deviant' individuals because they only identified with the 'poor' prisoner-hero anyway. Also, they are led to believe that brutal prison systems no longer exist because they have seen that these disciplinary institutions can become more progressive regimes. Prison narratives of the twentieth century do not only tell us that we need prisons because criminals exist. They also encourage ignorance of real prisons by suggesting that penal reform has already taken (or will soon take) place. Finally, they tell us that the 'real' criminals who have to be incarcerated in these allegedly so well-run institutions are colored or homosexual. Hence, they are openly racist and homophobic forms of pro-prison propaganda.

Endnotes

1. By contrast, most prison films about female prisoners construct the prison as a cultural space that allows women to deconstruct traditional gender roles. Female inmates often leave the prison as 'male' or 'masculine' women. Halberstam points out that in women-in-prison films like *Caged*, *Bad Girls' Dormitory* (1985) or *Caged Heat*, innocent women "enter prison as young ingenues but leave as street tough dykes" (202). Similarly, Walters notes that in such movies, "kick-ass women are both glamorized and contextualized; their strength and power is key to their liberation from the forces of patriarchal darkness that keep them submissive. Patriarchal wrongdoing, indeed, often provides the motivation for the violence in the first place, so that female violence is seen as morally justified (as well as sexy)" (106–7).
2. Apart from the examples I have discussed, one could mention Brendan Behan's *Borstal Boy* (1958); Norman Mailer's "The Killer: A Story" (1967); Chester Himes' *Cast the First Stone* (1972); J.M. Coetzee's *Waiting for the Barbarians* (1980); Jeanette Turner Hospital's "The Inside Story" (1987); Nayantara Sahgal's *Mistaken Identity* (1988); John Banville's *The Book of Evidence* (1989); Agnes Sam's "Sunflowers" (1989); Margaret Atwood's *Alias Grace* (1996); and Frederic Berthoff's "The Cupola" (2002). Nadine Gordimer's *Burger's Daughter* (1979) contains long stretches of interior monologue which familiarize us with the identity problems of the imprisoned Rosa Burger, and John Edgar Wideman's *Brothers and Keepers* (1985) is a first-person account about the narrator's imprisoned brother Robert. Furthermore, many prisoner autobiographies were written in the twentieth century. Important examples are Malcolm Little's *The Autobiography of Malcolm X* (1966); Jimmy Boyle's *A Sense of Freedom* (1977); Jack Henry Abbott's *In the Belly of the Beast* (1981); Breyten Breytenbach's *The True Confessions of an Albino Terrorist* (1984); Mumia Abu-Jamal's *Live from Death Row* (1995); and Leonard Peltier's *Prison Writings: My Life is My Sun Dance* (1999).
3. The term reflector-mode narrative roughly corresponds to the novel of consistent internal focalization. More specifically, in Stanzel's figural

narrative situation (1984: 59), i.e., in reflector-mode narratives, the narrative agency remains covert and the story is presented 'through the eyes' of a reflector character. Examples of reflector-mode prison narratives are Langston Hughes' "On the Road" (1935); Arthur Koestler's *Darkness at Noon* (1941); Vladimir Nabokov's *Invitation to a Beheading* (1959); Stanley Elkin's *A Bad Man* (1965); John Cheever's *Falconer* (1975); Norman Mailer's *The Executioner's Song* (1979); and Angela Carter's *Nights at the Circus* (1984).

Bibliography

Primary Texts

Prison Novels and Autobiographies

Anon. *Five Years' Penal Servitude: By One Who Has Endured It*. London: Richard Bentley and Son, 1877.

Abbott, Jack Henry. *In the Belly of the Beast*. With an Introduction by Norman Mailer. New York: Vintage Books, 1981.

Abu-Jamal, Mumia. *Live from Death Row*. New York: Avon, 1995.

Archer, Jeffrey. *A Prison Diary. Volume I: Hell*. London: Macmillan and Pan, 2003.

Atwood, Margaret. *Alias Grace*. London: Bloomsbury, 1996.

Balfour, Jabez Spencer. *My Prison Life*. London: Chapman and Hall, 1907.

Banville, John. *The Book of Evidence* [1945]. London: Secker and Warburg, 1989.

Behan, Brendan. *Borstal Boy* [1958]. London: Corgi Books, 1970.

Berthoff, Frederic. "The Cupola." *Genre* 35.3/4 (2002): 521–35.

Boyle, Jimmy. *A Sense of Freedom*. Basingstoke and London: Pan Books, 1977.

Braly, Malcolm. *On the Yard*. Boston: Little Brown, 1967.

Breytenbach, Breyten. *The True Confessions of an Albino Terrorist*. London and Boston: Faber and Faber, 1984.

Brontë, Charlotte. *Villette* [1853]. Ed. Herbert Rosengarten. Oxford: Clarendon Press, 1987.

Bruce, J. Campbell. *Escape from Alcatraz: Farewell to the Rock*. New York: McGraw-Hill, 1963.

Bunker, Edward. *The Animal Factory*. New York: Viking, 1977.

Burgess, Anthony. *A Clockwork Orange* [1962]. Stuttgart: Reclam, 1996.

Burns, Robert E. *I Am a Fugitive from a Georgia Chain Gang!* [1932]. Athens and London: Brown Thrasher Books. The University of Georgia Press, 1997.

Burns, Vincent, ed. *Female Convict*. New York: The Vanguard Press, 1934.

Carcaterra, Lorenzo. *Sleepers*. New York: Ballantine Books, 1995.

Carter, Angela. *Nights at the Circus*. London: Chatto and Windus, 1984.

Cheever, John. *Falconer*. New York: Knopf, 1975.

Coetzee, J.M. *Waiting for the Barbarians* [1980]. Harmondsworth: Penguin, 1982.

Collins, Wilkie. *Armadale* [1866]. Ed. with an introduction by Catherine Peters. Oxford: Oxford University Press, 1989.

Dickens, Charles. *Dombey and Son* [1847–48]. Ed. Alan Horsman. Oxford: Clarendon, 1974.

———. *Great Expectations* [1860–61]. Ed. Janice Carlisle. Boston, New York: Bedford Books, 1996.

———. *Little Dorrit* [1855–57]. Ed. Stephen Wall and Helen Small. London: Penguin, 1998.

———. *A Tale of Two Cities* [1859]. Ed. Richard Maxwell. London: Penguin, 2000.

Eliot, George. *Adam Bede* [1859]. Ed. Carol A. Martin. Oxford: Clarendon, 2001.

Elkin, Stanley. *A Bad Man*. New York: Dutton, 1965.

Gaddis, Thomas E. *Birdman of Alcatraz. The Story of Robert Stroud* [1955]. With an Epilogue by Phyllis E. Gaddis. San Francisco: Comstock Editions, 1989.

Galsworthy, John. "The Prisoner [1925]." *Caravan: The Assembled Tales of John Galsworthy*. Heinemann: London, 1963. 365–70.

Gordimer, Nadine. *Burger's Daughter* [1979]. London: Jonathan Cape, 1980.

Himes, Chester. *Cast the First Stone*. New York: New American Library, 1972.

Hospital, Janette Turner. "The Inside Story." *Dislocations*. Baton Rouge and London: Louisiana State University Press, 1987. 33–42.

Hughes, Langston. "On the Road [1935]." *Short Stories: Langston Hughes*. New York: Hill and Wang, 1996. 90–100.

Johnston, James A. *Alcatraz Island Prison*. New York and London: Charles Scribner's Sons, 1949.

King, Stephen. "Rita Hayworth and Shawshank Redemption [1982]." *Different Seasons*. New York: Warner Books, 1995. 9–113.

———. *The Green Mile*. 6 Vols. New York: Signet, 1996.

Koestler, Arthur. *Darkness at Noon*. Trans. by Daphne Hardy. New York: Macmillan, 1941.

Little, Malcolm. *The Autobiography of Malcolm X*. Ed. Alex Haley. New York: Grove Press, 1966.

Mailer, Norman. "The Killer: A Story." *Cannibals and Christians*. London: Andre Deutsch, 1967. 222–27.

———. *The Executioner's Song*. Boston and Toronto: Little, Brown and Company, 1979.

Nabokov, Vladimir. *Invitation to a Beheading*. Trans. by Dmitri Nabokov. London: Weidenfeld and Nicolson, 1959.

Oates, Joyce Carol. "A Legacy." *By the North Gate*. New York: Vanguard, 1961. 164–79.

O' Brien, Edna V. *So I Went to Prison*. New York: Stokes, 1938.

Peltier, Leonard. *Prison Writings: My Life is My Sun Dance*. Ed. Harvey Arden. New York, NY: St. Martin' s, 1999.

Reade, Charles. *It Is Never Too Late to Mend*. London: Chatto and Windus, 1895.

Sahgal, Nayantara. *Mistaken Identity*. Heinemann: London, 1988.

Sam, Agnes. "Sunflowers." *Jesus is Indian and Other Stories*. London: The Women's Press, 1989. 64–69.

Sillitoe, Alan. "The Loneliness of the Long-Distance Runner [1959]." *The Loneliness of the Long-Distance Runner*. London: W.H. Allen, 1969. 7–54.

Wideman, John Edgar. *Brothers and Keepers*. New York: Penguin Books, 1985.

Films (in chronological order; non-prison films [*] and British prison films are marked)

I Am a Fugitive from a Chain Gang. Dir. Mervyn LeRoy. Warner Bros., 1932.

20,000 Years in Sing Sing. Dir. Michael Curtiz. First National/Warner Bros., 1932.

Sing Sing Nights. Dir. Lew Collins. Monogram, 1935.

A Tale of Two Cities. Dir. Jack Conway. Metro-Goldwyn-Mayer, 1935.

Jailbreak. Dir. Nick Grinde. Warner Bros., 1936.

The Prisoner of Shark Island. Dir. John Ford. Twentieth-Century-Fox, 1936.

Alcatraz Island. Dir. William McGann. Warner Bros., 1937.

San Quentin. Dir. Lloyd Bacon. Warner Bros., 1937.

Convict 99. Dir. Marcel Varnel. Gainsborough, 1938. [British]

King of Alcatraz. Dir. Robert Florey. Paramount Pictures, 1938.

Over the Wall. Dir. Francis McDonald. Warner Bros., 1938.

Prison Break. Dir. Arthur Lubin. Universal, 1938.

Blackwell's Island. Dir. William McGann. Warner Bros., 1939.

Invisible Stripes. Dir. Lloyd Bacon. Warner Bros., 1939.

Those High Grey Walls. Dir. Charles Vidor. Columbia, 1939.

Castle on the Hudson (UK: *Years Without Days*). Dir. Anatole Litvak. Warner Bros., 1940.

Devil's Island. Dir. William Clemens. Warner Bros., 1940.

The House Across the Bay. Dir. Archie Mayo. United Artists, 1940.

Passport to Alcatraz. Dir. Lewis D. Collins. Columbia, 1940.

Men of San Quentin. Dir. William Beaudine. Producers Releasing Corp., 1942.

Seven Miles from Alcatraz. Dir. Edward Dmytryk. RKO Radios, 1942.

Road to Alcatraz. Dir. Nick Grindé. Republic Pictures Corporation, 1945.

Gilda. Dir. Charles Vidor. Columbia, 1946. [*]

Great Expectations. Dir. David Lean. Cineguild – Independent Producers, 1946. [British]

San Quentin. Dir. Gordon M. Douglas. RKO Radio, 1946.

Boys in Brown. Dir. Montgomery Tully. Gainsborough Pictures, 1948. [British]

Train to Alcatraz. Dir. Philip Ford. Republic Pictures Corporation, 1948.

Caged. Dir. John Cromwell. Warner Bros., 1949.

Now Barabbas was a Robber. Dir. Gordon Parry. Teddington Studios and Warner Bros., 1949. [British]

Experiment Alcatraz. Dir. Edward L. Cahn. RKO, 1950.

Inside the Walls of Folsom Prison. Dir. Crane Wilbur. Warner Bros., 1951.

Duffy of San Quentin. Dir. Walter Doninger. Warner Bros., 1954.

Riot in Cell Block Eleven. Dir. Don Siegel. Allied Artists, 1954.

The Steel Cage. Dir. Walter Doninger. United Artists, 1954.

Cell 2455 – Death Row. Dir. Fred F. Sears. Columbia, 1955.

Yield to the Night (US: *Blonde Sinner*). Dir. J. Lee-Thompson. ABP, 1956. [British]

Escape from San Quentin. Dir. Fred F. Sears. Columbia, 1957.

The Criminal. Dir. Joseph Losey. Anglo Amalgamated Film Distributors Ltd., 1960. [British]

Two Way Stretch. Dir. Robert Day. British Lion, 1960. [British]

Birdman of Alcatraz. Dir. John Frankenheimer. United Artists, 1962.

The Pot Carriers. Dir. Peter Graham Scott. Associated British, 1962.

The Quare Fellow. Dir. Arthur Dreifuss. British Lion and Bryanston, 1962. [British]

Reprieve (UK: *Convicts Four*). Dir. Millard Kaufman. Allied Artists, 1962.

The Loneliness of the Long Distance Runner. Dir. Tony Richardson. British Lion and Bryanston, 1964. [British]

Cool Hand Luke. Dir. Stuart Rosenberg. Warner Bros. and Seven Arts, 1967.

Riot. Dir. Buzz Kulik. Paramount, 1968.

A Clockwork Orange. Dir. Stanley Kubrick. Warner Bros., 1971. [British]

Papillon. Dir. Franklin J. Schaffner. Columbia Pictures, 1973.

Caged Heat. Dir. Jonathan Demme. New World, 1974.

Leadbelly. Dir. Gordon Parks Sr. Paramount, 1976.

Kill Me If You Can. Dir. Buzz Kulik. Columbia, 1977.

Midnight Express. Dir. Alan Parker. Columbia, 1978.

Escape from Alcatraz. Dir. Don Siegel. Paramount, 1979.

Penitentiary I. Dir. Jamaa Fanaka. Jerry Gross, 1979.

Porridge. Dir. Dick Clement. Black Lion Films, 1979. [British]

Scum. Dir. Alan Clarke. Berwyn Street Films, 1979. [British]

Alcatraz. The Whole Shocking Story. Dir. Paul Krasny. NBC-TV, 1980.

Brubaker. Dir. Stuart Rosenberg. Twentieth-Century-Fox, 1980.

McVicar. Dir. Tom Clegg. Polytel and Brent Walker, 1980. [British]

A Sense of Freedom. Dir. John Mackenzie. Scottish TV, 1981. [British]

The Sin Bin. Dir. John Gorrie. BBC TV, 1981. [British]

Penitentiary II. Dir. Jamaa Fanaka. Metro-Goldwyn-Mayer and United Artists, 1982.

Scrubbers. Dir. Mai Zetterling. Hand Made Films, 1982. [British]

Women of San Quentin. Dir. William Graham. NBC-TV, 1983.

Bad Girls' Dormitory. Dir. Tim Kincaid. Films Around the World, 1985.

Knockback. Dir. Piers Haggard. BBC-TV, 1985. [British]

Down by Law. Dir. Jim Jarmusch. Island, 1986.

Penitentiary III. Dir. Jamaa Fanaka. Cannon, 1987.

Little Dorrit. Part I: Nobody's Fault. Dir. Christine Edzard. Sands Film, 1987. [British]

Little Dorrit. Part II: Little Dorrit's Story. Dir. Christine Edzard. Sands Film, 1987. [British]

Malcolm X. Dir. Spike Lee. Largo International N.V., 1991.

Silent Scream. Dir. David Hayman. Antonine with the Assistance of The Scottish Film Production Fund, 1991. [British]

Alien III. Dir. David Fincher. Twentieth-Century Fox, 1992.

Death and the Maiden. Dir. Roman Polanski. Capitol Films, 1994.

The Shawshank Redemption. Dir. Frank Darabont. Castle Rock Entertainment, 1994.

Convict Cowboy. Dir. Rod Holcomb. Metro-Goldwyn-Mayer and United Artists, 1995.

Dead Man Walking. Dir. Tim Robbins. Working Title and Havoc, 1995.

Murder in the First. Dir. Marc Rocco. Le Studio Canal +, 1995.

The Chamber. Dir. James Foley. Universal Pictures, 1996.

Last Dance. Dir. Bruce Beresford. Touchstone Pictures, 1996.

The Rock. Dir. Michael Bay. Hollywood Pictures, 1996.

Sleepers. Dir. Barry Levinson. Propaganda Films and Baltimore Pictures, 1996.

Con Air. Dir. Simon West. Touchstone Pictures, 1997.

Wilde. Dir. Brian Gilbert. Samuelson Entertainment et al., 1997.

American History X . Dir. Tony Kaye. New Line Cinema, 1998.

Fight Club. Dir. David Fincher. Twentieth-Century-Fox, 1999. [*]

The Green Mile. Dir. Frank Darabont. Universal, 1999.

True Crime. Dir. Clint Eastwood. Warner Bros., 1999.

New Alcatraz. Dir. Phillip Roth. Cell Block Productions, 2000.

Stonehouse Reunion. Dir. Tony Johnson. Blunt Productions, 2000. [British]

A Beautiful Mind. Dir. Ron Howard. Universal, 2001. [*]

Stranger Inside. Dir. Cheryl Dunye. C-Hundred Film, HBO, and Stranger Baby, 2001.

Half Past Dead. Dir. Don Michael Paul. Screen Gems et al., 2002.

Secondary Literature

Anon. "Bird Man of Alcatraz." *Monthly Film Bulletin* 29.344 (1962): 122–23.

Adams, Robert, and Jo Campling. *Prison Riots in Britain and the USA*. New York: St. Martin's Press, 1992.

Alber, Jan. "Das Gefängnis im Hollywoodfilm: Strafvollzug zwischen Fiktion und Realität." *Zeitschrift für Strafvollzug und Straffälligenhilfe* 52.1 (2003): 31–40.

———. "Bodies Behind Bars: The Disciplining of the Prisoner's Body in British and American Prison Movies." *In the Grip of the Law. Prisons, Trials and the Space Between.* Ed. Monika Fludernik and Greta Olson. Frankfurt: Peter Lang, 2004. 241–69.

Albrecht, Hans-Jörg, Telemach Serassis, and Harald Kania, eds. *Images of Crime I: Representations of Crime and the Criminal in Politics, Society, the Media, and the Arts.* Freiburg: edition iuscrim, 2001.

———, eds. *Images of Crime II: Representations of Crime and the Criminal in Politics, Society, the Media, and the Arts.* Freiburg: edition iuscrim, 2004.

Alford, C. Fred. "What Would it Matter if Everything Foucault Said about Prison Were Wrong? *Discipline and Punish* after Twenty Years." *Theory and Society* 29 (2000): 125–46.

Altman, Rick. "Dickens, Griffith, and Film Theory Today." *Silent Film.* Ed. Richard Abel. New Brunswick, NJ: Rutgers University Press, 1996. 145–62.

Amnesty International. *USA. Hüter der Menschenrechte?* Bonn: Amnesty International, 1998.

Andrew, Dudley. *Concepts in Film Theory.* Oxford: Oxford University Press, 1984.

Armstrong, Richard B., and Mary Willems Armstrong, eds. *Encyclopedia of Film Themes, Settings and Series.* Jefferson, NC and London: McFarland, 2001.

Arnheim, Rudolf. *Film.* Trans. Louise Marie Sieveking and Ian F.D. Morrow. London: Faber and Faber, 1933.

Arnold, Frank. "Sleepers." *epd Film* 2 (1997): 42.

Bal, Mieke. "Notes on Narrative Embedding." *Poetics Today* 2.2 (1981): 41–59.

———. *Narratology. Introduction to the Theory of Narrative* [1985]. Second Edition. Toronto: University of Toronto Press, 1997.

Bammann, Kai. "Orte der Bestrafung. Wo Hollywood seine Verbrecher hinschickt und warum dies weit weniger Science-fiction ist, als es auf den ersten Blick scheint." *Zeitschrift für Strafvollzug und Straffälligenhilfe* 4 (2001): 233–38.

Bankston, Douglas. "Wrap Shot." *American Cinematographer* 80.12 (1999): 144.

Barman, Satyabhushan. *The English Borstal System: A Study in the Treatment of Young Offenders.* London: P.S. King and Son, 1934.

Baston, Jane. "Word and Image: The Articulation and Visualization of Power in *Great Expectations*." *Literature/Film Quarterly* 24.3 (1996): 322–31.

Bates, Sanford. *Prisons and Beyond.* New York: The Macmillan Company, 1938.

Baudry, Jean-Louis. "Ideological Effects of the Basic Cinematographic Apparatus [1974–75]." *Film Theory and Criticism. Introductory Readings*. Eds. Leo Braudy and Marshall Cohen. Oxford: Oxford University Press, 1980. 345–55.

Bauer, Erik. "Stephen King's Other Half. Interview with Frank Darabont." *Creative Screenwriting* 4.2 (1997): 3–16.

Baumgarten, Murray. "Writing the Revolution." *Dickens Studies Annual* 12 (1983): 161–76.

———. "Fictions of the City." *The Cambridge Companion to Charles Dickens*. Ed. John O. Jordan. Cambridge: Cambridge University Press, 2001. 106–19.

Beattie, John M. *Crime and the Courts in England 1660–1800*. Princeton, NJ: Princeton University Press, 1986.

Beaver, Frank E. *Dictionary of Film Terms. The Aesthetic Companion to Film*. New York: Twayne Publishers, 1994.

Beccaria, Cesare. *An Essay on Crimes and Punishments* [1767]. Second Edition. Boston: International Pocket Library, 1992.

Becker, Jörg. "Gefängnisbilder: Die Entlassung – Der Besuch." *Filmgeschichte* 15 (2001): 51–56.

Becker-Kavan, Ingo. *Alcatraz: Ein Synonym für Abschreckung*. Würzburg: Königshausen und Neumann, 1998.

Bender, John. *Imagining the Penitentiary. Fiction and the Architecture of Mind in Eighteenth-Century England*. Chicago, London: The University of Chicago Press, 1987.

———. "Making the World Safe for Narratology." *New Literary History* 26 (1995): 29–33.

Bentham, Jeremy. *The Panopticon Writings*. Ed. with Introduction by Miran Bozovic. London and New York: Verso, 1995.

Bialkowski, Brian. "Facing Up the Question of Fidelity: The Example of *A Tale of Two Cities*." *Literature/Film Quarterly* 29.3 (2001): 203–9.

Biressi, Anita. *Crime, Fear and the Law in True Crime Stories*. Houndmills: Palgrave, 2001.

Black, Barbara. "A Sisterhood of Rage and Beauty: Dickens' Rosa Dartle, Miss Wade, and Madame Defarge." *Dickens Studies Annual* 26 (1998): 91–106.

Black, David A. "Genette and Film: Narrative Level in the Fiction Cinema." *Wide Angle* 8.3–4 (1986): 19–26.

Black, David A. "Narrative." *Critical Dictionary of Film and Television Theory*. Ed. Roberta E. Pearson and Philip Simpson. London and New York: Routledge, 2001. 300–3.

Blandford, Steven, Barry Keith Grant, and Jim Hillier. *The Film Studies Dictionary*. London: Arnold, 2001.

Blaydes, Sophia B. and Philip Bordinat. "Blake's 'Jerusalem' and Popular Culture." *Literature/Film Quarterly* 11.4 (1983): 211–14.

Bluestone, George. *Novels into Film* [1957]. Berkeley and Los Angeles: University of California Press, 1973.

Bonta, James, and Paul Gendreau. "Reexamining the Cruel and Unusual Punishment of Prison Life [1990]." *Prison Violence in America*. Ed. Michael C. Braswell, Reid H. Montgomery, and Lucien X. Lombardo. Second Edition. Cincinnati, Ohio: Anderson, 1994. 39–68.

Booth, Wayne C. *The Rhetoric of Fiction*. Chicago: University of Chicago Press, 1961.

Bordwell, David. *Narration in the Fiction Film*. London: Routledge, 1985.

———. *Making Meaning. Inference and Rhetoric in the Interpretation of Cinema*. Cambridge, Mass.: Harvard University Press, 1989.

Bordwell, David, and Kristin Thompson. *Film Art. An Introduction*. Seventh edition. New York: McGraw Hill, 2003.

Branigan, Edward. *Point of View in the Cinema. A Theory of Narration and Subjectivity in Classical Film*. Berlin et al: Mouton, 1984.

——— *Narrative Comprehension and Film*. London and New York: Routledge, 1992.

Braswell, Michael C., Reid H. Montgomery, and Lucien X. Lombardo. *Prison Violence in America*. Second Edition. Cincinnati, Ohio: Anderson, 1994.

Braudy, Leo, and Marshall Cohen, eds. *Film Theory and Criticism. Introductory Readings*. Oxford: Oxford University Press, 1999.

Brodie, Allan, Jane Croom and James O' Davies. *English Prisons. An Architectural History*. Swindon: English Heritage, 2002.

Brombert, Victor. *The Romantic Prison: The French Tradition* [1975]. Princeton: Princeton University Press, 1978.

Brooks, Peter. "Repetition, Repression, and Return: The Plotting of *Great Expectations*." *Great Expectations*. Ed. Janice Carlisle. Boston, New York: Bedford Books, 1996. 481–501.

Brown, Carolyn. "'Great Expectations' : Masculinity and Modernity." *English and Cultural Studies*. Ed. Michael Green. London: Murray, 1987. 60–74.

Bryans, Shane, and David Wilson. *The Prison Governor: Theory and Practice* [1998]. Aylesbury, Bucks: Prison Service Journal, 2000.

Buckland, Warren, ed. *The Film Spectator: From Sign to Mind*. Amsterdam: Amsterdam University Press, 1995.

Buffard, Simone. *Le froid pénitentiaire: l'impossible réforme des prisons*. Paris: Editions du Seuil, 1973.

Büssing, Sabine. *Of Captive Queens and Holy Panthers. Prison Fiction and Male Homoerotic Experience*. Frankfurt: Lang, 1990.

Byars, John. "The Initiation of Alan Sillitoe's Long-Distance Runner." *Modern Fiction Studies* 22.4 (1976–77): 584–91.

Callahan, Lisa A. "Sing Sing Prison." *Encyclopedia of American Prisons*. Ed. Marilyn D. McShane and Frank R. Williams III. London and New York: Garland, 1996. 443–46.

Campbell, Russell. "I Am a Fugitive from a Chain Gang." *The Velvet Light Trap Review of Cinema* 1 (1971): 17–20.

Canby, Vincent. Rev. of *Little Dorrit*. *New York Times* 26 (1988): 11.

Caramango, Thomas Carmelo. "The Dickens Revival at the Bijou: Critical Reassessment, Film Theory and Popular Culture." *New Orleans Review* 15 (1988): 88–96.

Carlisle, Janice. "A Critical History of *Great Expectations*." *Great Expectations*. Ed. Janice Carlisle. Boston, New York: Bedford Books, 1996. 445–62.

Carnochan, W.B. *Confinement and Flight. An Essay on English Literature of the Eighteenth Century*. Berkeley: University of California Press, 1977.

———. "The Literature of Confinement." *The Oxford History of the Prison. The Practice of Punishment in Western Society*. Ed. Norval Morris and David J. Rothman. New York and Oxford: Oxford University Press, 1995. 427–55.

Carroll, Noël. "Visual Metaphor." *Aspects of Metaphor*. Ed. Jaakko Hintikka. Dordrecht: Kluwer, 1994. 189–213.

———. "A Note on Film Metaphor." *Theorizing the Moving Image*. Cambridge: Cambridge University Press, 1996. 212–23.

Cassetti, Francesco. *Inside the Gaze: The Fiction Film and its Spectator*. Trans. by Nell Andrew with Charles O' Brien. Bloomington, IN: Indiana University Press, 1998.

Champion, Dean J. "The Progressive Era." *Encyclopedia of American Prisons*. Ed. Marilyn D. McShane and Frank R. Williams III. London and New York: Garland, 1996. 237–39.

Chapman, James. "'A Bit of the Old Ultra-Violence.'" *British Science Fiction Cinema*. Ed. I.Q. Hunter. London and New York: Routledge, 1999. 128–37.

Chatman, Seymour. *Story and Discourse. Narrative Structure in Fiction and Film*. Ithaca, NY and London: Cornell University Press, 1978.

———. "What Novels Can Do That Films Can't (and Vice Versa)." *Critical Inquiry* 7.1 (1980): 121–40.

———. *Coming to Terms. The Rhetoric of Narrative in Fiction and Film*. Ithaca, NY and London: Cornell University Press, 1990.

———. "New Directions in Voice-Narrated Cinema." *Narratologies: New Perspectives on Narrative Analysis*. Ed. David Herman. Columbus: Ohio State University Press, 1999. 315–39.

Cheatwood, Derral. "Prison Movies: Films about Adult, Male, Civilian Prisons: 1929–1995." *Popular Culture, Crime, and Justice*. Ed. Frankie Y. Bailey and Donna C. Hale. Belmont et al.: Wadsworth, 1998. 209–31.

Chevigny, Bell Gale. *Doing Time: Twenty-Five Years of Prison Writing*. New York: Arcade Publishing, 1999.

———. "Writers with Convictions: Doing Time at Century's End." *Genre* 35.3/4 (2002): 495–509.

Chonco, N.R. "Sexual Assaults Among Male Inmates: A Descriptive Study." *The Prison Journal* 69 (1989): 72–82.

Churchill, Ward, and J.J. Vander Wall. *Cages of Steel. The Politics of Imprisonment in the United States*. Washington, DC: Maisonneuve Press, 1992.

Clark, John. "Barry Levinson. Baltimore's Favorite Son Takes on *Sleepers*, a Brutal Tale of Child Abuse and the Loyalty Between Friends." *Premiere* 10.3 (1996): 59–62.

Clay, Walter Lowe. *The Prison Chaplain: A Memoir of the Reverend John Clay, B.D., Late Chaplain of the Preston Gaol, with Selections from his Reports and Correspondence and a Sketch of Prison Discipline in England* [1861]. Montclair: Patterson Smith, 1969.

Clifton, N. Roy. *The Figure in Film*. Newark: University of Delaware Press, 1983.

Cockshut, A.O.J. "Prison Experiences in Dickens's Novels [1962]." *Readings on Charles Dickens*. Ed. Clarice Swisher. San Diego, CA: Greenhaven Press, 1998. 40–49.

Cohn, Dorrit. *Transparent Minds. Narrative Modes for Presenting Consciousness in Fiction*. Princeton, NJ: Princeton University Press, 1978.

———. "Optics and Power in the Novel." *New Literary History* 26 (1995): 3–20.

———. "Reply to John Bender and Mark Seltzer." *New Literary History* 26 (1995): 35–37.

Colatrella, Carol. "The Innocent Convict: Character, Reader Sympathy, and the Nineteenth Century Prison in *Little Dorrit*." *In the Grip of the Law. Prisons, Trials and the Space Between*. Ed. Monika Fludernik and Greta Olson. Frankfurt: Lang, 2004. 185–204.

Collins, Philip. *Dickens and Crime*. Cambridge Studies in Criminology Vol. XVII. Ed. L. Radzinowicz. London and New York: Macmillan and St. Martin's Press, 1962.

———. "A Tale of Two Novels: *A Tale of Two Cities* and *Great Expectations*." *Dickens Studies Annual* 2 (1972): 336–51.

———. "Little Dorrit: The Prison and the Critics." *TLS* (18 April 1980): 445–46.

Cooke, David J., Pamela J. Baldwin, and Jacqueline Howison. *Psychology in Prisons*. London and New York: Routledge, 1990.

Corrigan, Timothy. *Film and Literature: An Introduction and Reader*. New Jersey: Prentice Hall, 1999.

Craig, David. "The Crowd in Dickens." *The Changing World of Charles Dickens*. Ed. Robert Giddings. London: Vision and Barnes and Noble, 1983. 75–90.

Crouch, Ben M., and James W. Marquart. *An Appeal to Justice: Litigated Reform of Texas Prisons*. Austin, TX: University of Texas Press, 1989.

Crowther, Bruce. *Captured on Film: The Prison Movie*. London: Batsford, 1989.

Cullinan, John Thomas. "Anthony Burgess' *A Clockwork Orange*." *English Language Notes* 9 (1972): 287–92.

Dagrada, Elena. "The Diegetic Look. Pragmatics of the Point-of-View Shot." *The Film Spectator. From Sign to Mind*. Ed. Warren Buckland. Amsterdam: Amsterdam University Press, 1995. 236–49.

Daleski, H.M. "Large Loose Baggy Monsters and *Little Dorrit*." *Dickens Studies Annual* 21 (1992): 131–42.

Dante, Aligheri. *The Divine Comedy*. Text with Translation in the Metre of the Original by Geoffrey L. Bickersteth. Oxford: Shakespeare Head Press, 1965.

Dart, Peter. "Figurative Expression in Film." *Speech Monographs* 35 (1968): 170–74.

Davies, Ioan. *Writers in Prison*. Oxford: Blackwell, 1990.

Davis, Angela Yvonne. "Race, Gender, and Prison History: From the Convict Lease System to the Supermax Prison." *Prison Masculinities*. Ed. Don Sabo, Terry A. Kupers, and Willie London. Philadelphia: Temple University Press, 2001. 35–45.

Davis, Angela Yvonne, and Joy James. *The Angela Y. Davis Reader*. Malden, MA: Blackwell, 1998.

Davis, Laura. "Alcatraz Federal Penitentiary." *Encyclopedia of American Prisons*. Ed. Marilyn D. McShane and Frank R. Williams III. London and New York: Garland, 1996. 21–24.

Debona, Guerrie. "Doing Time; Undoing Time: Plot Mutation in David Lean's *Great Expectations*." *Literature/Film Quarterly* 20.1 (1992): 77–100.

Deleyto, Celestino. "Focalisation in Film Narrative [1991]." *Narratology*. Ed. Susana Onega and José Ángel García Landa. London and New York: Longman, 1996. 217– 33.

Depuy, Harry. "American Prisons and *A Tale of Two Cities*." *Cahiers Victoriens et Edouardiens* 25 (1987): 39–48.

DeRosia, Victoria R. *Living Inside Prison Walls. Adjustment Behavior.* Westport, Conneticut and London: Praeger, 1998.

Dickens, Charles. "In and Out of Jail." *Household Words* 7.164 (14 May 1853): 241–45.

———. "Philadelphia, and its Solitary Prison." *American Notes and Pictures from Italy.* London et al.: Oxford University Press, 1957. 97–111.

Dirks, Tim. "The Shawshank Redemption." <www.filmsite.org/shaw2.html>

Dixon, William Hepworth. *The London Prisons: With an Account of the More Distinguished Persons Who Have Been Confined in Them; to Which is Added a Description of the Chief Provincial Prisons* [1850]. Ed. Martin J. Wiener. Crime and Punishment in England, 1850–1922. New York and London: Garland, 1985.

Duncan, Martha Grace. *Romantic Outlaws, Beloved Prisons: The Unconscious Meanings of Crime and Punishment.* New York: New York University Press, 1996.

Edel, Leon. "Novel and Camera." *The Theory of the Novel: New Essays*. Ed. John Halperin. New York: Oxford University Press, 1974. 177–88.

Eisenstein, Sergei. *The Film Sense* [1942]. Trans. and ed. Jay Leyda. London: Faber, 1947.

———. *Film Form*. Trans. and ed. Jay Leyda. New York: Harcourt, Brace and World, 1949.

———. "Dickens, Griffith and Ourselves [Dickens, Griffith and Film Today [1942]." *Film Theory and Criticism. Introductory Readings*. Ed. Leo Braudy and Marshall Cohen. Oxford: Oxford University Press, 1999. 426–434.

Ek, Auli. *Race and Masculinity in Contemporary American Prison Narratives*. New York: Routledge, 2005.

Ekland-Olson, S., and W.R. Kelly. *Justice Under Pressure. A Comparison of Recidivism Patterns among four Successive Parolee Cohorts*. New York et al.: Springer, 1993.

Elliott, Kamilla. "Literary Film Adaptation and the Form-Content Dilemma." *Narrative Across Media: The Languages of Storytelling.* Ed. Marie-Laure Ryan. Lincoln and London: University of Nebraska Press, 2004. 220–43.

Ellmann, Richard. *Oscar Wilde*. London: Hamilton, 1987.

Elsässer, Thomas. "Screen Violence: Emotional Structure and Ideological Function in *A Clockwork Orange*." *Approaches to Popular Culture*. Ed. C.W.E. Bigsby. London: Arnold, 1976. 171–200.

Ericson, Richard V. et al. *Representing Order: Crime, Law And Justice in the News Media.* Milton Keynes: Open University Press, 1991.

Evans, Peter. *Prison Crisis*. Foreworded by Sir Robert Mark. London et al.: George Allen and Unwin, 1980.

Fell, John L. *Film and the Narrative Tradition* [1974]. Berkeley et al.: University of California Press, 1986.

Felperlin, Leslie. "Sleepers." *Sight and Sound* 7.1 (1997): 45–46.

Fisher, Bob. "*Murder in the First*. Probes Humanity's Dark Side. Cinematographer Fred Murphy and Director Marc Rocco Measure Man's Inhumanity to Man." *American Cinematographer* 76.5 (1995): 36–44.

Fitzgerald, Marian. "The Enemy. Rev. *Prison Gate*." *London Review of Books* (18 December 2003): 8–10.

Fitzgerald, Mike, and Joe Sim. *British Prisons*. Second Edition. Oxford: Basil Blackwell, 1982.

Fleishman, Avrom. *Narrated Films. Storytelling Situations in Cinema History*. Baltimore and London: The Johns Hopkins University Press, 1992.

Fludernik, Monika. *Towards a 'Natural' Narratology*. London and New York: Routledge, 1996.

———."Carceral Topography: Spatiality and Liminality in the Literary Prison." *Textual Practice* 13.1 (1999): 43–77.

———. "The Prison as Colonial Space." *Cycnos* 19.2 (2002): 175–90.

———. "The Prison as World - The World as Prison. Theoretical and Historical Aspects of Two Recurrent Topoi." *Symbolism* 3 (2003): 145–89.

———. "Caliban Revisited: Robben Island in the Autobiographical Record." *In the Grip of the Law. Prisons, Trials and the Space Between*. Ed. Monika Fludernik and Greta Olson. Frankfurt: Lang, 2004. 271–88.

———. "Fiction versus Reality: What is the Function of Prisons in Literary Texts?" *Images of Crime II. Representation of Crime and the Criminal in Politics, Society, the Media, and the Arts*. Eds. Hans-Jörg Albrecht, Telemach Serassis, and Harald Kania. Freiburg: edition iuscrim, 2004. 279–97.

———. "Prison Metaphors - The Carceral Imagery?" *In the Grip of the Law. Prisons, Trials and the Space Between*. Ed. Monika Fludernik and Greta Olson. Frankfurt: Lang, 2004. 145–67.

———. "Metaphorics and Metonymics of Carcerality: Reflections on Imprisonment as Source and Target Domain in Literary Texts." *English Studies* 86.3 (2005): 226–44.

———. "'Stone Walls Do (Not) a Prison Make' : Rhetorical Strategies and Sentimentalism in the Representation of the Victorian Prison Experience." *Captivating Subjects: Nineteenth-Century Writings by Prisoners, Slaves, and Captives*. Ed. Jason Haslam and Julia Wright. Toronto: University of Toronto Press, 2005. 144–74.

Fludernik, Monika, Donald C. Freeman, and Margaret Freeman. "Metaphor and Beyond: An Introduction." *Poetics Today* 20.3 (1999): 383–96.

Fludernik, Monika, and Greta Olson. "Introduction." *In the Grip of the Law. Prisons, Trials and the Space Between*. Ed. Monika Fludernik and Greta Olson. Frankfurt: Lang, 2004. xiii-liv.

Forceville, Charles. *Pictorial Metaphor in Advertising*. London and New York: Routledge, 1996.

———. "The Identification of Target and Source in Pictorial Metaphors." *Journal of Pragmatics* 34.1 (2001): 1–14.

Foster, John. "Review of *A Tale of Two Cities* [1859]." *Dickens. The Critical Heritage*. Ed. Philip Collins. London: Routledge and Kegan Paul, 1971. 424–26.

Foucault, Michel. "What is an Author? [1969]." *Language, Counter-Memory, Practice*. Ed. Donald F. Bouchard. Oxford: Blackwell, 1977. 113–38.

———. *Discipline and Punish. The Birth of the Prison* [1975]. Trans. by Alan Sheridan. New York: Vintage Books, 1979.

———. *Power – Knowledge. Selected Interviews and Other Writings 1972–1977*. Ed. Colin Gordon. Trans. by Colin Gordon et al. New York et al.: Prentice Hall, 1980.

———. "Of Other Spaces." *Diacritics* 16 (1986): 22–27.

———. *Politics, Philosophy, Culture. Interviews and Other Writings 1977–1984*. Ed. Lawrence D. Kritzman. Trans. by Alan Sheridan. New York, London: Routledge, 1988.

———. "Writing the Self." *Foucault and his Interlocutors*. Ed. Arnold I. Davidson. Chicago and London: University of Chicago Press, 1997.

Fox, Lionel W. *The English Prison and Borstal Systems*. London: Routledge, 1952.

Franklin, Howard Bruce. *Prison Literature in America. The Victim as Criminal and Artist* [1978]. Expanded Edition. New York and Oxford: Oxford University Press, 1989.

———, ed. *Prison Writing in Twentieth-Century America*. New York: Penguin, 1998.

French, Warren. "Fiction vs. Film 1960–1985." *Contemporary American Fiction*. Ed. Malcolm Bradbury and Sigmund Ro. London: Edward Arnold, 1987. 106–21.

Frey, Hans-Peter. *Stigma und Identität. Eine empirische Untersuchung zur Genese und Änderung krimineller Identität bei Jugendlichen*. Weinheim and Basel: Beltz, 1983.

Gaddis, Thomas E., and Karl Heinz Roth. "Zwei Zitate zu Alcatraz." *Filmkritik* 24.5 (1980): 197–99.

Gallagher, Catherine. "The Duplicity of Doubling in *A Tale of Two Cities*." *Dickens Studies Annual* 12 (1983): 125–46.

Garland, David. *Punishment and Modern Society. A Study in Social Theory*. Oxford: Clarendon Press, 1990

Genette, Gérard. *Narrative Discourse. An Essay in Method* [1972]. Trans. Jane E. Lewin Ithaca, NY: Cornell University Press, 1980.

———. *Narrative Discourse Revisited* [1983]. Trans. Jane E. Lewin. Ithaca, NY: Cornell University Press, 1988.

Ghent, Dorothy van. "The Dickens World: A View from Todger's." *Dickens. A Collection of Critical Essays*. Ed. Martin Price. Englewood Cliffs, NJ: Prentice-Hall, 1967. 24–38.

Gibbons, Don C. "Pennsylvania System." *Encyclopedia of American Prisons*. Ed. Marilyn D. McShane and Frank R. Williams III. London and New York: Garland, 1996. 351–53.

Giddings, Robert, Keith Selby, and Chris Wensley. *Screening the Novel. The Theory and Practice of Literary Dramatization*. Houndmills: Macmillan, 1990.

Goble, Alan, ed. *The Complete Index to Literary Sources in Film*. London: Bowker-Saur, 1999.

Goetsch, Paul. *Dickens: Eine Einführung*. München: Artemis, 1986.

Goffman, Erving. *Asylums: Essays on the Social Situation of Mental Patients and Other Inmates*. Garden City: Doubleday, 1961.

Goldberg, Michael. *Carlyle and Dickens*. Athens, GA: University of Georgia Press, 1972.

Gorbman, Claudia. *Unheard Melodies: Narrative Film Music*. Bloomington et al.: Indiana University Press, 1987.

Grass, Sean Christopher. *The Self in the Cell: Narrating the Victorian Prisoner*. New York and London: Routledge, 2003.

Greenstein, Michael. "Liminality in *Little Dorrit*." *Dickens Quarterly* 7.2 (1990): 275–83.

Greer, Chris. *Sex Crime and the Media: Sex Offending and the Press in a Divided Society*. Cullompton: Willan, 2003.

Griem, Julika, and Eckart Voigts-Virchow. "Filmnarratologie: Grundlagen, Tendenzen und Beispielanalysen." *Erzähltheorie transgenerisch, intermedial, interdisziplinär*. Ed. Ansgar Nünning and Vera Nünning. Trier: Wissenschaftlicher Verlag Trier, 2002. 155–83.

Grimm, Petra. *Filmnarratologie. Eine Einführung in die Praxis der Interpretation am Beispiel des Werbespots.* München: Diskurs-Film-Verlag Schaudig and Ledig, 1996.

Gross, John. "A Tale of Two Cities." *Dickens and the Twentieth Century.* Ed. John Gross and Gabriel Pearson. London: Routledge and Kegan Paul, 1962. 187–97.

———. Rev. of *Little Dorrit. New York Times* 30 Oct (1988): 22.

Hagan, Frank E. "Panopticon." *Encyclopedia of American Prisons.* Ed. Marilyn D. McShane and Frank R. Williams III. London and New York: Garland, 1996. 341–42.

Halberstam, Judith. *Female Masculinity.* Durham: Duke University Press, 2004.

Hale, Christopher. "Punishment and the Visible." *The Prison Movie.* Ed. Mike Nellis and Christopher Hale. London: Radical Alternatives to Prison, 1982. 50–64.

Hallinan, Joseph T. *Going Up the River: Travels in a Prison Nation.* New York: Random House, 2001.

Hamburger, Käte. *The Logic of Literature* [1973]. Trans. Marilynn J. Rose. Bloomington, IN: Indiana University Press, 1993.

Hampe, Barry. "Shawshank. Rambling Narrative to Dramatic Structure." *Creative Screenwriting* 4.2 (1997): 17– 25.

Hanway, Jonas. *Solitude in Imprisonment.* London: British Library, 1776.

Hardy, Phil, ed. *The BFI Companion to Crime.* Foreworded by Richard Attenborough. London: Cassell, 1997.

Haslam, Jason. "'They Locked the Door on my Meditations' : Thoreau and the Prison House of Identity." *Genre* 35.3/4 (2002): 449–78.

———. *Fitting Sentences: Identity in Nineteenth and Twentieth Century Prison Narratives.* Toronto: University of Toronto Press, 2005.

Haslam, Jason, and Julia Wright, eds. *Captivating Subjects: Writing Confinement, Citizenship, and Nationhood in the Nineteenth Century.* Toronto: University of Toronto Press, 2005.

Hayward, Susan. *Key Concepts in Cinema Studies.* London and New York: Routledge, 1996.

Helbig, Jörg. "Intermediales Erzählen: Baustein für eine Typologie intermedialer Erscheinungsformen in der Erzählliteratur am Beispiel der Sonatenform von Anthony Burgess' *A Clockwork Orange*." *Erzählen und Erzähltheorie im 20. Jahrhundert. Festschrift für Wilhelm Füger.* Ed. Jörg Helbig. Heidelberg: Winter, 2001. 131–52.

Heller, Arno. "Anthony Burgess, *A Clockwork Orange* (1962)." *Der Science-Fiction Roman in der angloamerikanischen Literatur. Interpretationen.* Ed. Hartmut Heuermann. Düsseldorf: Bagel, 1986. 236–52.

Hennelly, Mark M. Jr. "'The Games of the Prison Children' in Dickens's *Little Dorrit*." *Nineteenth-Century Contexts* 20.2 (1997): 187–213.

Hickethier, Knut. *Film- und Fernsehanalyse.* Third, revised edition. Stuttgart and Weimar: Metzler, 2001.

Hirst, John. "The Australian Experience: The Convict Colony." *The Oxford History of the Prison. The Practice of Punishment in Western Society.* Ed. Norval Morris and David J. Rothman. New York and Oxford: Oxford University Press, 1995. 263–95.

Hobsbawm, E.J. *Echoes of the Marseillaise. Two Centuries Look Back on the French Revolution.* London and New York: Verso, 1990.

Holmlund, Chris. *Impossible Bodies. Femininity and Masculinity at the Movies.* London and New York: Routledge, 2002.

Hooks, Bell. *Reel to Real: Race, Sex, and Class in the Movies.* New York: Routledge, 1996.

Hopf, Florian. "Down by Law." *epd Film* 11 (1986): 26.

Horne, William L. "'Greatest Pleasures': *A Taste of Honey* (1961) and *The Loneliness of the Long Distance Runner* (1962)." *The Cinema of Tony Richardson.* Ed. James M. Welsh and John C. Tibbetts. New York: State University of New York Press, 1999. 81–126.

House of Commons. *Report of an Enquiry by Her Majesty's Chief Inspector of Prisons for England and Wales into the Disturbances in Prison Service Establishments in England Between 29 April-2 May 1986.* London: Her Majesty's Stationery Office, 1987.

Howard, John. *The State of the Prisons in England and Wales* [1777]. London: Dent, 1929.

Howitt, Dennis. *Crime, the Media and the Law.* Chichester et al.: Wiley, 1998.

Human Rights Watch. *Prison Conditions in the United States.* A Human Rights Watch Report. New York et al.: Human Rights Watch, 1991.

Hurst, Matthias. *Erzählsituationen in Literatur und Film. Ein Modell zur vergleichenden Analyse von literarischen Texten und filmischen Adaptationen.* Tübingen: Niemeyer, 1996.

Hutchings, William. "The Work of Play: Anger and the Expropriated Athletes of Alan Sillitoe and David Storey." *Modern Fiction Studies* 33.1 (1987): 35–47.

Ignatieff, Michael. *A Just Measure of Pain. The Penitentiary in the Industrial Revolution, 1750–1850.* London: Macmillan, 1978.

Innes, Christopher. "Adapting Dickens to the Modern Eye: *Nicholas Nickleby* and *Little Dorrit*." *Novel Images. Literature in Performance.* Ed. Peter Reynolds. London and New York: Routledge, 1993. 64– 79.

Internet Movie Data Base. <http://www.imdb.com>

Isaacs, Neil D. "Unstuck in Time: *Clockwork Orange* and *Slaughterhouse-Five*." *Literature/Film Quarterly* 1.2 (1973): 122–31.

Isernhagen, Hartwig. "Alan Sillitoes 'The Loneliness of the Long-Distance Runner': Versuch einer literar- und genrehistorischen Einordnung." *Anglia* 99.1–2 (1981): 134–61.

Jackson-Retondo, Elaine. "Manufacturing Moral Reform: Images and Realities of a Nineteenth-Century American Prison." *People, Power, Places. Perspectives in Vernacular Architecture VIII.* Ed. Sally McMurry and Annmarie Adams. Knoxville: The University of Tennessee Press, 2000. 117–37.

Jackson, Thomas A. *Charles Dickens: The Progress of a Radical.* London: Lawrence and Wishart, 1937.

Jacobs, James B. *Stateville: The Penitentiary in Mass Society.* Chicago, IL: University of Chicago Press, 1977.

Jahn, Manfred. "A Guide to Narratological Film Analysis." <www.uni-koeln.de/~ame02/pppf.htm>

James, Joy. "Erasing the Spectacle of Racialized State Violence." *Resisting State Violence: Radicalism, Gender, and Race in US Culture.* Minneapolis: University of Minnesota Press, 1996. 24–43.

Jarvis, Brian. *Cruel and Unusual: Punishment and US Culture.* London and Sterling, Virginia: Pluto, 2004.

Jenkins, Steve. "Down by Law." *Monthly Film Bulletin* 54.636 (1986): 3–4.

Jewkes, Yvonne. *Captive Audience: Media, Masculinity and Power in Prisons.* Cullompton: Willan, 2002.

———. *Media and Crime*. London: Sage, 2004.

Johnson, Elmer H. "Auburn System." *Encyclopedia of American Prisons.* Ed. Marilyn D. McShane and Frank R. Williams III. London and New York: Garland, 1996. 46–49.

Johnston, Norman. *The Human Cage: A Brief History of Prison Architecture.* New York: Walker, 1973.

Joseph, Henry Samuel. *Memoirs of Convicted Prisoners: Accompanied by Remarks on the Causes and Prevention of Crime.* London: Wertheim, 1853.

Kaplan, Elizabeth Ann. *Women and Film: Both Sides of the Camera.* New York: Methuen, 1983.

Karpenstein-Eßbach, Christa. *Einschluß und Imagination. Über den literarischen Umgang mit Gefangenen.* Tübingen: Edition Diskord, 1985.

Kauffman, Sylvie. "Witness to Executions." *The New York Review of Books* 48.13 (2001): 25–26.

Kavanagh, James H. "Ideology." *Critical Terms for Literary Study.* Ed. Frank Lentricchia and Thomas McLaughlin. Chicago and London: The University of Chicago Press, 1995. 306–20.

Kawin, Bruce. *Mindscreen: Bergman, Godard, and First-Person Film.* Princeton, NJ: Princeton University Press, 1978.

Kemp, Philip. "Swamp Water: *Down by Law.*" *Sight and Sound* 56.2 (1987): 142–43.

Kermode, Mark. *The Shawshank Redemption.* BFI Modern Classics. London: The British Film Institute, 2003.

Kidd-Hewitt, David, and Richard Osborne. *Crime and the Media. The Post-Modern Spectacle.* London et al.: Pluto, 1995.

King, Roy D. "The Rise and Rise of the Supermax: An American Solution in Search of a Problem?" *Punishment and Society* 1.2 (1999): 163–86.

Klein, Michael, and Gillian Parker, eds. *The English Novel and the Movies.* New York: Ungar, 1981.

Konigsberg, Ira. *The Complete Film Dictionary.* Second Edition. London: Bloomsbury, 1997.

Kozloff, Sarah. *Invisible Storytellers: Voice-Over Narration in American Fiction Film*. Berkeley: University of California Press, 1988.

Kristeva, Julia. *Powers of Horror.* Trans. by Leon S. Roudiez. New York: Columbia University Press, 1982.

Kroll, Jack. Review of *Little Dorrit*. *Newsweek*, 7 Nov (1988): 118.

Kury, Helmut, and Martin Brandenstein. "Zur Viktimisierung (jugendlicher) Strafgefangener." *Zeitschrift für Straffälligenhilfe und Strafvollzug* 1 (2002): 22–33.

Lakoff, George, and Mark Johnson. *Metaphors We Live By.* Chicago and London: The University of Chicago Press, 1980.

Lakoff, George, and Mark Turner. *More than Cool Reason: A Field Guide to Poetic Metaphor*. Chicago: University of Chicago Press, 1989.

Lamb, John B. "Domesticating History: Revolution and Moral Management in *A Tale of Two Cities*." *Dickens Studies Annual* 25 (1996): 227–43.

Lauterbach, Frank. "Textual Errands into The Carceral Wilderness. Prison Autobiographies and the Construction of Cultural Hegemonies." *In the Grip of the Law. Prisons, Trials and the Space Between.* Ed. Monika Fludernik and Greta Olson. Frankfurt: Lang, 2004. 127–43.

———. "'From the Slums to the Slums': The Delimitation of Social Identity in Late Victorian Prison Narratives." *Captivating Subjects: Nineteenth-Century Writings by Prisoners, Slaves, and Captives.* Ed. Jason Haslam and Julia Wright. Toronto: University of Toronto Press, 2005. 113–43.

Lawrence, Jerome. *Actor: The Life and Times of Paul Muni*. New York: G.P. Putnam's Sons, 1974.

Leavis, F.R., and Q.D. Leavis. *Dickens the Novelist*. London: Chatto and Windus, 1970.

Ledbetter, Marc. *Victims and the Postmodern Narrative or Doing Violence to the Body.* Houndmills et al.: Macmillan, 1996.

Lehman, Peter, ed. *Masculinity: Bodies, Movies, Culture*. New York and London: Routledge, 2001.

Leitch, Thomas. *Crime Films*. Cambridge: Cambridge University Press, 2002.

Lejeune, Philippe. *Le pacte autobiographique* [1975]. Paris: Seuil, 1994.

Leonardi, Susan J. "The Long-Distance Runner (The Loneliness, Loveliness, Nunliness of)." *Tulsa Studies in Women's Literature* 13.1 (1994): 57–85.

Levinson, Jerrold. "Film Music and Narrative Agency." *Post-Theory. Reconstructing Film Studies*. Ed. David Bordwell and Noël Carroll. Madison: University of Wisconsin Press, 1996. 248–82.

Lewis, Randolph. "Black and White on the Chain Gang: Representing Race and Punishment." *Borderlines. Studies in American Culture* 3.3 (1996): 225–48.

Lichtenstein, Alex. "Chain Gangs, Communism, and the 'Negro Question': John L. Spivak's *Georgia Nigger*." *Georgia Historical Quarterly* 79.3 (1995): 633–58.

Lindgren, Ernest. *The Art of the Film*. London: Allen and Unwin, 1948.

Lloyd, Charles, George Mair, and Mike Hough. *Explaining Reconviction Rates: A Critical Analysis*. A Home Office Research and Planning Unit Report. London: HMSO, 1994.

Lloyd, Tom. "Language, Love and Identity: *A Tale of Two Cities*." *The Dickensian* (1992) 88: 154–70.

Lobrutto, Vincent. "The Old Ultra-Violence." *American Cinematographer* 80.10 (1999): 52–61.

Lohmeier, Anke-Marie. *Hermeneutische Theorie des Films*. Tübingen: Niemeyer, 1996.

Lothe, Jakob. *Narrative in Fiction and Film. An Introduction*. Oxford: Oxford University Press, 2000.

Lyon, David. *Surveillance Society: Monitoring Everyday Life*. Buckingham et al.: Open University Press, 2001.

Lyon, Juliet, Catherine Dennison, and Anita Wilson. *'Tell Them So They Listen': Messages from Young People in Custody. A Research, Development and Statistics Directorate Report. Home Office Research Study 201*. London: Home Office, 2000.

Luckett, Moya. "Performing Masculinities: Dandyism and Male Fashion in 1960s-70s British Cinema." *Fashion Cultures. Theories, Explorations and Analysis*. Ed. Stella Bruzzi and Pamela Church Gibson. London and New York: Routledge, 2000. 315–28.

McCahill, Michael. "Media Representations of Visual Surveillance." *Criminal Visions. Media Representations of Crime and Justice*. Ed. Paul Mason. Cullompton: Willan, 2003. 192–213.

McConville, Seán. *A History of English Prison Administration*. London and Boston: Routledge and Kegan Paul, 1981.

———. *English Local Prisons. Next Only to Death.* London and New York: Routledge, 1995.

———. "Local Justice: The Jail." *The Oxford History of the Prison. The Practice of Punishment in Western Society*. Ed. Norval Morris and David J. Rothman. New York and Oxford: Oxford University Press, 1995. 297–327.

———. "The Victorian Prison. England, 1865–1965." *The Oxford History of the Prison. The Practice of Punishment in Western Society*. Ed. Norval Morris and David J. Rothman. New York and Oxford: Oxford University Press, 1995. 131–67.

McCracken, Samuel. "Novel into Film: Novelist into Critic: *A Clockwork Orange*... Again." *The Antioch Review* 32.3 (1973): 427–36.

McDougal, Stuart Y. *Made into Movies: From Literature to Film*. New York: Holt, Rinehart, and Winston, 1985.

McFarlane, Brian. "David Lean's *Great Expectations*—Meeting Two Challenges." *Literature/Film Quarterly* 20.1 (1992): 68–76.

———. *Novel to Film. An Introduction to the Theory of Adaptation*. Oxford: Clarendon Press, 1996.

McGowen, Randall. "The Well-Ordered Prison. England, 1780–1865." *The Oxford History of the Prison. The Practice of Punishment in Western Society*. Ed. Norval Morris and David J. Rothman. New York and Oxford: Oxford University Press, 1995. 78–109.

Mackay, Carol Hanbery. "A Novel's Journey into Film: The Case of *Great Expectations*." *Literature/Film Quarterly* 13.2 (1985): 127–34.

McKnight, Natalie. *Idiots, Madmen, and Other Prisoners in Dickens*. New York: St. Martin's Press, 1993.

McLean, Adrienne L. "Star System." *Critical Dictionary of Film and Television Theory*. Ed. Roberta E. Pearson and Philip Simpson. London and New York: Routledge, 2001. 423–24.

McShane, Marilyn D. "Chain Gangs." *Encyclopedia of American Prisons*. Ed. Marilyn D. McShane and Frank R. Williams III. London and New York: Garland, 1996. 71–73.

———. "Films." *Encyclopedia of American Prisons*. Ed. Marilyn D. McShane and Frank R. Williams III. London and New York: Garland, 1996. 208.

———. "Marion Penitentiary." *Encyclopedia of American Prisons*. Ed. Marilyn D. McShane and Frank R. Williams III. London and New York: Garland, 1996. 317–18.

McShane, Marilyn D. and Frank R. Williams III. *Encyclopedia of American Prisons*. London and New York: Garland, 1996.

Magistrale, Tony. *Hollywood's Stephen King*. New York: Palgrave Macmillan, 2003.

Mahrenholz, Simone. "Die Verurteilten [The Shawshank Redemption]." *epd Film* 3 (1995): 34.

Maloff, Saul. "The Eccentricity of Alan Sillitoe." *Contemporary British Novelists*. Ed. Charles Shapiro. Carbondale: Southern Illinois Press, 1965. 95–113.

Maltby, Richard. "The Genesis of the Production Code." *Quarterly Review of Film and Video* 15.4 (1995): 5–32."

Mancini, Matthew J. "Foreword to the Brown Thrasher Edition." *I Am a Fugitive From a Georgia Chain Gang!* Robert E. Burns. Athens and London: Brown Thrasher Books. The University of Georgia Press, 1997. v–xxiv.

March, Joss. "Inimitable Double Vision: Dickens, *Little Dorrit*, Photography, Film." *Dickens Studies Annual* 22 (1993): 239–82.

Mariner, Joanne. *No Escape. Male Rape in U.S. Prisons*. New York: Human Rights Watch, 2001.

Marsh, Joss Lutz. "Dickens and Film." *The Cambridge Companion to Charles Dickens*. Ed. John O. Jordan. Cambridge: Cambridge University Press, 2001. 204–23.

Marzials, Frank T. *Life of Charles Dickens*. London: Scott, 1887.

Mason, Paul. "Systems and Process. The Prison in Cinema." *Images: Journal of Popular Culture and Film*. <www.imagesjournal.com/issue06/features/prison.htm>

———. "Men, Machines and the Mincer: The Prison in Cinema." *Picturing Justice*. <www.usfca.edu/pj/articles/Prison.htm>

———. "Watching the Invisible: Televisual Portrayal of the British Prison 1980–1990." *International Journal of the Sociology of Law* 28.1 (2000): 33–44.

———. "The Screen Machine: Cinematic Representations of Prison." *Criminal Visions. Media Representations of Crime and Justice*. Ed. Paul Mason. Cullompton: Willan, 2003. 278–97.

Massey, Dennis. *Doing Time in American Prisons: A Study of Modern Novels*. New York et al.: Greenwood, 1989.

Mathiesen, Thomas. "The Viewer Society: Michel Foucault's 'Panopticon' Revisited." *Theoretical Criminology* 2 (1997): 215–34.

Mathiesen, Thomas. *Prison on Trial.* Second edition. Ed. Andrew Rutherford. Criminal Policy Series. Winchester: Waterside Press, 2000.

Maxford, Howard. "The Science-Fiction Films of Stanley Kubrick." *Starbust* 263 (2000): 44–53.

Maxwell, Richard. "Introduction." *A Tale of Two Cities* [1859]. Ed. Richard Maxwell. London: Penguin, 2000. ix–xxxiii.

Mayhew, Henry and John Binny. *The Criminal Prisons of London and Scenes of Prison Life* [1862]. London: Frank Cass, 1971.

Melossi, Dario, and Massimo Patarini. *The Prison and the Factory: Origins of the Penitentiary System.* Trans. Glynis Cousin. London and Basingstoke: Macmillan, 1981.

Meranze, Michael. *Laboratories of Virtue: Punishment, Revolution, and Authority in Philadelphia, 1760–1835.* Chapel Hill: The University of North Carolina Press, 1996.

Metz, Christian. *Film Language. A Semiotics of Cinema* [1971]. Trans. by Michael Taylor. New York: Oxford University Press, 1974.

Millet, Kate. *The Politics of Cruelty: An Essay on the Literature of Imprisonment* [1994]. New York: Norton, 1995.

Miller, D.A. *The Novel and the Police.* Berkeley: University of California Press, 1988.

Mitry, Jean. "Remarks on the Problem of Cinematic Adaptation." *Bulletin of the Midwest Modern Language Association* 4.1 (1971): 1–9.

Monaco, James. *How to Read a Film. The World of Movies, Media, and Multimedia. Language, History, Theory* [1977]. Third Edition. Completely Revised and Expanded. New York and Oxford: Oxford University Press, 2000.

Montgomery, Reid H., and Gordon A. Crews. *A History of Correctional Violence: An Examination of Reported Causes of Riots and Disturbances.* Lanham, Maryland: American Correctional Association, 1998.

Morey, Anne. "'The Judge Called Me an Accessory.' Women's Prison Films, 1950–1962." *Journal of Popular Film and Television* 23.2 (1995): 80–87.

Morris, Christopher. "The Bad Faith of Pip's Bad Faith: Deconstructing *Great Expectations.*" *English Literary History* 54 (1987): 941–55.

Morris, Norval. "The Contemporary Prison. 1965-Present." *The Oxford History of the Prison. The Practice of Punishment in Western Society.* Ed. Norval Morris and David J. Rothman. New York and Oxford: Oxford University Press, 1995. 227–59.

Morris, Norval, and David J. Rothman, eds. *The Oxford History of the Prison. The Practice of Punishment in Western Society*. New York and Oxford: Oxford University Press, 1995.

Morrisette, Bruce. *Novel and Film: Essays in Two Genres*. Chicago and London: The Chicago University Press, 1985.

Mort, Frank. *Cultures of Consumption: Masculinities and Social Space in Late Twentieth Century Britain*. London: Routledge, 1996.

Morton, Jim. "Women in Prison Films." *Incredibly Strange Films*. Ed. Vivian Vale. San Francisco: Research Publ, 1986. 151–52.

Moynahan, Julian. "Seeing the Book, Reading the Movie." *The English Novel and the Movies*. Ed. Michael Klein and Gillian Parker. New York: Ungar, 1981. 143–54.

Mulvey, Laura. "Visual Pleasure and Narrative Cinema [1975]." *The Narrative Reader*. Ed. Martin McQuillan. London and New York: Routledge, 2000. 177–81.

Mundt, Michaela. *Transformationsanalyse. Methodologische Probleme der Literaturverfilmung*. Tübingen: Niemeyer, 1994.

Myers, Laura B., and Sue Titus Reid. "Modern Prisons: 1960 to the Present." *Encyclopedia of American Prisons*. Ed. Marilyn D. McShane and Frank R. Williams III. London and New York: Garland, 1996. 239–44.

Nasta, Dominique. *Meaning in Film. Relevant Structures in Soundtrack and Narrative*. Berne et al.: Lang, 1991.

Nau, Peter. "Die Zeit der Gefangenen." *Filmkritik* 24.5 (1980): 194–96.

Neier, Aryeh. "Confining Dissent. The Political Prison." *The Oxford History of the Prison. The Practice of Punishment in Western Society*. Ed. Norval Morris and David J. Rothman. New York and Oxford: Oxford University Press, 1995. 391–425.

Nellis, Mike. "Notes on the American Prison Film." *The Prison Movie*. Ed. Mike Nellis and Christopher Hale. London: Radical Alternatives to Prison, 1982. 5–49.

———. "British Prison Movies. The Case of 'Now Barabbas.'" *The Howard Journal* 27.1 (1988): 2–31.

———. "Prose and Cons: Offender Auto-Biographies, Penal Reform and Probation Training." *The Howard Journal of Criminal Justice* 41.5 (2002): 434–68.

Net, Mariana. "Representations of the Political Prison: Actual Spaces, Virtual Forms." *Spaces and Significations*. Ed. Roberta Kevelson. New York: Lang, 1996. 135–50.

Neubauer, Hans-Joachim. "Durch die Sonne gehen—Erzählen in Gefängnis." *Kursbuch* 153 (2003): 143–55.

Nichols, Bill, ed. *Movies and Methods. An Anthology*. Berkeley: University of California Press, 1976.

———. *Introduction to Documentary*. Bloomington: Indiana University Press, 2001.

Nicholson, Mervyn. "My Dinner With Stanley Kubrick: Food, and the Logic of Images." *Literature/Film Quarterly* 29.4 (2001): 279–89.

Nünning, Ansgar. "*Unreliable Narration* zur Einführung: Grundzüge einer kognitiv-narratologischen Theorie und Analyse unglaubwürdigen Erzählens." *Unreliable Narration. Studien zur Theorie und Praxis unglaubwürdigen Erzählens in der englischsprachigen Literatur*. Ed. Ansgar Nünning. Trier: WVT, 1998. 3–34.

O'Brien, Patricia. "The Prison on the Continent. Europe, 1865–1965." *The Oxford History of the Prison. The Practice of Punishment in Western Society*. Ed. Norval Morris and David J. Rothman. New York and Oxford: Oxford University Press, 1995. 199–225.

O'Donnell, Ian, and Kimmett Edgar. *Bullying in Prisons*. Oxford: Centre for Criminological Research, University of Oxford, 1998.

———. "Fear in Prison." *Prison Journal* 79 (1999): 90–99.

Olsen, Stein Haugom. "Understanding Literary Metaphor." *Metaphor. Problems and Perspectives*. Ed. David S. Miall. Sussex: Harvester Press, 1982. 36–54.

Orland, Leonard. *Prisons: Houses of Darkness*. New York and London: The Free Press, 1975.

Oshinsky, David. *Worse than Slavery: Parchman Farm and the Ordeal of Jim Crow Justice*. New York: Free Press, 1996.

O'Sullivan, Sean. "Representations of Prison in Nineties Hollywood Cinema: From *Con Air* to *The Shawshank Redemption*." *Howard Journal of Criminal Justice* 40.4 (2001): 317–34.

———. "Representing the 'Killing State': The Death Penalty in Nineties Hollywood Cinema." *Howard Journal of Criminal Justice* 42.5 (2003): 485–503.

Paech, Joachim. *Literatur und Film.* Stuttgart: Metzler, 1988.

Palermo, George B., and Maxine Aldridge White. *Letters from Prison. A Cry for Justice.* Springfield, Illinois: Charles C. Thomas, 1998.

Parish, James R. *Prison Pictures from Hollywood: Plots, Critiques, Casts and Credits for 293 Theatrical and Made-for Television Releases.* Jefferson, NC: McFarland, 1991.

Paroissien, David. "Dickens and the Cinema." *Dickens Studies Annual* 7 (1980): 68–80.

———. *The Companion to Great Expectations.* The Dickens Companions 7. The Banks: Helm Information, 2000.

Pawelczak, Andy. "The Shawshank Redemption." *Films in Review* 45.11/12 (1994): 55.

Perreault, Jeanne. "Chain Gang Narratives and the Politics of 'Speaking for.'" *Biography* 24.1 (2001): 152–71.

Peters, Jan Marie. *Pictorial Signs and the Language of Film.* Amsterdam: Rodopi, 1981.

Peters, Laura. "The Histories of Two Self-Tormentors: Orphans and Power in *Little Dorrit.*" *Dickensian* 91.3 (1995): 187–96.

Petzold, Dieter. "Der Moralist als Provokateur: Anthony Burgess' Erfolgsroman *A Clockwork Orange.*" *Anglistik und Englischunterricht* 19 (1983): 7–21.

Philpotts, Trey. "The Real Marshalsea." *Dickensian* 87.3 (1991): 130–45.

Pinar, William F. *The Gender of Racial Politics and Violence in America. Lynching, Prison Rape, and the Crisis of Masculinity.* New York et al.: Lang, 2001.

Pointer, Michael. *Charles Dickens on the Screen: The Film, Television, and Video Adaptations.* Lanham, MD: Scarecrow Press, 1996.

Poole, Mike. "Dickens and Films: 101 Uses of a Dead Author." *The Changing World of Charles Dickens.* Ed. Robert Giddings. London: Vision and Barnes and Noble, 1983. 148–62.

Powell, Dilys. "Postscript: Dickens on Film." *The Dickensian* 66. 361 (1970): 183–85.

Priestley, Philip, ed. *Jail Journeys. The English Prison Experience since 1918.* London, New York: Routledge, 1989.

Prince, Stephen. *Savage Cinema. Sam Peckinpah and the Rise of Ultraviolent Movies.* Austin: University of Texas Press, 1988.

Prince, Stephen. "Graphic Violence in the Cinema: Origins, Aesthetic Design, and Social Effects." *Screening Violence*. Ed. Stephen Prince. London: The Athlone Press, 2000. 1–44.

Probst, Chris. "Roger Deakins, ASC, BSC. The Shawshank Redemption." *American Cinematographer* 76.6 (1995): 62–68.

Pryluck, Calvin B. "The Film Metaphor Metaphor: The Use of Language-Based Models in Film Study." *Literature/Film Quarterly* 3.2 (1975): 119–30.

Pudovkin, Vsevolod I. *Film Technique and Film Acting* [1926]. Trans. and ed. Ivor Montagu. New York: Grove, 1970.

Querry, Ronald B. "Prison Movies: An Annotated Filmography 1921-Present." *The Journal of Popular Film* 2 (1973): 181–97.

———. "The American Prison as Portrayed in the Popular Motion Pictures of the 1930s." Diss. University of New Mexico, 1975.

Quirk, Eugene F. "Social Class as Audience: Sillitoe's Story and Screenplay 'The Loneliness of the Long-Distance Runner.'" *Literature/Film Quarterly* 9.3 (1981): 161–71.

Rafter, Nicole. *Shots in the Mirror. Crime Films and Society*. Oxford: Oxford University Press, 2000.

Ramsbotham, David. *Prison Gate: The Shocking State of Britain's Prisons and the Need for Visionary Change*. London: Free Press, 2003.

Rhyms, Deena. "Discursive Delinquency in Leonard Peltier's Prison Writings." *Genre* 35.3/4 (2002): 563–74.

Roberts, Bette B. "Travel versus Imprisonment: The 'Fellow Travellers' in *Little Dorrit*." *Dickens Studies Newsletter* 13.4 (1982): 109–12.

Rodensky, Lisa. *The Crime in Mind. Criminal Responsibility and the Victorian Novel*. Oxford: Oxford University Press, 2003.

Rodriguez, Dylan. "Against the Discipline of 'Prison Writing' : Toward a Theoretical Conception of Contemporary Radical Prison Praxis." *Genre* 35.3/4 (2002): 407–28.

Roffman, Peter, and Jim Purdy. *The Hollywood Social Problem Film. Madness, Despair, and Politics from the Depression to the Fifties*. Bloomington: Indiana University Press, 1981.

Rollins, Janet Buck. "Novel into Film: *The Loneliness of the Long-Distance Runner*." *Literature/Film Quarterly* 9.3 (1981): 172–88.

Rosen, David. "*A Tale of Two Cities*: Theology of Revolution." *Dickens Studies Annual* 27 (1998): 171–85.

Rosen, Philip, ed. *Narrative, Apparatus, Ideology. A Film Theory Reader.* New York: Columbia University Press, 1986.

Rothman, David J. "Perfecting the Prison. United States, 1789–1865." *The Oxford History of the Prison. The Practice of Punishment in Western Society.* Ed. Norval Morris and David J. Rothman. New York and Oxford: Oxford University Press, 1995. 111–29.

Rotman, Edgardo. "The Failure of Reform. United States, 1865–1965." *The Oxford History of the Prison. The Practice of Punishment in Western Society.* Ed. Norval Morris and David J. Rothman. New York and Oxford: Oxford University Press, 1995.168–97.

Rush, Benjamin. *Essays: Literary, Moral, and Philosophical* [1798]. Ed. Michael Meranze. Schenectady, NY: Union College Press, 1988.

Rush, Jeffery P. "Escapes." *Encyclopedia of American Prisons*. Ed. Marilyn D. McShane and Frank R. Williams III. London and New York: Garland, 1996. 197–98.

Ryan, Michael, and Douglas Kellner. *Camera Politica. The Politics and Ideology of Contemporary Hollywood Film.* Bloomington and Indianapolis: Indiana University Press, 1988.

Said, Edward S. "Two Commentaries on *Great Expectations*: From Deconstruction to Postcolonialism [1983 and 1993]." *Great Expectations*. Ed. Janice Carlisle. Boston, New York: Bedford Books, 1996. 518–26.

Samuel, Raphael. "Docklands Dickens." *Patriotism. The Making and Unmaking of British National Identity. Vol. III: National Fictions.* Ed. Raphael Samuel. London and New York: Routledge, 1989. 275–85.

Sarat, Austin. *When the State Kills*. Oxfordshire: Princeton University Press, 2001.

Schindler, Arlene. "*A Clockwork Orange*. Novel vs. Film." *Creative Screenwriting* 6.4 (1999): 38–41.

Schlossman, Steven. "Delinquent Children. The Juvenile Reform School." *The Oxford History of the Prison. The Practice of Punishment in Western Society.* Ed. Norval Morris and David J. Rothman. New York and Oxford: Oxford University Press, 1995. 363–89.

Schmidt, Johann N. "Didaktische Fabel und Kinofaszination: *A Clockwork Orange*." *Literaturverfilmungen*. Ed. Franz-Josef Albersmeier and Volker Roloff. Frankfurt: Suhrkamp, 1989. 300–23.

Schneider, Irmela. *Der verwandelte Text. Wege zu einer Theorie der Literaturverfilmung.* Tübingen: Niemeyer, 1981.

Schulz, William F. "Women in Prison." *The New York Review of Books* 48.9 (2001): 32–33.

Scraton, Phil, Joe Sim, and Paula Skidmore, eds. *Prisons Under Protest.* Milton Keynes, Philadelphia: Open University Press, 1991.

Sedgwick, Eve Kosofsky. *Between Men. English Literature and Male Homosocial Desire.* New York: Columbia University Press, 1985.

Segal, Lynn. *Slow Motion: Changing Masculinities, Changing Men* [1990]. Second Edition. New Brunswick, NJ: Rutgers University Press, 1995.

Seltzer, Mark. *Henry James and the Art of Power.* Ithaca and London: Cornell University Press, 1984.

———. "The Graphic Unconscious: A Response." *New Literary History* 26 (1995): 21–28.

Shaw, Harry E. "Realities of the Prison: Dickens, Scott, and the Secularization of their Eighteenth-Century Literature." *In the Grip of the Law. Prisons, Trials and the Space Between.* Ed. Monika Fludernik and Greta Olson. Frankfurt: Lang, 2004. 169–84.

Sheehan, Henry. "Escape from Alcatraz." *Sight and Sound* 1.2 (1991): 28–30.

Shelston, Alan, ed. *Charles Dickens. Dombey and Son and Little Dorrit. A Casebook.* Houndmills et al.: Macmillan, 1985.

Silberman, Matthew. *A World of Violence. Corrections in America.* Belmont, California: Wadsworth, 1995.

Silver, Alain. "The Untranquil Light: David Lean's *Great Expectations.*" *Literature/Film Quarterly* 2.2 (1974): 140–52.

Silverman, Ira J. "Diet and Food Service" *Encyclopedia of American Prisons.* Ed. Marilyn D. McShane and Frank R. Williams III. London and New York: Garland, 1996. 155–57.

Simonsen, Clifford E. "Federal Bureau of Prisons." *Encyclopedia of American Prisons.* Ed. Marilyn D. McShane and Frank R. Williams III. London and New York: Garland, 1996. 203–8.

Sinyard, Neil. *Filming Literature: The Art of Film Adaptation.* London: Croom Helm, 1986.

———. "Dickensian Visions in Modern British Film." *Dickensian* 85.2 (1989): 108–17.

Slack, John S. "A Sporting Chance: Sports, Delinquency, and Rehabilitation in 'The Loneliness of the Long-Distance Runner.'" *Aethlon* 17.2 (2000): 1–9.

Small, Helen. "The Marshalsea." *Little Dorrit*. Ed. Stephen Wall and Helen Small. London: Penguin, 1998. 835–39.

Smith, Grahame. "Novel Into Film: The Case of *Little Dorrit*." *Yearbook of English Studies* 7 (1988): 33–47.

———. "Dickens and Adaptation. Imagery in Words and Pictures." *Novel Images. Literature in Performance*. Ed. Peter Reynolds. London and New York: Routledge, 1993. 49–63.

———. "Dickens and the City of Light." *Dickens Quarterly* 16.3 (1999): 178–90.

———. *Dickens and the Dream of Cinema*. Manchester and New York: Manchester University Press, 2003.

Sobchack, Vivian C. "Décor as Theme: *A Clockwork Orange*." *Literature/Film Quarterly* 9.2 (1981): 92–102.

Sparks, Richard F. *Television and the Drama of Crime: Moral Tales and the Place of Crime in Public Life*. Buckingham et al.: Open University Press, 1992.

Stam, Robert. "Beyond Fidelity: The Dialogics of Adaptation." *Film Adaptation*. Ed. James Naremore. New Brunswick, NJ: Rutgers University Press, 2000. 54–76.

Stam, Robert, Robert Burgoyne, and Sandy Flitterman-Lewis. *New Vocabularies in Film Semiotics. Structuralism, Post-Structuralism, and Beyond*. London and New York: Routledge, 1992.

Stange, G. Robert. "Dickens and the Fiery Past: *A Tale of Two Cities* Reconsidered." *English Journal* 46.7 (1957): 381–90.

Stanzel, Franz Karl. *A Theory of Narrative* [1979]. Trans. Charlotte Goedsche, with a Preface by Paul Hernadi. Cambridge: Cambridge University Press, 1984.

Stein, Michael Eric. "The New Violence or Twenty Years of Violence in Films: An Appreciation." *Films in Review* 46.1/2 (1995): 40–48.

Stewart, Garrett. "Leaving History: Dickens, Gance, Blanchot." *The Yale Journal of Criticism* 2.2 (1989): 145–90.

Stroud, Robert F. *Stroud's Digest on the Diseases of Birds* [1943]. Jersey City, New Jersey: T.F.H. Publications, 1969.

Swan, Jim. "'Life Without Parole': Metaphor and Discursive Commitment." *Style* 36.3 (2002): 446–65.

Sweeney, Megan. "Provocations and Possibilities: Rethinking Prisoners' Discourse." *Genre* 35.3/4 (2002): 393–405.

Sweeney, Megan. "Legally Blind: Seeking Alternative Literacies from Prison." *Genre* 35.3/4 (2002): 599–624.

Tan, Ed S. *Emotion and the Structure of Narrative Film. Film as an Emotive Machine.* Trans. by Barbara Fasting. Mawah, NJ: Lawrence, 1996.

Tambling, Jeremy. "Prison-Bound: Dickens and Foucault [1986]." *Great Expectations. Charles Dickens.* Ed. Roger D. Sell. New Casebooks. Houndmills: Macmillan, 1994. 123–42.

———. *Dickens, Violence and the Modern State. Dreams of the Scaffold.* Houndmills: Macmillan, 1995.

Taylor, Doug. "From Slavery to Prison: Benjamin Rush, Harriet Jacobs, and the Ideology of Reformative Incarceration." *Genre* 35.3/4 (2002): 429–447.

Tharaud, Barry. "*Great Expectations* as Literature and Film." *The Dickensian* 87 (1992): 102–10.

Thüna, Ulrich von. "Murder in the First." *epd Film* 5 (1996): 37.

Timko, Michael. "Splendid Impressions and Picturesque Means: Dickens, Carlyle, and *The French Revolution.*" *Dickens Studies Annual* 12 (1983): 177– 95.

Tonry, Michael, ed. *The Handbook of Crime and Punishment.* New York and Oxford: Oxford University Press, 1998.

Trilling, Lionel. *The Opposing Self.* London: Secker and Warburg, 1955.

Turim, Maureen. *Flashbacks in Film: Memory and History.* New York and London: Routledge, 1989.

Turner, George. "Revenge Served Cold." *American Cinematographer* 77.10 (1996): 34–42.

Valier, Claire. *Crime and Punishment in Contemporary Culture.* London and New York: Routledge, 2004.

Van Dijk, Teun A. "Cognitive Processing of Literary Discourse." *Poetics Today* 1(1979): 143–160.

Van Voorhis, Patricia. "Rehabilitation Programs." *Encyclopedia of American Prisons.* Ed. Marilyn D. McShane and Frank R. Williams III. London and New York: Garland, 1996. 391–98.

Vaverka, Ronald Dee. *Commitment as Art. A Marxist Critique of a Selection of Alan Sillitoe's Political Fiction.* Studia Anglistica Upsaliensia 35. Upsala: Almqvist Wiksell, 1978.

Wagner, Geoffrey. "A Clockwork Orange (1972)." *The Novel and the Cinema*. Cranbury, New Jersey: Associated University Press, 1975. 307–13.

———. *The Novel and the Cinema*. Rutherford, New Jersey: Farleigh Dickinson University Press, 1975.

Waldrep, Shelton. "The Uses and Misuses of Oscar Wilde." *Victorian Afterlife. Postmodern Culture Rewrites the Nineteenth Century*. Ed. John Kucich and Dianne F. Sadoff. Minneapolis, London: University of Minnesota Press, 2000. 49–63.

Wall, Stephen. "Introduction." *Little Dorrit* [1855–57]. Ed. Stephen Wall and Helen Small. London: Penguin, 1998.vii–xxi.

Walmsley, Roy "World Prison Population List." *Research Findings* 88 (1999): 1–6.

———. "The World Prison Population Situation: Growth, Trends, Issues, and Challenges." <www. apaintl.org/Pub-Conf2000-PlenaryWalmsley-En.html>

Walsh, Susan. "Bodies of Capital: *Great Expectations* and the Climacteric Economy." *Victorian Studies* 37 (1993): 73–98.

Walters, Suzanna Danuta. "Caged Heat: The (R)evolution of Women-in-Prison Films." *Reel Knockouts. Violent Women in the Movies*. Ed. Martha McCaughey and Neal King. Austin: University of Texas Press, 2001. 106–23.

Ward, David A. "Alcatraz and Marion: Confinement in Super Maximum Custody." *Escaping Prison Myths. Selected Topics in the History of Federal Corrections*. Ed. John W. Roberts. Washington, D.C.: The American University Press, 1994. 81–93.

———. "Architecture." *Encyclopedia of American Prisons*. Ed. Marilyn D. McShane and Frank R. Williams III. London and New York: Garland, 1996. 34–39.

Watterson, Kathryn. *Women in Prison. Inside the Concrete Womb* [1973]. Boston: Northeastern University Press, 1996.

Webb, Sidney and Beatrice Webb. *English Prisons Under Local Government* [1922]. With a Preface by Bernard Shaw. London: Frank Cass, 1963.

Weigel, Sigrid. *"Und selbst im Kerker frei...!": Schreiben im Gefängnis: Zur Theorie und Gattungsgeschichte der Gefängnisliteratur (1750–1933)*. Marburg: Guttandin and Hoppe, 1982.

Welch, Michael. *Punishment in America. Social Control and the Ironies of Imprisonment*. London and New Delhi: Sage, 1999.

Welsh, Wayne N. "The Jacksonian Era." *Encyclopedia of American Prisons*. Ed. Marilyn D. McShane and Frank R. Williams III. London and New York: Garland, 1996. 234–37.

Whittock, Trevor. *Metaphor and Film*. Cambridge: Cambridge University Press, 1990.

Wilde, Oscar. "To the Editor of the Daily Chronicle. The Case of Warder Martin, Some Cruelties of Prison Life [1897]." *The Complete Letters of Oscar Wilde*. Ed. Merlin Holland and Rupert Hart-Davis. London: Fourth Estate, 2000. 847–55.

———. "To the Editor of the Daily Chronicle. Don't Read This If You Want to be Happy Today [1898]." *The Complete Letters of Oscar Wilde*. Ed. Merlin Holland and Rupert Hart-Davis. London: Fourth Estate, 2000. 1045–49.

Wilson, David. "Inside Observations." *Screen* 34.1 (1993): 76–79.

———. "The Cinematic Appeal of the Prison." *The Persistent Prison: Problems, Images and Alternatives*. Ed. Clive Emsley. London: Boutle, 2005. 74–90.

Wilson, David, and Sean O' Sullivan. *Images of Incarceration. Representations of Prison in Film and Television Drama*. Winchester: Waterside Press, 2004.

———. "Re-theorizing the Penal Reform Functions of the Prison Film: Revelation, Humanization, Empathy and Benchmarking." *Theoretical Criminology* 9.4 (2005): 471–91.

Wilson, George. *Narration in Light: Studies in Cinematic Point of View*. Baltimore and London: Johns Hopkins University Press, 1986.

Winn, Steve. "Dickens Story Lives in Potent Adaptation." *San Francisco Examiner* (25 Dec 1988): 27.

Witt, Mary Ann Frese. *Existential Prisons. Captivity in Mid-Twentieth Century French Literature*. Durham: Duke University Press, 1985.

Wlodarz, Joe. "Rape Fantasies: Hollywood and Homophobia." *Masculinity: Bodies, Movies, Culture*. Ed. Peter Lehman. New York and London: Routledge, 2001. 67–80.

Woolf, Virginia. "The Movies and Reality." *New Republic* 47 (1926): 308–10.

Wykes, Maggie. *News, Crime and Culture*. London et al.: Pluto, 2001.

Yeazell, Bernard R. "Do it or Dorrit." *Novel* 25 (1991): 33–49.

Young, Vernetta D. "Corporal Punishment." *Encyclopedia of American Prisons*. Ed. Marilyn D. McShane and Frank R. Williams III. London and New York: Garland, 1996. 115–17.

Zambrano, Ana Laura. "*Great Expectations*: Dickens and David Lean." *Literature/Film Quarterly* 2.2 (1974): 154–61.

———. "Charles Dickens and Sergei Eisenstein: The Emergence of Cinema." *Style* 9.4 (1975): 469–87.

Zambrano, Ana Laura. *Dickens and Film*. New York: Gordon Press, 1977.

Zedner, Lucia. "Wayward Sisters. The Prison for Women." *The Oxford History of the Prison. The Practice of Punishment in Western Society*. Ed. Norval Morris and David J. Rothman. New York and Oxford: Oxford University Press, 1995. 329–61.

Zelicovici, Dvora. "Circularity and Linearity in *Little Dorrit*." *Dickens Quarterly* 1.2 (1984): 50–53.

Zeller, Robert. "Running Away: 'The Loneliness of the Long-Distance Runner' Revisited." *Aethlon* 13.1 (1995): 45–52.

Zimbardo, Philip G. "The Prison Game." *Legal Process and Corrections*. Ed. N. Johnston and L.D. Savitz. New York: Wiley, 1982. 195–98.

———. "The Stanford Prison Experiment. A Simulation Study of the Psychology of Imprisonment Conducted at Stanford University." <www.prisonexp.org>

INDEX

www.ingramcontent.com/pod-product-compliance
Lightning Source LLC
Chambersburg PA
CBHW020946310726
48980CB00001B/79

* 9 7 8 1 9 3 4 0 4 3 6 0 8 *